Pediatric School Psychology

Routledge
Taylor & Francis Group

School Based Practice in Action Series
Series Editors
Rosemary B. Mennuti, EdD, NCSP
and
Ray W. Christner, PsyD, NCSP
Philadelphia College of Osteopathic Medicine

This series provides school-based practitioners with concise practical guidebooks that are designed to facilitate the implementation of evidence-based programs into school settings, putting the best practices *in action*.

Published Titles

Assessment and Intervention for Executive Function Difficulties
George McCloskey, Lisa A. Perkins, and Bob Van Divner

Resilient Playgrounds
Beth Doll

Comprehensive Planning for Safe Learning Environments: A School Counselor's Guide to Integrating Physical and Psychological Safety - Prevention through Recovery
Melissa A. Reeves, Linda M. Kanan, Amy E. Plog

Behavioral Interventions in Schools: A Response-to-Intervention Guidebook
David M. Hulac, Joy Terrell, Odell Vining, and Joshua Bernstein

The Power of Family-School Partnering (FSP): A Practical Guide for School Mental Health Professionals and Educators
Cathy Lines, Gloria Miller, and Amanda Arthur-Stanley

Implementing Response-to-Intervention in Elementary and Secondary Schools: Procedures to Assure Scientific-Based Practices, Second Edition
Matthew K. Burns and Kimberly Gibbons

A Guide to Psychiatric Services in Schools: Understanding Roles, Treatment, and Collaboration
Shawna S. Brent

Comprehensive Children's Mental Health Services in Schools and Communities
Robyn S. Hess, Rick Jay Short, and Cynthia Hazel

Responsive School Practices to Support Lesbian, Gay, Bisexual, Transgender, and Questioning Students and Families
Emily S. Fisher and Kelly S. Kennedy

Serving the Gifted: Evidence-Based Clinical and Psycho-Educational Practice
Steven I. Pfeiffer

Pediatric School Psychology: Conceptualization, Applications, and Leadership Development
Thomas J. Power and Kathy L. Bradley-Klug

Forthcoming Titles

Ecobehavioral Consultation in Schools: Theory and Practice for School Psychologists, Special Educators, and School Counselors
Steven W. Lee

Everyday Program Evaluation for Schools: Implementation and Outcomes
Diane Smallwood and Susan G. Forman

Early Childhood Education: A Practical Guide to Evidence-Based, Multi-Tiered Service Delivery
Gina Coffee, Corey E. Ray-Subramanian, G. Thomas Schanding, Jr., and Kelly A. Feeney-Kettler

Pediatric School Psychology: Conceptualization, Applications, and Strategies for Leadership Development

Thomas J. Power ■ Kathy L. Bradley-Klug

Routledge
Taylor & Francis Group
NEW YORK AND LONDON

First published 2013
by Routledge
711 Third Avenue, New York, NY 10017

Simultaneously published in the UK
by Routledge
27 Church Road, Hove, East Sussex, BN3 2FA

Routledge is an imprint of the Taylor & Francis Group, an informa business

Library of Congress Cataloging in Publication Data
Power, Thomas J.
   Pediatric school psychology : conceptualization, applications, and strategies for leadership development / Thomas J. Power & Kathy L. Bradley-Klug.
   p. cm.
   Includes bibliographical references and index.
   ISBN 978-0-415-87109-9 (hardcover : alk. paper) —
   ISBN 978-0-415-87110-5 (pbk. : alk. paper)
   1. School psychology. 2. Educational psychology. I. Bradley-Klug, Kathy L. II. Title.
   LB1027.55.P69 2013
   370.15—dc23
   2012008256

ISBN: 978-0-415-87109-9 (hbk)
ISBN: 978-0-415-87110-5 (pbk)
ISBN: 978-0-203-86975-8 (ebk)

Typeset in Melior
by EvS Communication Networx, Inc.

I thank my wife, Barbara, for the joy she brings to life and her patience with me as I do my work. And, I am grateful to my mentors, colleagues, mentees, and trainees at The Children's Hospital of Philadelphia who have nurtured and sustained me for essentially my entire career.

TJP

I dedicate this book to the memory of my mother, Janet L. Elwell, from whom I learned the importance of love and family support when faced with a terminal disease. Her valiant battle with cancer that ended when she was much too young has inspired me to educate others about the impact of health conditions on individuals and their families. I also dedicate this book to my husband, Tom, and my sons, Gregory and Alex—I am truly blessed by your patience, encouragement, and unconditional love. Thank you for always reminding me of the true treasures in life.

KBK

Contents

List of Tables

List of Figures

Series Editors' Foreword

The *School-Based Practice in Action* series grew out of a discussion between us several years ago while attending a professional conference. At that time, we were each at different points in our careers, yet we both realized and faced the same challenges for education and serving children and families. Acknowledging the transformations facing the educational system, we shared a passion and vision in ensuring quality services to schools, students, and families. This vision involved increasing the strong knowledge base of practitioners together with an impact on service delivery. This would require the need to understand theory and research, albeit we viewed the most critical element as having the needed resources bridging empirical knowledge to the process of practice. Thus, our goal for the *School-Based Practice in Action* series has been to truly offer resources for readers that are based on sound research and principles and can be set directly "into action."

Each book in our series offers information in a practice-friendly manner and has a companion CD with reproducible and usable materials. Within the text, readers will find a specific icon that will cue them to documents available on the accompanying CD. These resources are designed to have a direct impact on transitioning research and knowledge into the day-to-day functions of school-based practitioners. We recognize that the implementation of programs and the changing of roles come with challenges and barriers, and as such, these may take on various forms depending on the context of the situation and the voice of the practitioner. To that end, the books of the *School-Based Practice in Action* series may be used in their entirety and present form for a number of practitioners; however, for others, these books will help them find new ways to move toward effective action and new possibilities. No matter which style fits your practice, we hope that these books will influence your work and professional growth.

In this book, Tom Power and Kathy Bradley-Klug have brought us valuable information about the impact of health disorders on children's academic, social, and emotional progress. This up-to-date knowledge is critical to all individuals working with children in the school setting. The innovative ideas for intervention and prevention strategies are practical for school based practice yet they are rooted in strong theoretical foundations and research. Although this is not a simple issue to address within school settings, Power and Bradley-Klug are able to clearly identify and articulate the information needed for school personnel to be responsive and effective. In addition they offer valuable resources for grant writing, manuscript critiquing, and journal article preparation.

We are delighted to have this resource be a part of the *School-Based Practice in Action* series, and we trust this will be a valuable resource for those working in schools. Drs. Power and Bradley-Klug are leaders in the field of pediatric school psychology and we are honored to have had the opportunity to work together.

We must extend our gratitude to Mr. Dana Bliss and Routledge Publishing for their support and belief in the *School-Based Practice in Action* series. Their openness to our ideas and thoughts made this series possible. We hope that you enjoy reading and implementing the materials in this book and the rest of the series as much as we have enjoyed working with the authors on developing these resources. Best wishes in your work with schools, children, and families.

Rosemary B. Mennuti, EdD, NCSP
Ray W. Christner, PsyD, NCSP

Series Editors, School-Based Practice in Action Series

Preface

This book has been prepared for child-serving psychologists and trainees who are committed to promoting children's success in school. It is unique in that it is designed specifically for professionals whose investment in the education of children and youth is through promoting their health and development. The approach advanced in this text acknowledges that psychologists with a commitment to promote school success have training in many specialty areas and that each specialty has unique strengths related to the education of children. The concepts and applications presented are firmly grounded in multiple areas of child-serving psychology, including pediatric, child and adolescent clinical, school, community, developmental, and prevention psychology.

The focus of this book is equally balanced on intervention and prevention. Unlike other books in pediatric or health psychology that have a primary focus on specific health disorders, this book addresses cross-cutting topics. With regard to interventions for pediatric illnesses, the topics addressed include improving adherence, promoting successful school reintegration, reducing stress and enhancing coping skills, improving pain management, and enhancing quality of life. A conceptualization of intervention is described in chapter 2 and application strategies for real-world settings are presented in chapter 3. With respect to prevention programming to promote competence and resilience, the themes addressed include developing multitiered programs, establishing and maintaining critical partnerships for cross-system and cross-discipline collaboration, monitoring program effectiveness and quality of implementation, and programming for sustainability. A conceptual framework for prevention is described in chapter 4 and examples of how to apply this framework in community settings is presented in chapter 5.

A theme that permeates the text is that applications of a participatory action research approach are highly useful in developing and evaluating programs and measurement strategies. Also, the book places equal emphasis on theory and practice, including applications in diverse settings such as school, primary care, community, and hospital settings. In addition, although school obviously serves a critical function in the education of a high percentage of children in the United States and other countries, it is recognized that education occurs in multiple systems and that the family, in particular, serves a vital function in the schooling of children.

A unique feature of this text is its major emphasis on developing leaders in pediatric school psychology (i.e., psychology with a focus on the schooling of children by promoting their health and development). About half of the book is devoted to leadership development and addresses important topics for professionals and trainees who aspire to positions of leadership related to pediatric school psychology. These topics include program development and evaluation (chapter 6), measurement development (chapter 7), grant writing (chapter 8), manuscript reviewing and preparation (chapter 9), and training and research (chapter 10).

This book has been written as a guide for practitioners and researchers who are committed to the education of children by promoting their health and development. For professionals trained in health and clinical psychology, the book offers a model for conceptualizing the connections among health, family, and school systems as well as strategies for promoting cross-system linkages to foster student adaptation in educational settings. For professionals trained in school psychology, the book emphasizes the importance of children's health to their success in school, and offers strategies to connect health and school providers. Numerous examples are provided in each chapter to assist practitioners and researchers in understanding key concepts and applying these ideas to their work.

In addition, this book has been designed specifically for trainers in university and medical school settings. Each chapter includes tables and figures as well as discussion questions that can be used in class or training seminars. Multiple references are included in each chapter to direct students to further readings about important topics. Also, a CD with PowerPoint presentations, case examples, and guidelines for practice has been prepared to assist with lectures and describe strategies for application in clinical and school settings. In addition, the final chapter provides a description of two doctoral-level training programs dedicated to the preparation of pediatric school psychologists.

Acknowledgments

We are grateful to the school psychology students at Lehigh University and University of South Florida who have inspired and challenged us over the years. And, we are especially grateful to Ed Shapiro and George DuPaul for their vision and leadership in pediatric school psychology, and their support of our careers as colleague and mentor. In addition, we thank Kendall Jeffries for her assistance in researching the various topics covered in this book and her support in editing many draft chapters.

About the Authors

Thomas J. Power, PhD, Professor of School Psychology in Pediatrics, Psychiatry, and Education at the University of Pennsylvania, is Chief Psychologist and Director of the Center for Management of ADHD at The Children's Hospital of Philadelphia (CHOP). He has been principal investigator of research grants funded by NIMH and HRSA, Maternal and Child Health Bureau to evaluate the effectiveness of multisystemic interventions for children with ADHD. Also, since 1997 he has served as coprincipal investigator (with Edward Shapiro, PhD and George DuPaul, PhD) of a grant funded by the Department of Education to prepare doctoral students in the school psychology program at Lehigh University for leadership positions in pediatric school psychology. A Fellow in Divisions 16 (School Psychology) and 54 (Pediatric Psychology) of the American Psychological Association, Dr. Power has authored over 125 scholarly papers and is coauthor of *Promoting Children's Health: Integrating School, Family, and Community,* a book published in 2003 by Guilford Press. Dr. Power is past Editor of *School Psychology Review,* and currently Associate Editor of *School Mental Health* and President of the Society for the Study of School Psychology (2012).

Kathy L. Bradley-Klug, PhD, is Associate Professor, Graduate Programs in School Psychology and Associate Chair, Department of Psychological and Social Foundations at the University of South Florida (USF). She developed the Pediatric School Psychology doctoral area of specialization at USF. Dr. Bradley-Klug has been the principal investigator on several grants related to pediatric school psychology and has developed online training courses in the areas of pediatric health issues in the schools and pediatric psychopharmacology. Dr. Bradley-Klug is the Project Director of a collaborative, interdisciplinary program infusing principles of pediatric psychology, positive psychology, and public health in medical student education at USF Health. She also collaborates with Bringing Science Home, USF Health to develop methods to assess and promote health literacy and well-being in youth and young adults with chronic health conditions. Dr. Bradley-Klug has authored numerous book chapters and journal articles on topics related to pediatric school psychology and serves on the editorial board of several journals in the field of school psychology.

Other Contributors

Katherine Bevans, PhD, Research Assistant Professor of Pediatrics, The Children's Hospital of Philadelphia, Perelman School of Medicine at the University of Pennsylvania.

George J. DuPaul, PhD, Professor of School Psychology, Chair of the Department of Education and Human Services, Lehigh University.

Jessica A. Hoffman, PhD, Associate Professor, Department of Counseling and Applied Educational Psychology, Northeastern University.

Stephen S. Leff, PhD, Associate Professor of Clinical Psychology in Pediatrics, The Children's Hospital of Philadelphia, Perelman School of Medicine at University of Pennsylvania.

Emily Shaffer-Hudkins, PhD, Postdoctoral Fellow, Division of Child Development, Pediatrics, University of South Florida.

One

Background and Overview of Pediatric School Psychology

Success in school is critical for healthy child development. School promotes the learning of concepts and skills, the development of strategies for interacting with others, and fosters the growth of independence and a sense of self-efficacy. Failure in school is a strong risk factor for poor outcomes in life; it initiates a process of disengagement that can result in school dropout, increased risk for unhealthy patterns of behavior and psychopathology, and enhanced likelihood of relationship problems in adolescence and adulthood.

Being successful in school depends upon multiple factors, which include but are not limited to the following. First, a strong parent–child attachment prepares the child to relate effectively with teachers and classmates and regulate behavior and emotions in school. Second, parent involvement in education helps the child to appreciate the value of education, take advantage of educational opportunities at home and school, come prepared to learn in school, and master skills introduced in the classroom setting. Third, the climate of the school can create a context within which teachers are valued, professional development is emphasized, effective teaching strategies are modeled and affirmed, and students engage in supportive relationships with their teachers. Fourth, an ongoing relationship with a primary health care provider can prevent the emergence of illnesses that can serve as barriers to learning and social development.

What is Pediatric School Psychology?

Pediatric school psychology is a subset of child-serving psychology that is focused on the promotion of children's health and development through the coordination of efforts across systems, including family, school, health system, and community agencies, with a particular emphasis on fostering success in school. The essence of pediatric school psychology is to promote linkages among systems of care and interdisciplinary connections to enable children to be successful in school.

The domain of child-serving psychologists is quite diverse and includes professionals who place emphasis on varying aspects of child development. For example, clinical child and adolescent psychologists focus on mental health issues and they work to assess and treat problems, as well as to minimize and prevent risk. Clinical psychologists have an interest in resolving mental health problems or reducing risk so that children and youth can adjust well in the community, including school. Pediatric psychologists have a similar focus on assessment, intervention, and prevention but the targets of their efforts are health conditions, including acute and chronic illnesses. Pediatric psychologists, like clinical psychologists, focus on assisting children so that they can become integrated or reintegrated into normalized community environments. Community psychologists address the needs of children with a particular interest in how community-based agencies support the development of youth. They typically emphasize the importance of designing community organizations so that they are aligned with the cultural values and norms of the children and families served. School psychologists directly address the development of children in school. They have a principal focus on advancing the primary mission of schools to promote the cognitive and social development of students.

Child-serving psychologists often focus on a narrow range of systems in response to prevailing models of training or practice constraints, such as institutional priorities or billing policies. The term *pediatric school psychology* was coined to refer to the subset of child-serving psychologists who have a major focus on promoting child development within a wide range of systems (e.g., family, school, health system, mental health system, and other community systems), with a particular focus on the school, and facilitating the alignment of systems to promote school success (e.g., school–health system connection, school–mental health system connection, family–school connection; Power, DuPaul, Shapiro, & Parrish, 1995). The distinguishing feature of pediatric school psychologists is not the graduate program within which they receive their training (e.g., clinical vs. health vs. school), but the developmental/systems approach they use in understanding children and intervening to promote healthy and successful development especially in schools (Power, Shapiro, & DuPaul, 2003).

Pediatric school psychologists understand that promoting student success in school depends upon a wide range of variables, including school factors (e.g., content and method of instruction, teacher–student relationships, peer relationships), family factors (e.g., quality of the parent–child relationship, parental regulation of child behavior, family involvement in education), health system factors (e.g., access to health system, trust in health provider, quality of care), and the connections among these systems. The focus is on promoting the development of the whole child, supporting the multiple systems in which children function, and facilitating relationships between the school and family, and other systems in the child's life.

At its core, pediatric school psychology promotes interdisciplinary collaboration. In promoting connections among systems, professionals from multiple disciplines naturally intersect with one another. Strong intersystemic relationships require that professionals from various disciplines value one another's contributions and work to establish and maintain mutual partnerships.

Theoretical Foundations of Pediatric School Psychology

Because pediatric school psychologists work across systems and disciplines, it is essential that they understand and incorporate multiple theoretical models into their work. The following is a description of some of the more prominent models involved in practice and research related to pediatric school psychology.

Medical Model

This model is the prevailing paradigm used by health providers in medical settings. It is used to determine the presence or absence of a medical or mental health disorder. The *Diagnostic and Statistical Manual of Mental Disorders* is a system based on the medical model that is used to classify psychiatric disorders. In order to meet criteria for a diagnosis, one or more clusters of symptoms must be present and there generally needs to be evidence of functional impairment. For example, to receive a diagnosis of posttraumatic stress disorder, the person must have experienced an event that involved actual or threatened harm to self or others; demonstrate persistent symptoms related to reexperiencing the traumatic event, avoiding stimuli associated with the trauma, and being hyper-aroused; and show evidence that the disturbance is causing significant functional impairment (American Psychiatric Association, 2000).

The medical model has numerous advantages in that it spec-ifies useful guidelines for assessment, delineates conditions that have a somewhat predictable developmental course, and helps in identifying potentially effective interventions. Limi-tations of the model are that it identifies the person (child) as the source of the problem, may fail to identify varying levels of severity, and has limited utility in designing specific strate-gies for treatment (Power et al., 2003).

Psychometric Model

This model is based on decades of research demonstrating that individuals differ from one another on numerous dimen-sions of physical, cognitive, learning, behavioral, social, and emotional functioning. Measures based on a psychometric model provide an assessment of functioning along a contin-uum that does not clearly differentiate normal (adaptive) from abnormal (nonadaptive) functioning. As such, these methods afford an examination of the relative severity of a dimension of functioning (Achenbach & Rescorla, 2001). The psycho-metric model typically incorporates multiple methods and informants, including direct assessment of functioning (e.g., testing of a child), informant reports (e.g., parent and teacher ratings), self-reports, and direct observations of behavior. Decisions about severity are often determined based upon a comparison of an individual's functioning to that of peers of similar age and gender, although some assessment methods examine functioning in relation to an established criterion as a basis for decision making (i.e., criterion-referenced mea-surement). Although the psychometric model historically has focused on assessing deficits, recently there has been increasing emphasis on strength-based assessment.

The psychometric model addresses a limitation of the medical model in that it provides an assessment of the relative severity of a problem. It is highly useful for multimethod assessment of baseline functioning, as well as for progress monitoring and outcome assessment. Disadvantages may include its failure to account for contextual and cultural factors and its limited efficacy in designing intervention strategies (Power & Eiraldi, 2000).

Neuropsychological Model

Advances in neuroscience have been occurring at a breathtaking pace. Progress in neuroscience is elucidating mechanisms of action to explain individuals' learning and behavior and how educational, psychosocial, and pharmacological interventions have an effect on the developing brain. Neuropsychology provides a set of methods to understand linkages between structures and functions of the brain and processes of learning and execution (Levin & Hanten, 2005). Neuropsychology is especially useful with children who have disorders that are clearly linked to the central nervous system, including but not limited to traumatic brain injuries, brain tumors, and neurodevelopmental disorders, such as epilepsy, spina bifida, and cerebral palsy. Neuropsychological tests are applied to establish baseline levels of functioning, monitor progress over time, and evaluate responses to intervention.

The neuropsychological model has proven to be useful in understanding learning and behavioral processes that are strongly rooted in neuroscience. Also, this model can be useful in developing hypotheses about learning deficits and behavior problems that may be helpful in intervention planning (Hale et al., 2009). Potential disadvantages are that the application of neuropsychological methods may be time consuming and costly and the model is limited with regard to planning specific strategies for educational and behavioral intervention.

Behavior Analytic Model

The behavior analytic model as it is described for the purposes of this book is more accurately referred to as functional behavioral assessment (FBA). This model refers to the broad class of methods used to assess how environmental events elicit and maintain target behaviors. Environmental events typically are differentiated into those that are antecedents to target behaviors and those that are consequences. Tracking sequences of antecedent events, target behaviors, and consequences can be highly useful in understanding how target behaviors occur and are maintained. Further, identifying the function of behavior is important in understanding and predicting the occurrence of problem behaviors (Steege & Watson, 2009). In general, behavior has two major functions: (a) positive reinforcement (e.g., obtain adult attention, peer attention, access to privileges, concrete rewards), and (b) negative reinforcement (i.e., escape an undesirable situation). A functional behavioral approach typically includes an assessment of these two functions as well as an examination of potential skill deficits (e.g., memory or attention deficits, motor skills deficits, reading deficits) that may be contributing to the problem (Halle, Bambara, & Reichle, 2005). In addition, contextual factors that are more distal to antecedent events (i.e., setting events) are important to consider in predicting the occurrence of target behaviors.

The behavior analytic model has many assets, in particular its utility for intervention planning, progress monitoring, and outcome evaluation. Limitations include the time and effort involved in assessment and the difficulty in applying this approach to assess nonobservable behaviors, such as internalizing symptoms.

Cognitive-Behavioral Model

This model refers to the broad range of approaches based on the premise that an individual's perceptions and cognitions of environmental stimuli as well as the ways in which the person processes information, have an important impact on behavior. Included in this framework are approaches related to modeling (e.g., adult, peer, and self-modeling); self-instruction through internal self-talk and cognitive reframing; self-regulation including self-monitoring, self-evaluation, and self-reinforcement; coping and problem solving strategies (Mayer & Van Acker, 2009).

The cognitive-behavioral model has been highly useful in planning interventions for children with a range of health and mental health conditions, including aggression, anxiety and depression, posttraumatic stress, pain, and nonadherence (Power & Werba, 2006). Many of the established evidence-based treatments for health and mental health disorders can be classified as cognitive-behavioral interventions. Although many cognitive-behavioral interventions have been demonstrated to be effective and acceptable for use by providers and families, challenges remain with regard to disseminating these approaches for wide-scale use in the community. Also, this model is limited in that it may not account sufficiently for contextual and systemic factors that have an effect on development and performance.

Developmental-Ecological Model

This model is based on developmental-ecological theory (Bronfenbrenner, 1979) and provides a useful framework for understanding transactions between the developing child and the changing contexts in which the child develops. This framework is unique in its focus on the multiple systems in which children develop, including family, school, peer, health system, and other systems in the community (Kazak, Rourke, & Navsaria, 2009). Also, the model emphasizes the importance of intersystem dynamics, such as family–school relationship, family–health system interaction, and school–health system relationship. In addition, the model accounts for the impact of cultural and socioeconomic factors and broad systems issues that have an effect on the systems in which children are embedded, such as local, state, and federal policies regarding health care, education, and child welfare.

More so than the other models, the developmental-ecological model stresses interpersonal dynamics and intersystem connections. It is useful in identifying systemic risks and protective factors in developing programs to promote health and child development. The model is limited by a paucity of measurement methods to assess important interpersonal and intersystemic constructs (Power et al., 2003).

Hallmarks of Pediatric School Psychology

There are several features of pediatric school psychology that are hallmarks of this approach. These hallmarks include a focus on a continuum of services across varying levels of prevention and intervention, as well as an emphasis on positive psychology. In addition, pediatric school psychology is characterized by its incorporation of a multisystemic approach to working with children and adolescents, which involves building relationships across systems of care and across disciplines, and finally, the emphasis on the use of a partnership-based model to promote competence and solve problems.

Continuum of Services

The traditional approach to addressing the needs of youth has been to assess deficits and design interventions after a problem has emerged. A contemporary approach to working with youth involves an emphasis on preventive services. Service delivery is viewed along a continuum proceeding through varying stages of prevention and intervention. Promoting health and expanding the capacity of systems to address the needs of all individuals is essential in this approach. This continuum, described below and illustrated in Figure 1.1, is based upon the model of prevention developed by the Institute of Medicine (IOM; 1994). The focus on a continuum of care has also been emphasized in the context of school-based models of mental health service delivery (Weist, 2001).

The concentric circles presented in Figure 1.1 represent various levels of prevention and intervention. Proceeding from the outside circle, universal prevention efforts are offered to the entire population of children and youth prior

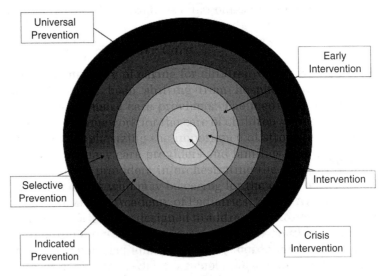

Figure 1.1 The continuum of prevention and intervention services, proceeding from universal prevention for all children to crisis intervention for children with urgent or emergent needs.

to the onset of problems. For example, the entire population of kindergarten students in a school district may be screened for the presence of sleep problems and disorders. The purpose would be to identify those children who may be predisposed to, or are demonstrating early signs of problems with sleep. Children identified as being at risk would then be targeted for the implementation of techniques to prevent further development of sleep problems (Luginbuehl, Bradley-Klug, Ferron, Anderson, & Benbadis, 2008).

The selective prevention level targets those individuals who may be at risk for a particular problem given their a priori membership in a particular group. For example, students attending a school situated in a low-income community in which there are high rates of obesity could be targeted for health promotion programming that included nutrition and fitness education. The Pathways program is an example of such a program. By working in partnership with school professionals and community members from several Native American communities, a team of university researchers was successful in developing a multicomponent, culturally effective obesity prevention initiative (Davis et al., 1999). Alternatively, selective prevention services can be provided to all children with a chronic illness such as sickle cell disease, given that these children generally are considered at risk for social and emotional difficulties by virtue of their health condition (Lemanek & Ranalli, 2009).

Indicated prevention targets individuals identified as being at risk for health or mental health problems. Alternatively, indicated prevention efforts can be targeted for children with health conditions who demonstrate evidence of risk for further complications (Kazak, Rourke, Alderfer, et al., 2007). For example, children with chronic health conditions such as cancer are often at risk for clinically significant levels of distress that may be associated with academic, social, and emotional impairments. Youth are identified for targeted prevention efforts when there is evidence of risk for stress and coping problems in order to decrease the likelihood that coping difficulties will evolve into more serious concerns.

With respect to the intervention components of this continuum, the first level encompasses early intervention and addresses youth who are in the beginning stages of coping with a problem. Early intervention services commonly are implemented when children are infants or preschoolers, although this level of care may be appropriate for children as they move through transitional stages of their development (e.g., advance from elementary to middle school) or for children in the early stages of coping with a problem after the onset of an illness.

The next level of intervention is designed for children who have an identified problem. In many cases, evidence-based interventions have been developed and validated to reduce symptoms and associated impairments. For example, for children identified with attention-deficit/hyperactivity disorder (ADHD), evidence-based interventions, including parent training, school-based behavioral approaches and medications (e.g., stimulants, atomoxetine, guanfacine) have been demonstrated to be effective. Finally, the innermost circle of Figure 1.1 represents crisis intervention. This level of intervention is intensive and designed for individuals with severe problems who need assistance on an emergency or urgent basis.

Positive Psychology

Consistent with the emphasis on prevention, pediatric school psychology embraces a positive psychology approach. The positive psychology movement has resulted in a shift from a focus on a one-dimensional, deficit-oriented view of health (e.g., the absence of disease or psychopathology), to a view that well-being is separate from disease and should be assessed and developed as such. Thus, rather than simply searching or waiting for problems related to illness to be observed, efforts must be directed to assist youth in coping with their illness and prevent additional negative outcomes.

The study of positive psychology, in its simplest form, may be termed the study of happiness. The study of happiness is also referred to as the investigation of one's subjective well-being, a more scientific term used in the empirical literature (Diener, Eunkook, & Lucas, 1999). The main components of subjective well-being include positive affect, negative affect, and life satisfaction. Positive and negative affect can be defined as one's stable emotions and mood states. Examples of positive affect may include such emotions as bliss, pleasure, and elation, whereas emotions such as sorrow, distress, and regret are examples of negative affect. The concept of life satisfaction is viewed as a more global construct and encompasses the overall evaluation of one's life (Diener, 1984). To illustrate, the types of questions asked on the Student's Life Satisfaction Scale (Huebner, 1991) include "I have a good life" and "My life is going well." Of these three components of subjective well-being, life satisfaction is proposed to be the most stable.

The traditional approach to assessing youth with physical or mental illness, which is consistent with the medical model, is to determine if the child meets criteria for an illness or disorder and to employ interventions designed to treat the identified condition(s). However, when applying the medical model, clinicians typically fail to explore factors that might promote wellness and prevent illness or at least a more serious illness. Patel and Goodman (2007) highlight the need to assess both protective and promoting factors related to wellness. Protective factors are group or individual factors that decrease the likelihood of developing problems. Life satisfaction is a prime example of a protective factor as studies have shown that life satisfaction can serve to facilitate adaptive responses to stressful life events in youth (Huebner, Suldo, & Gilman, 2006). Promoting factors, clearly aligned with the focus of positive psychology, enhance psychological well-being. These factors may include family communication, peer relationships, participation in activities that are meaningful (i.e., extracurricular activities in school, positive employment experiences), and relationships with teachers. Research to date demonstrates the importance of support across multiple contexts (i.e., family, school, community) to reduce risk and promote wellness in youth (Youngblade et al., 2007).

With respect to the application of positive psychology to youth with mental health difficulties, it is useful for psychologists to assess components that comprise subjective well-being. Although the interaction between subjective well-being and physical health makes intuitive sense, research investigating this relationship is still in its infancy. Bray, Kehle, Peck, Theodore, and Zhou (2004) proposed a theory explaining the reduction in emotionally triggered asthma attacks through treatments consistent with the basic tenets of positive psychology. If this proposed theory is generalized broadly to other chronic health conditions, the suggestion is that strategies to promote positive affect and life satisfaction while decreasing negative affect may result in positive physical health outcomes for youth. Further research needs to be conducted to test this theory.

Multisystemic Approach

The promotion of child development within multiple systems (e.g., family, school health, community) is clearly a hallmark of pediatric school psychology. The theory supporting a multisystemic approach is rooted in the developmental-ecological model (Bronfenbrenner, 1979). Bronfenbrenner describes several levels of functioning within this framework, including (a) the individual (i.e., child); (b) the microsystem (i.e., the child's interactions with others in their immediate surroundings, such as parents, peers, and teachers); (c) the mesosystem (i.e., the context within which multiple interactions are occurring, such as the family and classroom, as well as the interface of microsystems, such as the family–school connection and the family–health system connection); (d) the exosystem (i.e., social systems that affect the child indirectly such as parent's workplace, school district, social services); (e) the macrosystem (i.e., aspects of society and culture that impact the child such as educational and health care laws and local customs); and (f) the chronosystem (i.e., significant changes that occur throughout the lifespan such as beginning school and the birth of a sibling). Figure 1.2 provides a streamlined version of the developmental-ecological model highlighting child development within the context of the family, school, and health systems.

The developmental-ecological model highlights the importance of contextual and relational factors within systems and the effect of within-system dynamics on functioning in other systems. For example, research has demonstrated that the

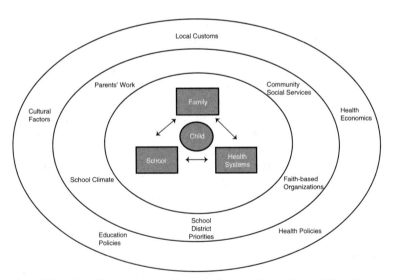

Figure 1.2   The multiple systems that have an effect on child development. The outer ring reflects macrosystemic factors, the middle ring reflects exosystemic factors, and the inner triangle represents the factors within and between systems of care.

quality of the parent–child relationship not only has an effect on self-control in the family environment, but also has an impact on the quality of adult-directed and peer-directed relationships in school (Pianta, 1997). Similarly, family involvement in education in the home environment has repeatedly been demonstrated to have an effect on students' educational performance in school (Power & Mautone, 2008).

The developmental-ecological model also emphasizes the importance of between-system dynamics. For example, the quality of the family-school connection has a strong impact on how children function in school and can serve as the basis for effective problem solving between parents and teachers (Sheridan & Kratochwill, 2008). Similarly, there is evidence that the quality of the relationship between family and health care provider can have a beneficial effect on the management of children with special health care needs (Starfield & Shi, 2004). Further, Kazak, Simms, and Rourke (2002) discuss the importance of systems level connections to enhance collaboration and communication between the child, parent, and health care team to promote positive outcomes. Also, contemporary models of school integration and reintegration for children with chronic health conditions, such as TBI and cancer, highlight the importance of a strong connection between the health system and school (DuPaul, Power, & Shapiro, 2009). These strategies all emphasize the importance of recognizing the child's total ecology as well as the detailed assessment required in planning prevention and intervention strategies.

This model accounts for broader systemic, policy, and cultural factors that have an indirect effect on the ways in which children are provided with services in health systems, educated in schools, and access social services in the community. For example, health policies have a major effect on whether families have health insurance, how they gain access to preferred care, and the extent of coverage for mental health services. Educational policies can strongly influence priorities within a school district and school, emphasis on related services such as health and mental health care, and attitudes about connecting with agencies in the community.

Partnership-Based Programming

Partnership-based programming is critical to the success of any prevention or intervention effort. An example of a partnership-based framework is the participatory intervention model (PIM) proposed by Nastasi, Moore, and Varjas (2004). A fundamental principle of PIM is that all key stakeholders (e.g., child, caregivers, teacher, and primary care physician) must be actively involved in the process of designing, implementing, and evaluating the intervention.

Another principle of a partnership-based approach is that the relationship between consultant (researcher) and participants is nonhierarchical and fully collaborative. Each party in the process has an equal role and brings unique expertise to the partnership (Power et al., 2005). For example, in a partnership among family, school, and primary care, parents contribute expertise about the unique assets and personality traits of the child; the teacher has a distinct perspective on the learning and peer relation skills of the child; the primary care provider has a unique perspective on the medical and developmental history of the child; and the consultant brings skills related to building partnerships and fostering a collaborative problem solving process. The active involvement of participants throughout the course of program development and evaluation virtually assures a high level of treatment acceptability and increases the likelihood that participants will become engaged and stay engaged throughout the process. Also, a partnership process helps to promote buy-in over time so that intervention and prevention initiatives will be sustained (Nastasi et al., 2004).

A third premise of a partnership model is that program development and implementation is an iterative process. The program is continually modified and refined over time in response to progress monitoring and feedback from contributing stakeholders. The iterative nature of the process enables initiatives to be responsive to shifts in perspectives and changes in resources and priorities over time.

Finally, the partnership framework not only is useful for the outcomes it promotes (i.e., acceptable and culturally effective programs), but also for the empowerment process it fosters among participants. Throughout the process, all stakeholders (including parents, youth, and community members) are placed in significant roles as child advocates and social change agents. This approach sharply contrasts with expert-driven models of consultation and research that perpetuate a process of disempowerment, keeping participants in powerless roles during the course of program design, implementation, and evaluation (Fantuzzo, Coolahan, & Weiss, 1997).

Unique Features of This Book

This book is unique in that it is designed specifically for psychologists and other mental health professionals who work in and with schools to serve the needs of children. The information contained in this text will enable professionals to address the broad range of health issues that can have an effect on student functioning in schools, including academic, social, and emotional functioning. The following is a brief description of distinguishing features of this book.

Integrates Multiple Frameworks and Perspectives

The book is designed to reflect a broad vision of psychology that promotes child health and development across a wide range of systems and through the collaborative efforts of professionals from multiple disciplines and training backgrounds. Unlike many books that emphasize one or a limited number of theoretical frameworks (e.g., applied behavior analysis, cognitive-behavioral intervention, neuropsychology), this book integrates multiple theoretical models and the perspectives of child serving professionals from many disciplines. It is recognized that each of these models reflects critical domains of child functioning and has contributed to the development of a range of evidence-based practices for improving children's health and promoting their development.

Emphasizes Prevention and Intervention

This book addresses the broad continuum of needs of youth, including programs for healthy youth, those at risk, youth with identified problems, and those with an emerging need for intervention. As such, the book strikes a balance between focusing on intervention services for children who are coping with an illness or disorder and focusing on prevention programming for children who are healthy or at risk for illness or disorder. In addition, we recognize that children with a physical or mental health condition often need intervention for the presenting disorder and prevention efforts due to their risk for comorbid disorders. As such, this text integrates an intervention and prevention perspective into treatment planning for children with identified health concerns.

Highlights Cross-Cutting Themes and Concepts

Most books about pediatric psychology focus on specific health disorders, describing clinical presentation, causes and developmental course, assessment strategies, and methods of intervention. This book takes a different perspective by addressing cross-cutting themes related to a wide range of pediatric conditions (e.g., treatment adherence, pain management, coping with illness, pharmacological management, and prevention of comorbid conditions). As such, this text serves as a complement to books that include in-depth coverage of a range of disorders (e.g., Brown, 2004; Phelps, 2006; Roberts & Steele, 2009).

Emphasizes Strategies for Practitioners

Although this text presents conceptual models for promoting child development, linking systems, and promoting interdisciplinary collaboration, there is an emphasis on strategies that will be useful for practice. This book includes specific guidelines for applying models of intervention and prevention to promote children's health and address problems when they arise. Also, the text describes methods of program development and evaluation that are practical for use by professionals serving the health needs of children in schools.

Provides Aids for Teaching

For each chapter we have included tools that can assist university professors and continuing education instructors in conveying critical themes and models of prevention and intervention described in this text. The teaching tools provide specific guidelines and examples for applying conceptual models in practice. The teaching tools include PowerPoint presentations and handouts for students or seminar participants.

Offers Strategies for Leadership Development

A major focus of this book is on developing leaders in the field of pediatric school psychology. The largest section of the book is devoted to leadership development and includes chapters on program development, program evaluation, measurement development, grant writing, and manuscript critiquing and journal article preparation. "How to" guides, worksheets, and a variety of other materials are included for direct application to practice.

Questions for Discussion

1. What aspects of your training have prepared you to be effective as a pediatric school psychologist?
2. What are the gaps in your training that affect your ability to function as a pediatric school psychologist, and how can you address these gaps?
3. Linkages between the health and school systems typically are grossly underdeveloped. Can you think of an example that illustrates a strong connection between the health and school systems? What were the challenges in developing this partnership?
4. What are the barriers to promoting intersystemic collaborations? What strategies can be used to overcome these barriers?

Additional Teaching Aids

PowerPoint slides that provide an introduction to pediatric school psychology are included in the attached CD.

References

Achenbach, T. M., & Rescorla, L. A. (2001). *Manual for the ASEBA school-age forms and profiles.* Burlington: University of Vermont, Research Center for Children, Youth, and Families.

American Psychiatric Association. (2000). *Diagnostic and statistical manual of mental disorders—Text revision* (4th ed.). Washington, DC: Author.

Bray, M. A., Kehle, T. J., Peck, H. L., Theodore, L. A., & Zhou, Z. (2004). Enhancing subjective well-being in individuals with asthma. *Psychology in the Schools, 41,* 95–100.

Bronfenbrenner, U. (1979). *The ecology of human development.* Cambridge, MA: Harvard University Press.

Brown, R. T. (Ed.). (2004). *Handbook of pediatric psychology in school settings.* Mahwah, NJ: Erlbaum.

Davis, S. M., Going, S. B., Helitzer, D. L., Teufel, N. I., Snyder, P., Gittelsohn, J., ... Altaha, J. (1999). Pathways: A culturally appropriate obesity-prevention program for American Indian schoolchildren. *American Journal of Clinical Nutrition, 69*(Supplement), 796S–802S.

Diener, E. (1984). Subjective well-being. *Psychological Bulletin, 95,* 542–575.

Diener, E., Eunkook, M., & Lucas, R. E. (1999). Subjective well-being: Three decades of progress. *Psychological Bulletin, 125,* 276–302.

DuPaul, G. J., Power, T. J., & Shapiro, E. S. (2009). Schools and reintegration into schools. In M. C. Roberts & R. G. Steele (Eds.), *Handbook of pediatric psychology* (4th ed., pp. 689–702). New York: Guilford.

Fantuzzo, J. W., Coolahan, K., & Weiss, A. (1997). Resiliency partnership-directed research: Enhancing the social competencies of preschool victims of physical abuse by developing peer resources and community strengths. In D. Cicchetti & S. Toth (Eds.), *Development perspective on trauma: Theory, research and intervention* (pp. 463–514). Rochester, NY: University of Rochester Press.

Hale, J. B., Reddy, L. A., Decker, S. L., Thompson, R., Henzel, J., Teodori, A., ... Denckla, M. B. (2009). Development and validation of an ADHD executive function and behavior rating screening battery. *Journal of Clinical and Experimental Neuropsychology, 1,* 1–16.

Halle, J., Bambara, L. M., & Reichle, J. (2005). Teaching alternative skills. In L. M. Bambara & L. Kern (Eds.), *Designing positive behavior supports for students* (pp. 237–274). New York: Guilford.

Huebner, E. S. (1991). Initial development of the Students' Life Satisfaction Scale. *School Psychology International, 12,* 231–240.

Huebner, E. S., Suldo, S. M., & Gilman, R. (2006). Life satisfaction. In G. G. Bear & K. M. Minke (Eds.), *Children's needs: Vol. 3. Development, prevention, and intervention* (pp. 357–368). Bethesda, MD: National Association of School Psychologists.

Institute of Medicine (IOM). (1994). *Reducing risks for mental disorders: Frontiers for preventive intervention research.* Washington, DC: National Academy Press.

Kazak, A. E., Rourke, M. T., Alderfer, M. A., Pai, A., Reilly, A. F., & Meadows, A. T. (2007). Evidence-based assessment, intervention and psychosocial care in pediatric oncology: A blueprint for comprehensive services across treatment. *Journal of Pediatric Psychology, 32*(9), 1099–1110. doi: 10.1093/jpepsy/jsm031

Kazak, A. E., Rourke, M. T., & Navsaria, N. (2009). Families and other systems in pediatric psychology. In M. C. Roberts & R. G. Steele (Eds.), *Handbook of pediatric psychology* (4th ed., pp. 656–671). New York: Guilford.

Kazak, A. E., Simms, S., & Rourke, M. T. (2002). Family systems practice in pediatric psychology. *Journal of Pediatric Psychology, 27,* 133–143.

Lemanek, K. L., & Ranalli, M. (2009). Sickle cell disease. In M. C. Roberts & R. G. Steele (Eds.), *Handbook of pediatric psychology* (4th ed., pp. 303–318). New York: Guilford.

Levin, H. S., & Hanten, G. (2005). Executive functions after traumatic brain injury in children. *Pediatric Neurology, 33,* 79–93.

Luginbuehl, M., Bradley-Klug, K. L., Ferron, J., Anderson, W. M., & Benbadis, S. R. (2008). Pediatric sleep disorders: Validation of the Sleep Disorders Inventory for Students. *School Psychology Review, 37,* 409–431.

Mayer, M. J., & Van Acker, R. (2009). Historical roots, theoretical and applied developments, and critical issues in cognitive-behavior modification. In M. J. Mayer, R. Van Acker, J. E. Lochman, & F. M. Gresham (Eds.), *Cognitive-behavioral interventions for emotional and behavioral disorders: School-based practice* (pp. 3–28). New York: Guilford.

Nastasi, B. K., Moore, R. B., & Varjas, K. M. (2004). *School-based mental health services: Creating comprehensive and culturally specific programs.* Washington, DC: American Psychological Association.

Nastasi, B. K., Varjas, K., Schensul, S. L., Silva, K. T., Schensul, J. J., & Ratnayake, P. (2000). The participatory intervention model: A framework for conceptualizing and promoting intervention acceptability. *School Psychology Quarterly, 15,* 207–232.

Patel, V., & Goodman, A. (2007). Researching protective and promotive factors in mental health. *International Journal of Epidemiology, 36,* 703–707.

Phelps, L. (Ed.). (2006). *Chronic health-related disorders in children: Collaborative medical and psychoeducational interventions.* Washington, DC: American Psychological Association.

Pianta, R. C. (1997). Adult–child relationship processes and early schooling. *Early Education and Development, 8,* 11–26.

Power, T. J. (2006). Collaborative practices for managing children's chronic health needs. In L. Phelps (Ed.), *Chronic health-related disorders in children: Collaborative medical and psychoeducational interventions* (pp. 7–23). Washington, DC: American Psychological Association.

Power, T. J., Blom-Hoffman, J., Clarke, A. T., Riley-Tillman, T. C., Kelleher, C., & Manz, P. (2005). Reconceptualizing intervention integrity: A partnership-based framework for linking research with practice. *Psychology in the Schools, 42*(5), 495–507.

Power, T. J., DuPaul, G. J., Shapiro, E. S., & Parrish, J. M. (1995). Pediatric school psychology: The emergence of a subspecialty. *School Psychology Review, 24,* 244–257.

Power, T. J., & Eiraldi, R. E. (2000). Educational and psychiatric classification systems. In E. S. Shapiro & T. R. Kratochwill (Eds.), *Behavioral assessment in schools: Theory, research, and clinical foundations* (2nd ed., pp. 464–488). New York: Guilford.

Power, T., & Mautone, J. (2008). Best practices in linking families and schools to manage children with attention problems. In A. Thomas & J. Grimes (Eds.), *Best practices in school psychology*

(Vol. 5, pp. 839–851). Bethesda, MD: National Association of School Psychologists.

Power, T. J., Shapiro, E. S., & DuPaul, G. J. (2003). Preparing psychologists to link the health and educational systems in managing and preventing children's health problems. *Journal of Pediatric Psychology, 28,* 147–155.

Power, T. J., & Werba, B. (2006). Interventions for health problems: A cognitive behavioral approach. In R. Mennuti, A. Freeman, & R. Christner (Eds.), *Cognitive behavioral interventions in educational settings* (pp. 323–342). New York: Routledge.

Roberts, M. C., & Steele, R. G. (Eds.). (2009). *Handbook of pediatric psychology* (4th ed.). New York: Guilford.

Sheridan, S. M., & Kratochwill, T. R. (2008). *Conjoint behavioral consultation: Promoting family-school connections and interventions* (2nd ed.). New York: Springer.

Starfield, B., & Shi, L. (2004). The medical home, access to care, and insurance: A review of evidence. *Pediatrics, 113*(Supplement 5), 1493–1498.

Steege, M. W., & Watson, T. S. (2009). *Conducting school-based functional behavioral assessments: A practitioner's guide* (2nd ed.). New York: Guilford.

Weist, M. D. (2001). Toward a public mental health promotion and intervention system for youth. *Journal of School Health, 71,* 101–104.

Youngblade, L. M., Theokas, C., Schulenberg, J., Curry, L., Huang, I., & Novak, M. (2007). Risk and promotive factors in families, schools, and communities: A contextual model of positive youth development in adolescence. *Pediatrics, 119,* 47–53.

Two

A Conceptual Model for Understanding Health Problems and Developing Interventions

with Emily Shaffer-Hudkins

The purpose of this chapter is to present a model for under-standing pediatric health problems that can guide the develop-ment and implementation of effective and useful interventions. The model proposed is based on developmental-ecological psychology and integrates aspects of social learning theory and cognitive-behavioral psychology. The chapter begins with a consideration of the developing child who is coping with an illness that can change over time in response to disease course, developmental and systemic factors, and treatments. Next, we consider child and system resources that can support child coping and form the basis for intervention planning. Finally, we describe a model of intervention development and imple-mentation that is based upon multisystemic collaboration and focuses on competence enhancement and problem solving using strategies derived from social learning and cognitive-behavioral psychology.

Understanding the Developing Child with a Health Condition

When a typically developing child is suddenly diagnosed with a health condition, the lives of that child and his or her caregivers and extended family members suddenly change. Life generally becomes less predictable; day-to-day events in the lives of these individuals as well as future plans are governed to some extent by the disease process, which depends on the nature and course of the health condition, systems of care, and approaches used to treat the condition.

Disease Process and Symptoms

Vrijmoet-Wiersma et al. (2008) suggest the following stages of a condition: initial diagnosis, time period following initial diagnosis, treatment, complications, and maintenance or post-treatment. Each one of these stages may result in a change in level of stress, ability to cope, and overall impairment not only for the affected child but for all members of the family system.

The developmental-ecological model provides a framework to help us understand the impact of the disease process on the interactions between the developing child and his or her family (Kazak, Rourke, & Navsaria, 2009). Upon initial diagnosis of a child with an illness, the caregivers take primary responsibility for understanding the diagnosis, the trajectory of the illness, and decisions related to treatment. A gradual shift in decision making and understanding of the illness typically occurs as a child matures and enters adolescence and becomes more autonomous. Families should plan for how the increasing independence of the child changes their roles in treatment of the illness. For instance, a plan for when an adolescent with diabetes may begin monitoring blood sugar level without supervision needs to be discussed. Such decisions must be addressed on an individual basis, based on illness and treatment severity, stage of the condition, and psychosocial variables (e.g., parent–child relationship and the child's decision-making capabilities).

The illness may also impact a child's relationships with peers differently across developmental stages. Children coping with an initial diagnosis and treatment for their illness may fear social rejection from peers (La Greca, 1990), especially as they transition to adolescence. By the same token, over the course of the disease and its treatment, positive peer relationships can serve a primary role in helping a child cope with illness-related stressors (Hartup, 1996), particularly as socialization with peers becomes more important during adolescence.

Dynamic Nature of Effect

The effect of an illness on the child and systems of care may vary depending upon the health issue and whether the condition is acute or chronic. An acute health condition is defined as one that has sudden onset. The course of the condition may vary substantially over a relatively short period of time. For example, a child who has sustained a sudden traumatic brain injury (TBI) will need frequent assessment following the initial trauma based upon the fact that recovery from a TBI is unpredictable and outcomes may vary with maturation (Wade, Walz, & Bosques, 2009). Thus, frequent progress monitoring of functioning across settings is required to promote positive outcomes. In contrast, a child diagnosed with a chronic condition that may have less variability over time, such as diabetes, may not require the same frequency of monitoring.

The course of an illness also may vary depending upon the treatment regimen. A child receiving radiation treatment for a brain tumor may demonstrate frequent changes in cognitive functioning and academic performance as treatment progresses, thus requiring frequent monitoring. In contrast, a child diagnosed with obstructive sleep apnea who has undergone surgery to remove his or her tonsils and adenoids may change less frequently and require less frequent monitoring.

As complications arise due to variations in the progression of a disease or treatment, data must be collected to determine functional changes for the individual. For example, children with allergies and asthma may experience an exacerbation of symptoms as a result of certain environmental triggers (e.g., pollen, changes in temperature). These variations may result in absences from school as well as changes in treatment that may directly impact a child's academic and behavioral performance across settings (McQuaid & Abramson, 2009).

Impairment and Perceived Impairment

In the medical literature, the term *impairment* typically refers to a situation in which one's functioning is compromised due to a change in physical, cognitive, or social ability. Functional impairment is often directly assessed through the use of such tools as behavioral observations as well as measures of cognitive and academic performance. Perceived impairment refers to one's perception of the impact of an illness on functioning.

Tools used to assess perceived impairment include self-report measures and behavior rating scales. A number of factors may influence perceived impairment including knowledge of the illness, disease prognosis, and the individual treatment plan (Pai et al., 2007).

Perceived impairment is important to assess as it may directly impact intervention planning. In a study comparing the views of patients diagnosed with somatoform disorder or asthma and their respective caregivers regarding health- and illness-related symptoms, Goldbeck and Bundschuh (2007) found very little similarity in the perceptions of youth and their parents. These authors discuss the importance of collecting data related to symptom perceptions from the child with the illness as well as the caregivers so that psychologists better understand this relationship and can use these data for intervention planning. Although this recommendation is consistent with best practice in obtaining data from multiple informants across multiple settings, the fact that agreement across raters is often lacking can make it difficult for clinicians to interpret these data. Studies have shown a greater likelihood of agreement on reports of observable symptoms (aggressive behavior) as compared to internal symptoms (subjective well-being). Rather than expecting agreement across raters, Garber, Van Slyke, and Walker (1998) suggest that clinicians anticipate disagreement and then determine how best to use this information for decision-making purposes. For example, when the illness perception ratings from mothers are significantly higher than those of the child, the treatment plan may include strategies to address symptoms of maternal distress.

Mishel (1990) coined the term illness uncertainty (IU) to define one's perception of illness when its course and outcomes are unknown or unpredictable. IU has been found to be a critical factor in the ability of children and adolescents to adapt to and cope with chronic health conditions. In a research study evaluating the factor structure of the Children's Uncertainty in Illness Scale (Mullins & Hartman, 1995) with a sample of children and adolescents with a variety of chronic illnesses, Pai and colleagues found two factors related to illness uncertainty: (a) the illness itself, given that some illnesses are highly variable in their course or unpredictable in terms of outcomes, and (b) the child's ability to understand his or her illness. These two factors can directly impact a youth's perception of the illness in question and should be considered as part of the assessment of a condition with respect to the development of strategies to enhance a child's ability to cope with it.

Another concept that relates to perceived impairment is illness intrusiveness, which is defined as "the extent to which illness restrictions (including, but not limited to disability) are seen as precluding involvement in and/or access to disease-unrelated activities" (Andrews et al., 2007, p. 1260). Comparing illness intrusive-adjustment across samples of European American and Native American parents of children with juvenile rheumatic disease (JRD), Andrews and colleagues found that race moderated the influence of illness intrusiveness and adjustment. Specifically, there was a direct relationship between degree of illness intrusiveness and psychological distress for the Native American parent sample. This relationship was not replicated in the European American sample. This finding is important for pediatric psychologists in considering how impairment and perceived impairment may differ across diverse populations and directly impact the adjustment of those in the immediate environment to a child's chronic illness.

Health-Related Quality of Life

Quality of life (QOL) is a construct that has received considerable attention in the medical and psychological literatures over the years; however, its definition varies considerably depending on the referent group or research focus. QOL refers to the personal appraisal of one's well-being (Haas, 1999). Assessment of QOL and similar concepts, such as life satisfaction and well-being, has been studied over the past several decades, primarily among adults. Much of this research has focused on domains such as economic, social, or psychological well-being. Across these studies, physical health status has been identified as a moderator accounting for many differences found among individuals' well-being appraisals (Eiser & Morse, 2001). Thus, the measurement of health-related quality of life (HRQOL) has emerged as a priority in both research and practice (Taylor, Gibson, & Franck, 2008).

Factors Determining HRQOL among Youth

The extension of HRQOL research into younger samples started in the early 1990s as researchers began to examine how different perceptions and experiences may influence well-being across the life span (Huebner, 1991). Developmental issues are central to the assessment of HRQOL among youth and have become particularly relevant when determining the role that physical health has on an individual's well-being during various stages of childhood and adolescence. Specifically, developmental tasks such as peer relationships, autonomy, and abstract thinking are central to how HRQOL is viewed among youth and play a key role in determining how physical health conditions impact well-being (Taylor et al., 2008). Assessment tools sensitive to these developmental factors have been developed specifically for use with pediatric populations and are discussed in further detail below.

The influence that a physical health condition has on one's overall HRQOL is multidimensional. Chronic illness may play a role in appearance, coping, and relationships with friends, family, and community (Taylor et al., 2008). Importantly, HRQOL is a subjective appraisal of well-being; the actual degree of impairment that health has on one's functioning across domains is not the focus but rather how the illness impacts one's perception of quality of life.

Well-developed, psychometrically sound measures of HRQOL assessment for use with pediatric populations have only emerged in the last several years. Some measures tap factors generic to a broad range of health concerns, whereas other instruments are condition-specific and intended for use with specific clinical samples such as oncology patients or youth with cystic fibrosis (Palermo et al., 2008). Table 2.1 provides a summary of some of the widely used measures of HRQOL.

Child and System Resources for Coping with Illness

Children with illnesses and injuries demonstrate remarkable variability with regard to their ability to cope with and thrive in the face of adversity. Variations in ability to cope with adversity are reflected in the extensive research base that has investigated childhood resilience. There is a range of factors related to resilience in the midst of adversity including those within the child, factors in the systems in which children develop, and intersystemic dynamics.

Child Resources for Coping with Illness

The child's knowledge and understanding of his or her illness are important factors related to coping with illness. Other

Table 2.1   Measures of Health-Related Quality of Life

	Generic Measures	Condition-Specific Measures
Examples	Child Health and Illness Profile (CHIP; Starfield, Riley & Green, 1999)	Pediatric Quality of Life Inventory disease-specific modules (PedsQL; Varni, Seid, & Rode, 1999)
	Child Health Questionnaire (CHQ; Landgraf, Abetz, & Ware, 1996)	Pediatric Asthma Quality of Life Questionnaire (PAQLQ; Juniper et al., 1996)
	Pediatric Quality of Life Inventory (PedsQL; Varni, Seid, & Rode, 1999)	Quality of Life in Epilepsy Inventory (QOLIE-AD-48; Cramer et al., 1999)
Strengths	Multiple response formats	Fewer items (i.e., less than 50 items)
	Multidimensional	
	Comparisons across disease types	Items clinically relevant to a specific illness
Drawbacks	Numerous items can make administration and scoring difficult	Data on psychometric properties of scales vary
	Lack of sensitivity to illness-specific factors	No comparisons across disease types

factors include the child's developmental ability, the social support network available to the child, and the child's perceived peer support. These factors not only contribute to the child's ability to adapt to an illness, but also affect adherence to specific treatment regimens.

With respect to their understanding of illness, studies have found that the amount of information shared with youth by a physician regarding their illness may vary based upon a number of factors including maturity, cognitive functioning, gender, age, and environment (Quinn et al., 2011). The type and amount of medical information to share with a child or adolescent is not without controversy, particularly with respect to knowledge that may influence decisions about one's treatment and long-term quality of life issues. For example, researchers are currently investigating the ethical and practical concerns of discussing negative, long-term side-effects of therapies with pediatric oncology patients who may undergo treatments that could potentially compromise their fertility (Quinn et al., 2011). Clearly, variables related to the child's ability to understand long-term consequences as well as cultural and religious issues must be considered when addressing such a potentially sensitive topic.

Evaluating children's knowledge and understanding of their condition is important to determine if they are able to recognize the symptoms of their illness and communicate these symptoms accurately and honestly with parents and health care providers. It also is critical to assess whether children understand the consequences of the decisions made about their condition. In other words, are youth making data-based decisions or socially acceptable decisions (Klaczynski, 2001)? For example, children may decide not to report symptoms to parents if they are concerned about activity restrictions being imposed (e.g., not being allowed to attend a party), in this case perhaps failing to consider that a particular activity may result in a medical crisis. Unfortunately, to date there are few disease-specific tools available to determine children's knowledge of their disease. Appendix A provides a sample list of questions derived from the *Youth Knowledge and Understanding of Chronic Illness Questionnaire* (Bradley-Klug et al., 2011) that may be used to determine a child's health literacy.

Similarly, children's developmental ability is related to the capability of making decisions regarding the management of their health. In the elementary years, parents typically are charged with making all management decisions. However, as children mature and enter adolescence, they may seek to become more involved in decisions related to treatment and ongoing disease management. Miller (2009) recommends that caregivers model and teach their children how to make these decisions through collaborative decision making (CDM). In a qualitative study of youth ages 8 to 19 years and their parents, Miller found that parent–child collaborative decision making is more likely to occur when there is sufficient time to make decisions. In other words, the decision should not be made during a moment of crisis, but instead at a time when those involved can share and reflect on the decision options and subsequent consequences of these options. Other factors that contribute to collaborative decision making include the child's level of trust in the parent, the availability of options related to the decision that are acceptable to the parent, the child's knowledge of the illness, and the relative seriousness of the decision, with more serious decisions involving more parental input.

Positive outcomes related to CDM include a general sense of satisfaction by children and parents, a shared understanding of the illness and why decisions were made, and an increase in children's perception of their ability to control the situation. Modeling of the decision-making process by parents provides a learning opportunity for youth and prepares them for independent decision making in the future. Increased compliance with disease management strategies as a result of CDM also has been reported (Miller, 2009). Currently, there are no available tools designed to assess CDM, although research is underway to develop this type of measurement tool.

Perceived social support has been shown to positively correlate with indicators of subjective well-being and overall social-emotional adjustment (Eccleston, Wastell, Crombez, & Jordan, 2008; Suldo & Shaffer, 2008). Thus, assessing a child's perception of social support is critical to gaining an understanding of their ability to cope with a physical or mental health issue. An example of an empirically validated measure of perceived social support developed for use with children and adolescents is the Child and Adolescent Social Support Scale (CASSS; Malecki & Demaray, 2002). This 40-item multidimensional scale asks youth to respond to items related to perceived social support from parent, teachers, classmates, and friends. Results from this assessment tool can assist psychologists to focus interventions on those particular areas in which youth perceive less support, while strengthening areas that are perceived as positive sources of social support. Some disease-specific social support measures also are available, such as the Diabetes Social Support Questionnaire (Bearman & LaGreca, 2002), and these may be helpful in treatment planning related to specific conditions.

Family Resources for Coping with Illness

When a child or adolescent is diagnosed with a chronic illness, the entire family is affected, including parents, siblings, and extended family members. There is extensive research describing the impact, both negative and positive, of a child's chronic illness on the family. Some of the negative effects reported by families include financial impact, overwhelming time commitments to maintain required treatment regimens and attend medical appointments, loss of employment, disruption of family and daily routines, unpredictability of the child's prognosis, and loss of control and helplessness (Brown et al., 2008; Robinson, Gerhardt, Vannatta, & Noll, 2007). Some families also experience positive growth from dealing with a pediatric health issue, such as parents of pediatric oncology patients who report having a more positive outlook on life, treating other people in a more positive manner, and having an improved ability to make positive plans for the future (Kazak, Stuber, Barakat, & Meeske, 1996).

A relatively unexplored area related to families is the comparison of two-parent to single-parent units. Brown and colleagues (2008) reported that very little research has examined the unique challenges experienced by single parents of children with chronic illness. Part of the reason for this may be the definition of a single parent. Some parents may identify themselves as being single, yet they have a partner or extended family member(s) living with them in the home. Brown and colleagues recommend using the term *lone parent* (p. 416) to clarify whether or not this is a parent who truly is without any additional support in the home. Similarly, Powell and Holmes (2008) argue that blended families appear to be a distinct group and may experience unique stressors and difficulties related to having a child with a health issue.

Adlerfer and colleagues (2008) provided a review of evidence-based measures that can be used to assess family resources and functioning within the family system. The assessment tools reviewed address marital and couple relationships, parent–child relationships, and sibling relationships. Specific instruments designed for families coping with a medical illness also are discussed.

School Resources for Coping with Illness

The availability of resources for youth within the school also can have an impact on a child's ability to cope with illness. Children with chronic illnesses usually return to the academic setting and are expected to be integrated back into the educational system with little guidance provided (Clay, 2004). Often the classroom teacher, as well as other educators and school staff, have little information about the impact of the illness on the child's ability to perform in the educational setting, a lack of knowledge with regard to treatment side effects, and limited understanding of how to set appropriate expectations for the child with respect to academic, behavioral, and social/emotional outcomes.

School personnel (e.g., school psychologist, school nurse, classroom teacher) can be helpful in all stages of the assessment and treatment of a health condition. The biopsychoeducational model (Grier & Bradley-Klug, 2011), which involves a collaborative problem-solving process, was developed to provide support in the educational setting for youth with pediatric health issues. Designed to be facilitated by the school psychologist, this model promotes interdisciplinary communication and collaboration across systems including the child, family, school, and medical professionals. Incorporating a team of individuals from these systems throughout each stage, the steps of this model include identification of the student's problem, focused data collection across settings using an ecological framework, development of prevention or focused intervention strategies, and monitoring of interventions to determine the student's response (Bradley-Klug, Grier, & Ax, 2006). The model can be used proactively to address the myriad of concerns that may impact a student with a chronic illness (e.g., transition back to school, academic skills problems, behavior issues, peer relationships, mental health concerns, school attendance). Additionally, the need for targeted interventions may be determined, including services such as occupational therapy or physical therapy.

In some cases youth may require interventions designed for specific impairments related to chronic health conditions. These interventions may include cognitive behavior therapy, academic skills interventions, or pharmacological interventions. Such interventions should be developed collaboratively and monitored with respect to treatment integrity, acceptability, compliance, and overall effectiveness. For example, a common issue experienced by up to 30% of youth is chronic pain (Logan, Catanese, Coakley, & Scharff, 2007). Chronic pain in students can result in high rates of absenteeism, poor academic performance, and difficulty sustaining the level of attention and effort needed for successful educational outcomes. A group-based intervention program designed for use with adolescents, such as "Coping with Pain in School" (CPS; Logan & Simons, 2010), may be provided in the school setting to teach these students methods for coping with pain, enabling them to improve their school performance.

If necessary, availability and quality of homebound instruction should be evaluated, and instruction for youth should be coordinated with school personnel to ensure appropriate curriculum coverage. The policies and procedures related to these instructional options need to be explored relative to the specific school district or county educational system. In terms of quality, Shaw and McCabe (2008) identified barriers to effective delivery of services through homebound instruction, including student eligibility criteria, requirements for parent involvement, lack of flexibility in delivery of services, and the significant costs incurred by the educational system for the provision of these services. The use of technology (e.g., e-mail, chat sessions, online classes, text messages) to enhance communication between home and school may offset the barriers identified in the more traditional model of homebound instruction.

Community Resources for Coping with Illness

The family cannot be expected to function and cope in isolation. Resources available in the community for families should be identified and connections with these organizations can be facilitated. Families will have greater access to health services if medical and mental health clinics are within the geographic vicinity and offer reduced fees for families in financial need. Access to health services is often related to whether the family resides in an urban or rural area. Accurate assessment of condition and subsequent availability of treatment and adherence to that treatment may be impacted by the amount of travel required to attend medical appointments.

Connections among Systems

Consistent with a developmental-ecological framework, child adaptation within a system is impacted by transactions that occur between that system and other systems. For example, a child's development in school is strongly influenced by the quality of the family–school relationship. A strong family–school partnership can set the stage for effective problem solving at the point when problems arise (Sheridan & Kratochwill, 2008). In a similar vein, a strong connection between the family and health system is important to promote effective adjustment in the community. When the family has a trusting relationship with the child's primary care providers, it is possible for them to collaborate in designing treatment plans that are feasible and have the potential to be effective (Power et al., 2003).

Implications for Intervention: Multisystemic Collaboration and Competence Enhancement

Based upon systems-ecological and resilience models of child development, we offer the following guidelines for developing intervention plans for children with acute and chronic illnesses.

Strengthen Systems

Children develop successfully to the extent that major systems in their lives are aligned to promote adaptive functioning. Within the family, a strong attachment between caregivers and the child fosters self-regulation, which in turn promotes successful adjustment outside the family (Pianta, 1997). Also, careful monitoring of child behavior and consistent use of positive parenting strategies promote successful child functioning in multiple settings. In school, warm, responsive teacher–student relationships are critically important and help to promote academic and social competence (Hamre & Pianta, 2001). Further, individuals who have a trusting and enduring relationship with their PCP tend to be more engaged in health care and are likely to receive higher quality services (Sia, Tonniges, Osterhus, & Taba, 2004).

Connecting Systems

Two models available in the literature that specifically promote communication and collaboration across systems for youth with pediatric health conditions are the conjoint behavioral consultation model (CBC; Sheridan & Kratochwill, 2008) and the biopsychoeducational model (Grier & Bradley-Klug, 2011). The CBC model emphasizes the importance of parents and teachers working together to help children with problems in school. Recently, the original CBC model was adapted and applied to children with medical conditions, including attention-deficit/hyperactivity disorder (ADHD; Sheridan et al., 2009). Also, the biopsychoeducational model was developed based upon a problem solving approach to prevention and intervention. This model incorporates a structured guide to promote communication and collaboration among family members, educators, and medical professionals, facilitated by a school psychologist. This model informs the process of assessment and treatment for youth with pediatric health issues.

Strengthening Competencies

Although providers typically spend considerable effort identifying and solving problems, such as through the use of cognitive-behavioral therapy (discussed later in this chapter), significant attention must also be paid to the prevention of problems. Both prevention and intervention efforts must be developed and implemented with consideration among stakeholders across systems in order to be effective in promoting competence and health.

Power and DeRosa (2012) developed the multisystemic cognitive-behavior intervention model (MCBIM) as a framework for competence enhancement and intervention for youth with chronic illness. Development of interventions within the context of the child's family, school, medical, and community systems are at the center of this model. In addition, promoting resilience and building competencies are critical, rather than focusing only on the treatment of problems once they have developed. MCBIM emphasizes that behavioral and cognitive-behavioral strategies are most effective when developed in the context of collaborative relationships.

Initial steps in the MCBIM model of intervention include identifying strengths and resources of the child, family, and surrounding systems (i.e., school, medical, community) and finding factors that promote healthy behaviors. Although not developed specifically for populations with acute or chronic illness, the strategies presented below are applicable to enhance the competence of youth and families. For instance, a strength-based assessment of youth may include a focus on identifying factors associated with resiliency, such as commitment to learning, problem solving, and family communication (Oman et al., 2002; Scales & Leffert, 2004).

In an effort to identify the developmental factors that are most closely linked to resilience during childhood and adolescence, researchers have developed a framework of developmental assets that has received significant attention in positive youth development literature over the past two decades (Lerner & Benson, 2003; Scales, Benson, & Leffert, 2000). Researchers have studied surveys of nearly 150,000 youth and have identified a set of 40 developmental assets that relate to both the prevention of high-risk behaviors and resiliency in the face of adversity among youth (Oman et al., 2002). Examples of each category of developmental assets are listed in Table 2.2. The Search Institute has developed survey instruments to assess these assets at both a community level, such as a school or medical outreach program, and an individual level. Studies of how these developmental assets are linked to resiliency in clinical samples of youth have focused on adversities that

Table 2.2   Categories of the 40 Developmental Assets (Search Institute, 2007)

Type of Developmental Asset	Examples
External Assets	
Support	Positive family communication, caring school climate
Empowerment	Child contributes to family decisions, child feels safe at home, school, and in the neighborhood
Boundaries and Expectations	Clearly defined family rules and consequences, positive adult role models
Constructive Use of Time	Involvement in creative activities outside the school day, high-quality interaction at home
Internal Assets	
Commitment to Learning	Active engagement in learning at school, reading outside of school
Positive Values	Parents teach personal responsibility for behavior, adults teach and model honesty
Social Competencies	Peaceful conflict resolution, interpersonal skills to build and maintain friendships
Positive Identity	Optimism about the future, sense of purpose

include risk of academic failure (Edwards, Mumford, Shillingford, & Serra-Roldan, 2007), substance use (Atkins, Oman, & Vesely, 2002), and sexual activity (Perkins, Luster, Villarruel, & Small, 1998). High levels of self-reported developmental assets have been found to be associated with lower levels of health risk. Further investigation is needed to determine the assets most closely linked to increased resiliency and strengths in samples of chronically ill youth.

Increasing Quality of Life and Subjective Well-Being

Prevention research also underscores the importance of attending to quality of life (QOL) and subjective well-being (SWB) to bolster resilience (Haas, 1999). Although researchers have called for prevention efforts aimed at increasing QOL, few methods for promoting mental wellness in children and adolescents have been proposed (Suldo & Shaffer, 2008). Among adults, QOL has been improved via interventions focused on helping individuals attain their goals, encouraging them to engage in acts of kindness, and developing a learned optimism approach (Seligman, 2002; Sheldon & Lyubomirsky,

2006). Use of these interventions with chronically ill youth may also be effective, given that multiple studies demonstrate a link between mental wellness and better physical health (e.g., Hampton, 2004; Zullig, Valois, Huebner, & Drane, 2005).

Building Adaptive Coping Strategies

Promoting developmental assets and quality of life are prevention approaches that provide a first line of support to foster health and resilience. A second level of prevention is centered on teaching coping strategies and increasing knowledge and skills to prevent further illness (Grey et al., 2009; Waller et al., 2004). Adaptive forms of coping include taking deliberate cognitive or behavioral actions to understand a situation and managing stress through problem solving (Rudolph, Dennig, & Weisz, 1995). This form of coping has been linked with fewer sick days and self-reported health benefits among clinical adult populations (Carels et al., 2004; Roth & Cohen, 1986); however, the evidence base is limited for children and adolescents (Venning, Eliott, Wilson, & Kettler, 2008). Conversely, the use of emotionally reactive coping, defined as trying to regulate moment-by-moment emotional states associated with a stressor (Ebata & Moos, 1991), has been linked with poorer health adjustment, including lower pain tolerance (Piira, Taplin, Goodenough, & von Baeyer, 2002) and increased anxiety (Compas et al., 2006) in children and adolescents. Among a sample of nearly 50 children aged 10 to 13 with a range of parent-reported chronic disabilities including cerebral palsy and blindness, decreased use of emotionally reactive coping was demonstrated to be related to higher levels of life satisfaction (Dahlbeck & Lightsey, 2008). Significant links were not demonstrated between adaptive coping and positive psychosocial outcomes; however, replication with larger samples and children with other chronic illness is needed to understand how adaptive coping strategies relate to outcomes for these youth.

In a noteworthy study designed to teach and improve coping strategies in a pediatric population, Grey and colleagues (2005) delivered a group-based family intervention for elementary-aged children diagnosed with Type 1 diabetes and their parents. Specific coping skills taught included problem solving, conflict resolution, stress management, and communication skills. When compared with a control group of children receiving only education about diabetes, results suggested that the children taught specific coping skills reported a somewhat higher level of life satisfaction and family functioning. Researchers hypothesized that teaching coping skills may be beneficial as an intervention for families already experiencing significant psychosocial stressors as a result of child illness, and it may be less helpful as a prevention strategy for those at risk.

Educating Caregivers and Children

Educational programs can provide youth and their caregivers with valuable knowledge regarding an illness, long-term outcomes, and strategies for coping with the condition. These programs can be delivered at a broad prevention level as well as at a targeted level for specific clinical populations already diagnosed with a disease. At a targeted level, education is treatment-focused and centered on improving specific knowledge and self-care of an illness (Waller et al., 2004). Education directed to parents is typically provided when children are younger and treatment adherence is managed primarily by caregivers. Didactic strategies range from basic disease and treatment information via brochures or booklets to small-group trainings focused on a specific care strategy with follow-up support (Huth, Broome, Mussatto, & Morgan, 2003; Warschburger, von Schwerin, Buchholz, & Petermann, 2003).

Education programs have been found to result in knowledge gains and an increased sense of self-efficacy in managing disease or preventing further illness. For instance, parents of postoperative youth provided with a pain education booklet showed significant increases in knowledge of pain management, but child and parent pain ratings only decreased slightly (Huth et al., 2003). Focused intervention provided through an 8-week program designed to teach caregivers specific cognitive-behavioral coping skills showed more promising results in terms of decreasing severity of symptoms at 6-month follow-up (Warschburger et al., 2003). These studies support the notion that brief educational programming for caregivers may lead to knowledge gains, but that targeted interventions focused on skills to be developed are needed to reduce symptoms and improve quality of life.

As children progress toward adolescence, they generally develop greater understanding and the ability to manage their own health and treatment. In response to this developmental change, educational strategies have been tailored specifically for adolescent youth. Interventions vary in intensity, ranging from one to several sessions and most often empha-size the use of self-management strategies (Barlow & Ellard, 2004). Although similar to the didactic strategies used with adult populations, significant emphasis is placed on address-ing peer relationships and reducing the stigma related to disease (Houston, Cunningham, Metcalfe, & Newton, 2000). For instance, Waller and colleagues (2004) proposed an edu-cational group-based intervention for adolescents (mean age of 13 years) with Type 1 diabetes. During feedback sessions to assess treatment acceptability, youth indicated that sessions held in a community setting with a focus on social relation-ships and adherence to their treatment regimen would be most beneficial for them.

Applying Competence Enhancement Strategies to Practice

Research on competence enhancement strategies to prevent future health concerns is limited yet gaining increased atten-tion in the pediatric literature. Consistent with the framework outlined by Kazak and colleagues (2006), our contention is that research and practice should be guided by a prevention framework that capitalizes on the strengths of youth and fami-lies to promote resilience, rather than a model that is based on a "wait-to-fail" approach. Engaging parents and children to focus on assets in their relationships and environment requires a shift in practice, given that existing paradigms focus primar-ily on symptom reduction and problem resolution.

Cognitive-Behavioral Therapy: Enhancing Competencies and Solving Problems

Cognitive-behavioral therapy (CBT) is one of the most widely used, empirically supported approaches to enhance medi-cal and psychosocial outcomes for patients of all ages with chronic illness (Christner, Stewart, & Freeman, 2007; Taylor, 2006; White, 2001). This approach to therapy is based on the theoretical framework that cognition affects behavior, and behavior change can be mediated by restructuring cognitions (Dobson & Dozios, 2001). CBT typically includes a combination of cognitive (i.e., focused on beliefs) and behavioral (i.e., ante-cedent-based or reinforcement-based) strategies for changing behavior (Power & DeRosa, 2012). CBT has been used to assist patients with chronic illness in numerous ways, including reducing pain symptoms, improving adherence, and managing anxiety and stress.

CBT Strategies for Reducing Pain

Recurrent pain is a primary symptom of many pediatric conditions. Although pharmacological treatments can be useful in managing pain, families and providers often prefer nonpharmacological pain management strategies used separately or in combination with medication. An advantage of CBT strategies, such as relaxation training, coping self-statements, and biofeedback, is that they assist children in developing a sense of autonomy in managing their pain (Dahlquist & Nagel, 2009). Gil and colleagues (Gill, Abrams, Phillips, & Williams,1992) found that youth taught to use active coping strategies to manage pain (i.e., relaxation, positive self-talk) experienced less severe pain episodes, reported less stress, and used hospital services at a lower rate than patients who used passive coping strategies (i.e., ignoring, withdrawing from activity). Understanding the family context related to recurrent pain is also an important aspect of treatment. Parents may unintentionally support nonadaptive responses to pain by reinforcing children for playing the "sick role" by avoiding school or other age-appropriate activities. It is important for parents to promote adaptive responses to pain behaviors by reinforcing children for the use of adaptive strategies, such as relaxation skills and positive self-statements (Power & DeRosa, 2012).

CBT Strategies for Improving Adherence

CBT strategies play a significant role in promoting treatment adherence. Recent conceptualizations of adherence have emphasized the importance of collaborative management, involving an ongoing partnership among health providers, school professionals, and the family (Power et al., 2003). As children mature, it is critically important that they become increasingly active in planning and implementing treatment strategies (Sperry, 2009). Motivational interviewing strategies, contingency management approaches, and self-management techniques (e.g., self-monitoring and self-reinforcement) can be useful in improving and sustaining adherence to medical regimens (La Greca & Mackey, 2009).

CBT Strategies for Reducing Anxiety and Posttraumatic Stress

Anxiety is one of the most prevalent psychosocial concerns associated with chronic illness, with prevalence rates nearly twice as high among samples of youth with asthma, cystic fibrosis, or other conditions as compared to the general population (Katon et al., 2007; White, Miller, Smith, & McMahon, 2009). Often, CBT is the indicated treatment for teaching youth coping skills and cognitive restructuring strategies to reduce anxious thoughts and feelings associated with their illness (Warner, Reigada,, Fisher, Saborsky, & Benkov, 2009). Delivered via an individual, group, or family context, therapy combines cognitive approaches (e.g., problem solving) with behavioral strategies (e.g., exposure, role-play; Kendall, 2000). Although numerous empirical investigations support CBT as an effective treatment for anxiety in youth, further research on ways to address anxiety specific to pediatric illness is still needed (Christner et al., 2007).

Posttraumatic stress (PTS) following chronic illness or treatment has received increasing attention following the American Psychiatric Association's recognition of disease as a traumatic event in 1994, with the publication of DSM-IV. Among pediatric samples, PTS has been investigated primarily among survivors of pediatric cancer and their families (Stoppelbein, Greening, & Elkin, 2006). Young survivors may report symptoms of avoidance and reexperiencing of the trauma of the illness, for which CBT may be warranted (Walker, Harris, Baker, Kelly, & Houghton., 1999). Therapy techniques overlap with anxiety treatment, and include cognitive restructuring and relaxation training at a developmentally appropriate level (Stoppelbein et al., 2006).

Overcoming Barriers to Treatment

There are numerous challenges involved in providing interventions in hospital and community settings. One of the most frequent barriers encountered is getting families engaged in treatment and maintaining their involvement. Based on a review of 40 CBT interventions for children with chronic illness provided in the context of research, mean refusal rate for participation in therapy was 37%, and mean attrition rate was 20% at initial follow-up and 32% at extended follow-up (Karlson & Rapoff, 2009). To address this issue, Karlson and Rapoff recommend that providers plan ahead to prevent attrition and use strategies such as emphasizing the personal benefits of intervention, minimizing family burden, providing incentives, and being persistent yet flexible in using engagement strategies. Additional barriers include maintaining adequate integrity through adherence of therapists to manualized therapy protocols and implementation of strategies by patients and their families (Walco, Sterling, Conte, & Engel, 1999). Collaboration between providers and families at the outset and throughout the course of intervention is critically important to promote and sustain engagement and foster high quality implementation of intervention strategies.

Designing Developmentally Appropriate and Culturally Effective Interventions

Designing developmentally appropriate strategies requires that providers take into account the child's cognitive, social/emotional, and physical abilities. In order to accomplish this, it is important to involve children in the intervention planning process in a manner that is appropriate for their developmental level. For young children, this might involve a brief conversation in the context of a family meeting to understand their preferences and perceptions. For older elementary and secondary school children, it may be appropriate to include them in meetings with the family and providers to design plans. Youth may find these meetings to be intimidating so it is important to prepare them for participation and support them in giving voice to their preferences and needs.

Young children typically require active involvement from caregivers in the intervention program. As children mature, they are typically able to take a more active role by using self-management strategies, such as self-monitoring, self-evaluation, self-statements, and self-reinforcement. For elementary age children, nonetheless, it is important for caregivers to identify the appropriate level of adult support needed for successful implementation. To avoid public knowledge of their illness, Burns, Durkins, and Nicholas (2009) advocate for an Internet-based resource to provide information and support to adolescents. Components of this online resource available to youth include fact sheets on health issues, access to a supervised virtual community, the opportunity to role-play scenarios using an online game called *Reach Out Central*, and podcasts containing information on specific topics related to mental health. Burns and colleagues conducted a survey of users to determine the effectiveness of the website. The results indicated that sites such as these often are able to reach adolescents and provide them with information and skills to improve their mental health.

In addition to developmental factors, it is critically important for practitioners to keep in mind and account for cultural factors that may influence the perceptions and understanding of health conditions and the development of interventions. The help-seeking model is highly useful for understanding cultural factors that influence service use. Eiraldi, Mazzuca, Clarke, and Power (2006) adapted a help-seeking model that is applicable to families seeking services for children with ADHD, and this model is relevant to pediatric populations dealing with all types of chronic illness. In the next chapter, this model is described and illustrated. Reference to a help-seeking model can help to inform providers about how to design intervention strategies that are culturally effective. For example, strategies may be needed to build trust between family and provider, promote family engagement in intervention, and support the development of a social network for youth and their families. Practitioners also need to be aware that as children become adolescents, they may become more independent in seeking help. In some cases, adolescents may be negatively influenced by peers who discourage help-seeking behaviors. Similarly, adolescents may be influenced by parents and other family members whose cultural values and lack of trust of mental health professionals may preclude their accessing such services (Barker, Olukoya, & Aggleton, 2005).

Conclusions

Developmental-ecological psychology, social learning theory, and cognitive-behavioral psychology provide the theoretical foundation for the conceptualization of interventions in pediatric school psychology. Interventions are designed to promote child development in systems, understanding that connections among systems are critical in this process. In the context of systems that are properly aligned, behavioral and cognitive-behavioral interventions are more likely to be effective and feasible to implement. The approach to intervention recommended in this chapter emphasizes the use of a prevention framework to foster resilience and prevent the emergence of further impairment.

Discussion Questions

1. Studies have shown that youth's knowledge and understanding of their chronic illness are important factors linked to coping. Discuss how a physician and medical team would work with the child and family to determine what information to share and discuss. What family, cultural, disease-specific, or developmental factors impact the decision of what information is shared with the child?

2. Robert, a fifth-grade student diagnosed with sickle cell disease, has been absent from school for several days each month. In a previous conversation with the school social worker, Robert's parents have explained that he often just doesn't feel up to going to school. Explain how the school team (teachers, support staff, administrators) may work together with Robert's family to address this concern using the steps of the biopsychoeducational model (Grier & Bradley-Klug, 2011). What child and system resources should be considered in the development of interventions for Robert?

3. Explain the rationale for assessing health-related quality of life (HRQOL) among youth with chronic illness. In what ways might information gathered from an HRQOL assessment be used to strengthen competencies for a child or adolescent with a specific illness or disease?

4. Discuss some of the ways in which cognitive-behavioral therapy (CBT) can assist patients in coping with chronic illness. How might developmental factors impact the effectiveness of CBT?

Additional Teaching Aids

PowerPoint slides pertaining to interventions for children with health conditions are included in the attached CD.

References

Alderfer, M. A., Fiese, B. H., Gold, J. I., Cutuli, J. J., Holmbeck, G. N., Goldbeck, L., … Patterson, J. (2008). Evidence-based assessment in pediatric psychology: Family measures. *Journal of Pediatric Psychology, 33,* 1046–1061.

American Psychiatric Association. (2000). *Diagnostic and statistical manual of mental disorders—Text revision* (4th ed.). Washington, DC: Author.

Andrews, N. R., Chaney, J. M., Mullins, L. L., Wagner, J. L., Hommel, K. A., & Jarvis, J. N. (2007). Brief report: Illness intrusiveness and adjustment among Native American and Caucasian parents of children with juvenile rheumatic diseases. *Journal of Pediatric Psychology, 32,* 1263.

Atkins, L. A., Oman, R. F., & Vesely, S. K. (2002). Adolescent tobacco use: The protective effects of developmental assets. *American Journal of Health Promotion, 16*(4), 198–205.

Barakat, L. P., Kunin-Batson, A., & Kazak, A. E. (2003). Child health psychology. In A. Nezu, C. Nezu, & P. Geller (Eds.), *Handbook of psychology: Health psychology* (Vol. 9, pp. 439–464). New York: Wiley.

Barker, G., Olukoya, A., & Aggleton, P. (2005). Young people, social supports, and help-seeking. *International Journal of Adolescent Medicine and Health, 17,* 315–335.

Barlow, J. H., & Ellard, D. R. (2004). Psycho-educational interventions for children with chronic illness, parents, and siblings: An overview of the research evidence base. *Child: Care, Health, & Development, 30*(6), 637–645.

Barry, J. B. A., & von Baeyer, C. L. (1997). Brief cognitive-behavioral group treatment for children's headache. *Clinical Journal of Pain, 13*(3), 215–220.

Bearman, K. J., & LaGreca, A. M. (2002). Assessing friend support of adolescents' diabetes care: The Diabetes Social Support Questionnaire-Friends version. *Journal of Pediatric Psychology, 27,* 417–428.

Bradley-Klug, K. L., Bateman, L., Cunningham, J., Nadeau, J., St. John Walsh, A., Sundman-Wheat, A., & Jeffries, K. (2011). *Youth knowledge and understanding of chronic illness questionnaire.* Unpublished manuscript.

Bradley-Klug, K. L., Grier, E. C., & Ax, E. E. (2006) Chronic illness. In G. Bear & K. Minke (Eds.), *Children's needs* (Vol. 3, pp. 857–869). Bethesda, MD: National Association of School Psychologists.

Brown, R. T., Weiner, L. Kupst, M. J., Brennan, T., Behrman, R., Compas, B. E., … Zeltzer, L (2008). Single parents of children with chronic illness: An understudied phenomenon. *Journal of Pediatric Psychology, 33*(4), 408–421.

Burns, J. M., Durkins, L. A., & Nicholas, J. (2009). Mental health of young people in the United States: What role can the internet play in reducing stigma and promoting help seeking? *Journal of Adolescent Health, 45,* 95–97.

Carels, R. A., Musher-Eizenman, D., Cacciapaglia, H., Pérez-Benítez, C. I., Christie, S., & O'Brien, W. (2004). Psychosocial functioning and physical symptoms in heart failure patients: A within individual approach. *Journal of Psychosomatic Research, 56,* 95–101.

Cramer, J. A., Perrine, K., Devinsky, O., Bryant-Comstock, L., Meador, K., & Hermann, B. (1998), Development and cross-cultural translations of a 31-item quality of life in epilepsy inventory. *Epilepsia, 39,* 81–88.

Christner, R. W., Stewart, J. L., & Freeman, A. (2007). *Handbook of cognitive-behavior group therapy with children and adolescents: Specific settings and presenting problems.* New York: Routledge.

Clay, D. L. (2004). *Helping schoolchildren with chronic health conditions: A practical guide.* New York: Guilford.

Compas, B. E., Boyer, M. C., Stanger, C., Colletti, R. B., Thomsen, A. H., Dufton, L. M., … Cole, D. A. (2006). Latent variable analysis of coping, anxiety/ depression, and somatic symptoms in adolescents with chronic pain. *Journal of Consulting and Clinical Psychology, 74,* 1132–1142.

Dahlbeck, D. T., & Lightsey Jr., O. R. (2008). Predictors of adjustment among children with chronic illness. *Children's Health Care, 37,* 293–315.

Dahlquist, L. M., & Nagel, M. S. (2009). Chronic and recurrent pain. In M. C. Roberts & R. G. Steele (Eds.), *Handbook of pediatric psychology* (4th ed., pp. 153–170). New York: Guilford.

Dobson, K. S., & Dozois, D. J. A. (2001). Historical and philosophical bases of the cognitive-behavioral therapies. In K. S. Dobson (Ed.), *Handbook of cognitive-behavioral therapies* (2nd ed., pp. 3–39). New York: Guilford.

Ebata, A. T., & Moos, R. H. (1991). Coping and adjustment in distressed and healthy adolescents. *Journal of Applied Developmental Psychology, 12,* 33–54.

Eccleston, C., Wastell, S., Crombez, G., & Jordan, A. (2008). Adolescent social development and chronic pain. *European Journal of Pain, 12,* 765–774.

Edwards, O. W., Mumford, V. E., Shillingford, M. A., & Serra-Roldan, R. (2007). Developmental assets: A prevention framework for students considered at risk. *Children and Schools, 29*(3),145–153.

Eiraldi, R. B., Mazzuca, L. B., Clarke, A. T., & Power, T. J. (2006). Service utilization among ethnic minority children with ADHD: A model of help-seeking behavior. *Administration and Policy in Mental Health & Mental Health Services Research, 33,* 607–622.

Eiser, C., & Morse, R. (2001). Quality-of-life measures in chronic diseases of childhood. *Health Technology Assessment, 5,* 1–157.

Elkin, T. D., & Stoppelbein, L. (2008). Evidence-based treatments for children with chronic illness. In R. G. Steele, T. D. Elkin, & M. C. Roberts (Eds.), *Handbook of evidence-based therapies for children and adolescents: Bridging science and practice* (pp. 297–309). New York: Springer.

Garber, J., Van Slyke, D. A., & Walker, L. S. (1998). Concordance between mothers' and children's reports of somatic and emotional symptoms in patients with recurrent abdominal pain or emotional disorders. *Journal of Abnormal Child Psychology, 26,* 381–391.

Gil, K. M., Abrams, M. Phillips, G., & Williams, D. A. (1992). Sickle cell disease pain: 2. Predicting health care use and activity level at 9 months follow-up. *Journal of Consulting and Clinical Psychology, 60,* 267–273.

Goldbeck, L., & Bundschuh, S. (2007). Illness perception in pediatric somatization and asthma: Complaints and health locus of control beliefs. *Child and Adolescent Psychiatry and Mental Health, 1, 1*(5). doi:10.1186/1753-2000-1-5

Grey, M., Whittemore, R., Jaser, S., Ambrosino, J., Lindemann, E., Liberti. L., ... Dziura, J. (2009). Coping skills training for youth with diabetes. *Research in Nursing & Health, 32,* 405–418.

Grier, E. C., & Bradley-Klug, K. L. (2011). A biopsychoeducational model of consultation for students with pediatric health disorders. *Journal of Educational and Psychological Consultation, 21,* 88–105.

Haas, B. K. (1999). A multidisciplinary concept analysis of quality of life. *Western Journal of Nursing Research, 21,* 728–742.

Hamre, B. K., & Pianta, R. C. (2001). Early teacher–child relationships and the trajectory of children's school outcomes through eighth grade. *Child Development, 72,* 625–638.

Hampton, N. (2004). Subjective well-being among people with spinal cord injuries: The role of self-Efficacy, perceived social support, and perceived health. *Rehabilitation Counseling Bulletin, 48*(1), 31–37.

Hartup, W. W. (1996). The company they keep: Friendships and their developmental significance. *Child Development, 67,* 1–13.

Houston, E. C., Cunningham, C. C., Metcalfe, E., & Newton, R. (2000). The information needs and understanding of 5–10 year old children with epilepsy, asthma, or diabetes. *Seizure, 9*(5), 340–343.

Huebner, E. S. (1991). Correlates of life satisfaction in children. *School Psychology Quarterly, 6*(2), 103–111.

Huth, M. M., Broome, M. E., Mussatto, K. A., & Morgan, S. W. (2003). A study of the effectiveness of a pain management education booklet for parents of children having cardiac surgery. *Pain Management Nursing, 4*(1), 31–39.

Juniper, E. F., Guyatt, G. H., Feeny, D. H., & Ferrie, P. J. (1996). Measuring quality of life in children with asthma. *Quality Of Life Research: An International Journal of Quality of Life Aspects of Treatment, Care & Rehabilitation, 5*(1), 35–46.

Karlson, C. W., & Rapoff, M. A. (2009). Attrition in randomized controlled trials for pediatric chronic conditions. *Journal of Pediatric Psychology, 34*(7), 784–793.

Katon, W., Lozano, P., Russo, J., McCauley, E., Richardson, L., & Bush, T. (2007). The prevalence of DSM-IV anxiety and depressive disorders in youth with asthma compared with controls. *Journal of Adolescent Health, 41,* 455–463.

Kazak, A., Kassam-Adams, N., Schneider, S., Zelikovsky, N., Alderfer, M., & Rourke, M. (2006). An integrative model of pediatric medical traumatic stress. *Journal of Pediatric Psychology, 31,* 343–355.

Kazak, A. E., Rourke, M. T., & Navsaria, N. (2009). Families and other systems in pediatric psychology. In M. C. Roberts, R. G. Steele

(Eds.), *Handbook of pediatric psychology* (4th ed.; pp. 656-671). New York: Guilford Press.

Kazak, A. E., Stuber, M. L., Barakat, L. P., & Meeske, K. (1996). Assessing posttraumatic stress related to medical illness and treatment: The Impact of Traumatic Stressors Interview Schedule (ITSIS). *Families, Systems, and Health, 14,* 365–380.

Kendall, P. C. (Ed.) (2000). *Child and adolescent therapy: Cognitive-behavioral procedures.* New York: Guilford.

Klaczynski, P. (2001). Analytic and heuristic processing influences on adolescent reasoning and decision-making. *Child Development, 72*(3), 844–861.

La Greca, A. M. (1990). Social consequences of pediatric conditions: Fertile area for future investigation and intervention? *Journal of Pediatric Psychology, 15,* 285–307.

La Greca, A. M., & Mackey, E. R. (2009). Adherence to pediatric treatment regimens. In M. C. Roberts & R. G. Steele (Eds.), *Handbook of pediatric psychology* (4th ed., pp. 130–152). New York: Guilford.

Landgraf, J. M., Abetz, L., & Ware, J. E. (1996). *The CHQ user's manual.* Boston, MA: The Health Institute, New England Medical Center.

Lerner, R. M., & Benson, P.L. (2003). *Developmental assets and asset-building communities.* New York: Kluwer Academic/Plenum.

Logan, D. E., Catanese, S. P., Coakley, R. M., & Scharff, L. (2007). Chronic pain in the classroom: Teachers' attributions about the causes of chronic pain. *Journal of School Health, 77,* 248–256.

Logan, D. E., & Simons, L. E. (2010). Development of a group intervention to improve school functioning in adolescents with chronic pain and depressive symptoms: A study of feasibility and preliminary efficacy. *Journal of Pediatric Psychology, 35,* 823–836.

Malecki, C. K., & Demaray, M. K. (2002). Measuring perceived social support: Development of the Child and Adolescent Social Support Scale (CASSS). *Psychology in the Schools, 39,* 1–18.

McQuaid, E. L., & Abramson, N. W. (2009). Pediatric asthma. In M. C. Roberts & R. G. Steele (Eds.), *Handbook of pediatric psychology* (4th ed., pp. 254–270). New York: Guilford.

Miller, V. A. (2009). Parent–child collaborative decision-making for management of chronic illness: A qualitative analysis. *Families, Systems, & Health, 27,* 249–266.

Mishel, M. H. (1990). Reconceptualization of the uncertainty in illness theory. *Journal of Nursing Scholarship, 22,* 256–262.

Mullins L. L., & Hartman V. L. (1995). *Children's uncertainty in illness scale.* University of Oklahoma Health Sciences Center; Norman. *Unpublished manuscript.*

Pai, A. L. H., Mullins, L. L., Drotar, D., Burant, C., Wagner, J., & Chaney, J. M. (2007). Exploratory and confirmatory factor analysis of the Child Uncertainty in Illness Scale among children with chronic illness. *Journal of Pediatric Psychology, 32,* 288–296.

Palermo, T. M., Long, A. C., Lewandowski, A. S., Drotar, D., Quittner, A. L., & Walker, L. S. (2008). Evidence-based assessment of health-related quality of life and functional impairment in pediatric psychology. *Journal of Pediatric Psychology, 33*(9), 983–996.

Perkins, D. F., Luster, T., Villarruel, F. A., & Small, S. (1998). An ecological, risk-factor examination of adolescents' sexual activity in three ethnic groups. *Journal of Marriage and the Family, 60,* 660–673.

Pianta, R. C. (1997). Adult–child relationship processes and early schooling. *Early Education and Development, 8,* 11–26.

Piira, T., Taplin, J. E., Goodenough, B., & von Baeyer, C. L. (2002). Cognitive-behavioural predictors of children's tolerance of laboratory-induced pain: Implications for clinical assessment and future directions. *Behaviour Research and Therapy, 40,* 571–584.

Powell, P., & Holmes, C. (2008). Single parents of children with chronic illnesses: An under studied phenomenon [Letter to the editor]. *Journal of Pediatric Psychology, 33,* 797–798.

Power, T. J., DuPaul, G. J., Shapiro, E. S., & Kazak, A. E. (2003). *Promoting children's health: Integrating school, family, and community.* New York: Guilford.

Power, T. J., & DeRosa, B. E. (2012). Interventions for children with chronic health problems: A multisystemic cognitive-behavioral approach. In R. B. Mennuti, A. Freeman, & R. W. Christner (Eds.), *Cognitive-behavioral interventions in educational settings: A handbook for practice* (2nd ed., pp. 531–556). New York: Routledge.

Oman, R. F., Vesely, S. K., & McLeroy, K. R., Harris-Wyatt, V., Aspy, C. B., Rodine, S., & Marshall, L. (2002). Reliability and validity of the Youth Asset Survey (YAS). *Journal of Adolescent Health, 31*(3), 247–255.

Quinn, G. P., Murphy, D., Knapp, C., Stearsman, D., Bradley-Klug, K. L., Sawcyn, K., & Clayman, M. L. (2011). Who decides? Decision making and fertility preservation in teens with cancer: A review of the literature. *Journal of Adolescent Health, 49,* 337–346.

Robinson, K. E., Gerhardt, C. A., Vannatta, K., & Noll, R. B. (2007). Parent and Family factors associated with child adjustment to pediatric cancer. *Journal of Pediatric Psychology, 32*(4), 400–410.

Roth, S., & Cohen, L. J. (1986). Approach, avoidance, and coping with stress. *American Psychologist, 41,* 813–819.

Rudolph, K. D., Dennig, M. D., & Weisz, J. R. (1995). Determinants and consequences of children's coping in the medical setting: Conceptualization, review, and critique. *Psychological Bulletin, 118,* 328–257.

Scales, P. C., Benson, P. L., & Leffert, N. (2000). Contribution of developmental assets to the prediction of thriving among adolescents. *Applied Developmental Science, 4*(1), 27–46.

Scales, P. C., & Leffert, N. (2004). *A synthesis of the scientific research on adolescent development.* Minneapolis, MN: Search Institute.

Seligman, M. E. P. (2002). *Authentic happiness.* New York: Simon & Shuster.

Shaw, S. R., & McCabe, P. C. (2008). Hospital-to-school transition for children with chronic illness: Meeting the new challenges of an evolving health care system. *Psychology in the Schools, 45,* 74–87.

Sheldon, K. M., & Lyubomirsky, S. (2006). Achieving sustainable gains in happiness: Change your actions, not your circumstances. *Journal of Happiness Studies, 7*(1), 55–86.

Sheridan, S. M. & Kratochwill, T. R. (2008). *Conjoint behavioral consultation: Promoting family-school connections and interventions* (2nd ed.). New York: Springer.

Sheridan, S. M., Warnes, E. D., Woods, K. E., Blevins, C. A., Magee, K. L., & Ellis, C. (2009). An exploratory evaluation of conjoint behavioral consultation to promote collaboration among family, school, and pediatric systems: A role for pediatric school psychologists. *Journal of Educational and Psychological Consultation, 19,* 106–129.

Sia, C., Tonniges, T. F., Osterhus, E., & Taba, S. (2004). History of the medical home concept. *Pediatrics, 113,* 1473–1478.

Sperry, L. (2009). *Treatment of chronic medical conditions: Cognitive-behavioral therapy strategies and integrative treatment protocols.* Washington, DC: American Psychological Association.

Starfield, B., Riley, A. W., & Green, B. F. (1999). *Manual for the child health and illness profile: Adolescent edition (CHIP-AE).* Baltimore, MD: Johns Hopkins University Press.

Stoppelbein, L., Greening, L., & Elkin, T. (2006). Risk of posttraumatic stress symptoms: A comparison of child survivors of pediatric cancer and parental bereavement. *Journal of Pediatric Psychology, 31*(4), 367–376.

Suldo, S. M., & Shaffer, E. J. (2008). Looking beyond psychopathology: The Dual-Factor Model of mental health in youth. *School Psychology Review, 37,* 52–68.

Taylor, R. R. (2006). *Cognitive behavioral therapy for chronic illness and disability.* New York: Springer.

Taylor, R. M., Gibson, F., & Franck, L. S. (2008). A concept analysis of health-related quality of life in young people with chronic illness. *Journal of Clinical Nursing, 17,* 1823–1833.

Varni, J. W., Seid, M., & Rode, C. A. (1999). The PedsQL: Measurement model for the pediatric quality of life inventory. *Medical Care, 37*(2), 126–139.

Venning, A., Eliott, J., Wilson, A., & Kettler, L. (2008). Understanding young peoples' experience of chronic illness: A systematic review. *International Journal of Evidence Based Health, 6,* 321–336.

Vrijmoet-Wiersma, C. M. J., van Klink, J. M. M., Kolk, A. M., Koopman, H. M., Ball, L. M., & Egeler, R. M. (2008). Assessment of parental psychological stress in pediatric cancer: A review. *Journal of Pediatric Psychology, 37,* 694–706.

Wade, S. L., Walz, N. C., & Bosques, G. (2009). Pediatric traumatic brain injury and spinal cord injury. In M. C. Roberts & R. G. Steele, *Handbook of pediatric psychology* (4th ed., pp. 334–349). New York: Guilford.

Walco, G. A., Sterling, C. M., Conte, P. M., & Engel, R. G. (1999). Empirically supported treatments in pediatric psychology: Disease-related pain. *Journal of Pediatric Psychology, 24*(2), 155–167.

Waller, H., Eiser, C., Heller, S., Knowles, J., & Price, K. (2004). Adolescents' and their parents' views on the acceptability and design of a new diabetes education programme: A focus group analysis. *Child: Care, Health, & Development, 31*(3), 283–289.

Walker, A., Harris, G., Baker, A., Kelly, D., & Houghton, J. (1999). Post-traumatic stress responses following liver transplantation in older children. *Journal of Child Psychology And Psychiatry, 40*(3), 363–374.

Warner, C., Reigada, L. C., Fisher, P. H., Saborsky, A. L., & Benkov, K. J. (2009). CBT for anxiety and associated somatic complaints in pediatric medical settings: An open pilot study. *Journal of Clinical Psychology in Medical Settings, 16*(2), 169–177.

Warschburger, P., von Schwerin, A. D., Buchholz, H. T., & Petermann, F. (2003). An educational program for parents of asthmatic preschool children: Short- and medium-term effects. *Patient Education and Counseling, 51*(1), 83–91.

White, C. A. (2001). *Cognitive behaviour therapy for chronic medical problems: A guide to assessment and treatment in practice.* New York: Wiley.

White, T., Miller, J., Smith G. L., & McMahon W. M. (2009). Adherence and psychopathology in children and adolescents with cystic fibrosis. *European Child & Adolescent Psychiatry, 18* (2), 96 104.

Zullig, K. J., Valois, R. F., Huebner, E. S., & Drane, J. (2005). Adolescent health-related quality of life and perceived satisfaction with life. *Quality of Life Research, 14*, 1573–1584.

APPENDIX A

Youth Knowledge and Understanding of Chronic Illness Questionnaire

Select sample of questions from Youth Knowledge and Understanding of Chronic Illness Questionnaire

- What do <u>you</u> call your health condition?
- Tell me about _____.
- How do people get the condition that you have?
- How did you get _____?
- How does having _____ make you feel?

- Tell me about the symptoms people can have with
  _____.
  - What does _____ do to the inside of your body?
  - What does _____ do to the outside of your body?
- Who first told you that you had _____? (e.g., parent, pediatrician, etc.)
- How did he/she/they explain it to you?
- What did they tell you about it?
- What part of what they told you made sense to you?
- What was confusing to you about what you were told?
- What sources do you use to get information about _____?
  - Prompt for parent, pediatrician, teacher, specialty doctor, Internet, counselor/psychologist, etc.
  - Where do you get <u>most</u> information about _____?
- Other than your parents (if your parents do know), do other people know you have _____?
- Do <u>you</u> tell people outside of your family that you have _____?
  - If yes, who do you tell?
  - When you do tell, how do you explain it to them?
  - What would be the most important things for them to know?
- How does having _____ affect your day-to-day life?
- Are there things that are different for you than for other kids?
- How does _____ impact your learning?
  - Attendance?
  - Homework completion?
  - Memory?
- How does _____ impact your friendships?
- How are you being treated for _____?
  - Do you have to take any medications for _____?
  - What other types of treatments do you have?

Three

Interventions in Pediatric School Psychology

Applications of a Multisystemic Model

A major role of the expert in pediatric school psychology is to design, implement, and evaluate intervention strategies when children with health conditions experience functional impairments in school settings, including academic, social, and behavioral problems. As a rule, empirical evidence is required to guide intervention decisions with regard to determining whether intervention is needed, when to intervene, what the targets of treatment will be, who ought to be involved in the process, what strategies to use, how to monitor progress, and how to evaluate outcomes. Intervention strategies can be applied by psychologists in multiple settings, including hospital, pediatric primary care, and school.

This chapter describes hallmarks of intervention based upon fundamental principles of pediatric school psychology discussed in the previous two chapters. In addition, the chapter describes empirical methods useful in designing interventions, monitoring progress, and evaluating outcomes; key components of a multisystemic model of intervention; and examples of how interventions based on a multisystemic model can be applied in multiple settings, including hospital, primary care, and school settings.

Foundation for Intervention

Intervention approaches used in pediatric school psychology are grounded in numerous models that are complementary to one another. These models include developmental-ecological, partnership, help-seeking, cognitive-behavioral, and behavioral.

Developmental-Ecological Model

As indicated in chapter 2, pediatric school psychology is firmly rooted in the developmental-ecological model. This model emphasizes the critical importance of relationships and contexts for the successful development of the person (Kazak, Rourke, & Navsaria, 2009). According to this framework, a primary goal of intervention is to strengthen relationships within systems (e.g., family, school, health system) and to foster partnerships between systems. In addition, this model highlights the importance of considering policy, cultural, and economic issues that have an effect on system functioning. A developmental-ecological model often supports the need for professionals to assume an advocacy role to address policy issues at a local, state, and national level that might be contributing to barriers to care (e.g., policies governing the health insurance industry) or creating an unjust situation for a child or family (e.g., disparities in health care as a function of the socioeconomic or minority status of the family; Power, Eiraldi, Clarke, Mazzuca, & Krain, 2005).

Partnership Model

Intervention that is based in pediatric school psychology involves key participants (e.g., child, parents or caregivers, school professionals, health professionals) as essential partners in every phase of the treatment process (De Civita & Dobkin, 2004). The essence of partnership is that there is a collaborative, nonhierarchical relationship among parties that have the ability to influence the intervention process. Partnership promotes the empowerment of all participants involved in the collaboration so that each party—doctor, teacher, family—has a strong voice in determining the goals, strategies, and roles of participants in the process (Nastasi, Moore, & Varjas, 2004). At the same time, a partnership model acknowledges the unique and complementary expertise of each participant and the authority of each party in his or her own domain. For example, physicians are experts in diagnosing and treating health conditions; teachers are experts in academic instruction; and parents are experts in their own child's developmental strengths and limitations. Further, a partnership model accounts for the likelihood that effective health care requires adaptation over the course of time and that the process of collaboration needs to be dynamic and responsive to evolving needs and circumstances.

Help-Seeking Model

Intervention can only be effective if participants are ready to seek help and become actively engaged in the process. Four stages of help seeking have been identified: (a) problem recognition, (b) decision to seek help, (c) service selection, and (d) intervention implementation (Andersen, 1995). Individuals typically advance through the stages in a sequential manner. For example, they typically will not be ready to select services and intervention strategies until they accept that there is a problem and they need help. This model was originally developed to explain adult behavior related to help seeking for health services, but it has subsequently been adapted for youth and specifically families coping with health conditions (Eiraldi, Mazzuca, Clarke, & Power, 2006). Numerous factors have an influence on the ability of families to successfully advance through each stage of the help-seeking process; examples are included in Table 3.1. This model can be useful in examining systems of service delivery, identifying potential barriers to service use, and developing strategies to overcome barriers and promote greater use of services. Further, the model has implications for the delivery of services at the individual family level and may be useful in developing strategies to promote intervention engagement.

Cognitive-Behavioral Model

Interventions that incorporate components designed to improve one's understanding of an illness or its treatment, change perceptions of symptoms, or alter one's approach to problem solving have been used with great success in treating health conditions and mental health disorders (Power & Werba, 2006). Interventions that provide education to children and families to increase knowledge and improve coping strategies are commonly used in pediatric psychology. In fact, education about an illness and its management is an element of many cognitive-behavioral interventions for children's health conditions. A core element of many cognitive-behavioral interventions is

Table 3.1   Stages of the Help-Seeking Model and Factors Contributing
to Progression at Each Stage

Stage of Help Seeking	Factors Contributing to Progression
Stage I: Problem Recognition	Functional impairment Perceived family burden Parent–child relationship Parental psychopathology Marital conflict
Stage II: Decision to Seek Help	Stigma of mental health care Family trust in health system Acculturation Health locus of control Knowledge of disorder
Stage III: Service Selection	Accessibility of services Social and economic resources of family Social support Treatment acceptability Cultural sensitivity of clinical staff
Stage IV: Service Utilization	Staff support in overcoming barriers Quality of care Coordination of services Demands of treatment Side effects

Note: Information in this table was derived in part from Eiraldi et al. (2006) and Power et al. (2005).

the identification and reframing of cognitive distortions linked
to maladaptive patterns of behavior (e.g., Rofey et al., 2008).
In addition, cognitive-behavioral interventions often include a
focus on problem solving strategies, such as problem identification, generation of alternative solutions, selection of the most
appropriate option, implementation, and evaluation (e.g., Seid,
Varni, Gidwani, Gelhard, & Slymen, 2010).

Behavioral Model

Interventions based on principles of behavioral psychology
have been demonstrated repeatedly to be effective in treating
health and mental health conditions. Behavioral interventions
generally are designed to address both the antecedents and
consequences of behavior (Steege & Watson, 2009). Antecedents include environmental circumstances that are proximal
and distal to behaviors targeted for change. Proximal circumstances occur close in time to the target behavior and serve as
triggers for the behavior. For example, being in a room where

there is a television may trigger actions by the child that lead to the avoidance of homework behaviors. Distal circumstances refer to setting events that may set the stage for one or more proximal events. As an example, performing homework after school when no parents are available in the home to provide supervision may be setting events or distal circumstances resulting in the avoidance of work. Behavioral interventions also address the consequences of behavior, including those that increase the likelihood of behavior occurring (positive and negative reinforcement) and those that decrease the likelihood of behavior (punishment). Examples of positive reinforcement are providing adult or peer attention and offering tangible rewards, such as privileges and desired objects, contingent on the occurrence of targeted behaviors. As an example, token reinforcement systems have been used successfully to increase adherence with exercise regimens recommended for children with cystic fibrosis (Bernard, Cohen, & Moffett, 2009). Negative reinforcement is provided by terminating an aversive situation (e.g., homework) and serves as the basis for avoidant behavior. Punishment can be provided in numerous ways (e.g., corrective feedback, privilege removal) and can be highly effective and acceptable to intervention participants if provided in the context of a system offering primarily positive reinforcement (Power, Karustis, & Habboushe, 2001).

Empirical Basis for Intervention Decision Making

Providing intervention in an effective manner requires the collection and examination of data throughout the process. The following is a brief description of assessment approaches that can be useful in shaping intervention design, implementation, modification, and evaluation. Table 3.2 describes some of the strengths and limitations of each approach.

Intervention Design

Numerous approaches to assessment are useful in designing interventions for children and youth coping with health conditions. Each approach has strengths and limitations and generally speaking the methods are complementary to one another.

Categorical Assessment. Categorical methods of assessment are based on the medical model and are designed to answer

Table 3.2 Examples of Strengths and Limitations of Assessment
Paradigms Useful in Intervention Planning

Paradigm	Strengths	Limitations
Categorical	Identifies diagnostic status that can point to potential evidence-based treatments	Fails to account for gender and age of child
	Identifies comorbid conditions that may serve as moderators of treatment effect	Limited utility for tailoring interventions to the specific needs of the child
Dimensional	Assesses severity in relation to gender and age of child	Fails to account for important contextual factors
	Useful in obtaining information from multiple informants	Limited utility for tailoring interventions to the specific needs of the child
Functional Behavioral	Accounts for important contextual variables	Limited utility for addressing relational and cultural factors
	Useful for tailoring interventions to address the specific circumstances of the child	Limited utility for addressing child stress, anxiety, depression, and pain
Social-Cognitive	Identifies beliefs that are linked to emotions and behaviors	Limited utility for addressing relational and cultural factors
	Useful in addressing child stress, anxiety, depression, and pain	Fails to account for contextual factors that may prompt or reinforce behavioral responses
Ecological	Accounts for important contextual variables	Fails to account for important child psychological factors
	Focuses on relational processes within and between systems	Limited in understanding mechanisms that trigger and maintain maladaptive behaviors

Note: Information in this table was derived in part from Power et al. (2003).

questions about whether a disorder exists. For example,
structured and semistructured diagnostic interviews, such
as the *Schedule for Affective Disorders and Schizophrenia
for School Age Children—Present State—DSM IV Version
(K-SADS-P IVR*; Ambrosini, 2000) and the *Anxiety Disorders
Interview Schedule for Children for DSM-IV* (Silverman &
Albano, 1996), are commonly used to determine whether one
or more mental health disorders are present. These methods
have been refined so that they have reasonably strong levels
of interclinician agreement and they are useful in identifying
disorders and evidence-based methods for treating specific

conditions. They are also helpful in identifying comorbid conditions that may be helpful in determining response to intervention (Multimodal Treatment Study of ADHD Cooperative Group, 1999). Limitations are that they identify the child as the source of the problem; they fail to account for gradations in disorder severity, and they have little utility in designing specific components of treatment (Power & Eiraldi, 2000).

Dimensional Assessment. Dimensional approaches provide an assessment of functioning along a continuum ranging from adaptive to nonadaptive with no definitive cut-point for determining the presence of disorder. Data derived from these methods generally are compared to normative information about children of similar gender and age. Dimensions assessed by these methods have been identified by empirical, theoretical, or combined approaches (Achenbach & Rescorla, 2001). Rating scales, including self-reports and other informant reports, are the procedures typically used to conduct dimensional assessments. These methods have been used to assess narrow bands of functioning, such as pain severity or duration, and level of functional impairment associated with a disorder, as well as broad bands of functioning, such as dimensions of internalizing and externalizing functioning. These approaches generally have strong psychometric properties and are useful in assessing severity of disorders or impairments. They are limited with regard to assessing contextual factors that may contribute to presenting problems and planning components of intervention (Power & Eiraldi, 2000).

Functional Behavioral Assessment. This type of assessment is based on principles of applied behavior analysis and is designed to identify functions of behavior that can be used to generate hypotheses useful in treatment design (Steege & Watson, 2009). The most common functions of behavior are: (a) avoid or escape task demands, (b) obtain attention from adults or peers, (c) obtain tangible rewards, or (d) obtain stimulation or produce arousal. Although many behaviors can be linked to a single function, most behaviors that are difficult to change have two or more functions. Knowing the function(s) of behavior is very helpful in designing interventions. For example, if the primary function of maladaptive behavior is avoidance, an intervention approach that includes strategies that offer a choice of tasks, decrease the burden of a task (perhaps by providing break periods), and increase the reinforcement obtained by performing the task generally are effective (DuPaul & Ervin, 1996). Despite its utility for treatment planning, this approach is limited in that it typically does not focus on broad contextual factors, such as school climate and relationship issues within and between systems.

Social-Cognitive Assessment.   Child and parent beliefs about health conditions and their treatment can have a significant effect on the course of intervention. It can be useful to understand these beliefs in designing cognitive-behavioral components of intervention. Examples of health-related beliefs are health locus of control and self-efficacy. Locus of control refers to the belief that following a set of actions will lead to an improvement in health status. Research has shown that an external locus of control or belief that little can be done to improve health status is associated with greater distress in reaction to an illness and poorer child outcomes (Barakat, Lutz, Nicolaou, & Lash, 2005). Self-efficacy refers to a person's belief about his or her ability to improve health status by following a course of action. It has been shown that a strong sense of self-efficacy with regard to accessing and working with health providers is predictive of greater service use and engagement in intervention (Janicke & Finney, 2003). The Parent Health Locus of Control Scale is an example of a measure used to assess locus of control with regard to a parent's belief about the mutability of health outcomes (DeVellis et al., 1993). The Self-Efficacy for Accessing Physician Assistance Scale has been used to assess parents' perceptions of their ability to access their child's physician and enlist the assistance of the provider (Janicke & Finney, 2003). Although these measures may have some value with regard to treatment planning, generally they have been developed for research purposes and their utility for clinical practice needs to be demonstrated.

Ecological Assessment.   Understanding contextual and relational variables within and across systems is important for the design of comprehensive intervention plans. Within the family, it is critical for the child to have a strong attachment with caregivers. The strength of the relationship between caregivers in the family and their ability to work effectively in their role as parents also has an effect on the developing child. Numerous measures of family functioning have been

developed, including measures of the parent–child relationship (e.g., Parent–Child Relationship Questionnaire; Furman & Giverson, 1995), the marital relationship (e.g., Dyadic
Adjustment Scale; Spanier, 1976), and the parenting partnership (e.g., Parenting Alliance Inventory; Abidin & Brunner,
1995). With regard to the school system, contextual and relational variables also have a strong effect on educational performance. In particular, classroom climate and the quality of
the teacher–student relationship are important to examine. A
useful measure of classroom climate is the Classroom Assessment Scoring System, a direct observation technique (Pianta,
La Paro, & Hamre, 2008), and a helpful tool for assessing the
quality of the student–teacher relationship is the Student–
Teacher Relationship Scale (Pianta, 2002).

Research related to understanding intersystem connections
is less developed. Measures of trust may be helpful in understanding the relationship between family and health providers (Hall, Camacho, Dugan, & Balkrishnan, 2002), and the
Parent–Teacher Involvement Questionnaire may have utility
in assessing quality of the home–school relationship (Kohl,
Lengua, McMahon, & Conduct Problems Prevention Research
Group, 2000). Measures of ecological variables have been
developed primarily for research purposes and their clinical
utility requires further investigation.

Assessment of Intervention Integrity

Intervention integrity or fidelity refers to the extent to which
a set of treatment strategies is implemented as designed.
Assessing integrity is a method for checking whether the
intervention has been applied in a valid manner, so that it
is reasonable to hypothesize that changes occurring during
the course of intervention are attributable to key components
and not to other aspects of the treatment. Although the relationship between intervention integrity and outcomes is not
straightforward, research generally indicates that higher
levels of integrity are associated with more favorable outcomes (Durlak & DuPre, 2008). The assessment of integrity
clearly is critical for evaluating treatment validity and promoting treatment effectiveness, but intervention studies often
fail to assess integrity or do so in a highly inadequate manner
(Perepletchikova, Treat, & Kazdin, 2007). Further, the assessment of integrity is rarely conducted in practice settings.

Integrity is usually assessed by examining the extent to which the steps of intervention have been implemented by the clinician. Although the assessment of the content of intervention delivery is important, there are other dimensions of intervention implementation that are also critical to assess. At this point, it is widely recognized that integrity is a multidimensional construct that incorporates the process of implementation as well as its content. Dane and Schneider (1998) identified five distinct dimensions of integrity: (a) adherence, which refers to the extent to which the steps of the intervention are implemented as intended; (b) exposure, referring to the amount of treatment received; (c) program differentiation, which is the inclusion of unique aspects of the intervention and exclusion of elements of other treatments; (d) quality, which refers to the effectiveness of intervention delivery; and (e) participant responsiveness, which is the level of participant engagement in intervention. In conceptualizing integrity, it is useful to differentiate dimensions related to how intervention is delivered (e.g., clinician adherence to treatment protocols and quality of implementation) from how intervention is received (e.g., dosage received, participant responsiveness, and participant enactment of treatment recommendations; Schulte, Easton, & Parker, 2009). Treatment acceptability, which refers to participants' views about the appropriateness and reasonableness of an intervention program, is a dimension of participant engagement that has been found to have substantial utility in research and practice (Krain, Kendall, & Power, 2005).

Table 3.3 presents a range of strategies for assessing dimensions of integrity, including aspects of intervention delivery and participant engagement. Useful information regarding integrity can be collected in a variety of ways, including attendance data, dosage data (minutes in clinical sessions), clinician self-report ratings, participant self-reports, clinician ratings of participants, direct observations of clinician and participant behavior, and review of permanent products generated during the course of treatment (e.g., child and parent diaries, teacher ratings on daily report cards; Sheridan, Swanger-Gagne, Welch, Kwon, & Garbacz, 2009).

Progress Monitoring

Monitoring progress during the course of intervention is important because it yields ongoing information about the

Table 3.3 Methods for Assessing Dimensions of Clinician Integrity
and Participant Engagement

Dimension of Integrity/ Engagement	Method of Assessment
Clinician adherence	Self-reports using integrity checklists
	External ratings using integrity checklists based on live, video, or audio observations
Clinician competence	External ratings of quality of implementation based on live, video, or audio observations
	Child and parent ratings of therapeutic alliance
Program differentiation	External ratings of the occurrence of prohibited components based on live, video, or audio observations
Participant exposure	Attendance at face-to-face sessions; frequency of telephone contact with clinician
	Amount of time spent in face-to-face sessions and on the telephone with clinician
Participant adherence	Percent and quality of homework assignments completed
Participant responsiveness	External ratings of participation in face-to-face sessions based on live, video, or audio observations
	Self-reports using measures of treatment acceptability

Note: Information in this table was derived in part from Jones, Clarke, and Power (2008).

effectiveness of intervention and the need for modifications,
and in some cases can provide information about rate of
change. Hallmarks of effective progress monitoring tools are
that they are psychometrically reliable and valid, brief and
efficient to use, suitable for repeated administration, and
adaptable for use with a wide range of target behaviors and
intervention programs (Chafouleas, Volpe, Gresham, & Cook,
2010).

    There have been substantial advances in the development
of tools to track progress in academic functioning, especially
with regard to reading. This approach has been referred to as
curriculum-based measurement. Recently, there has been an
increased focus on developing progress monitoring tools for
tracking changes in behavior and social functioning. Although
direct observation methods and rating scales are often used
to assess behavioral and social functioning, these tools typically are not efficient to use and not amenable to repeated use
for progress monitoring. To address this gap in research and

practice, researchers have been investigating brief rating scales or direct behavior ratings (DBRs) to examine their validity and utility for use in progress monitoring of behavioral and social functioning.

Several approaches have been used to develop DBRs. One method is to ask intervention participants (e.g., children, parents, teachers) to select items for inclusion in the DBR. A second approach is for the clinician to administer a standard rating scale at baseline and select those items that are rated as most problematic by informants. A third approach is to examine the factor coefficients derived from factor analyses of a standardized behavioral measure and to select a subset of items with the highest loadings on one or more relevant dimensions. The fourth approach that has been investigated is to administer a standardized rating scale and to select those items that have been demonstrated to be most sensitive to change over time in response to intervention (Volpe & Gadow, 2010). The advantage of the first two approaches is that they are tailored to the problems and concerns of a specific child and therefore may have a high level of social validity for intervention participants. However, because these approaches are designed to be individualized, they are not adaptable for use with a broad range of children with varying target behaviors and intervention programs. There are clear advantages to developing general outcome measures that are adaptable for multiple purposes. The third and fourth approaches have utility for the development of generic progress monitoring measures and increasingly researchers are working on validating these types of approaches (e.g., Gresham et al., 2010).

Outcome Assessment

Whereas progress monitoring is useful for ongoing formative assessment of intervention effects, comprehensive outcome assessment is necessary for in-depth evaluation of effectiveness. Outcome assessment generally consists of the evaluation of effects across multiple domains of functioning. For example, the evaluation of interventions to manage pain might include assessment across the domains of perceived pain intensity, frequency, and duration, functional impairments in the family, school, and social interaction, utilization of medical services, and school absences (Robins, Smith, Glutting, & Bishop, 2005). As another example, an examination of interventions to address the distress experienced by the parents of children diagnosed with cancer might include an evaluation of the domains of acute and posttraumatic stress, state and trait anxiety, and functional impairment (Stehl et al., 2009).

If possible, multiple methods of assessment ought to be used in assessing each outcome domain, given the limitations of single methods of assessment. For example, the assessment of behaviors related to the domain of adherence might include self-reports, diaries, provider ratings, drug assays, pill counts, and electronic monitoring devices (La Greca & Mackey, 2009). Further, the assessment of behaviors related to attention-deficit/hyperactivity disorder (ADHD) might include parent reports, teacher reports, direct observations of behavior, and evaluation of work samples to examine productivity and efficiency (DuPaul & Stoner, 2004).

Multisystemic Intervention

Interventions based in pediatric school psychology are intrinsically multisystemic; that is, they involve multiple systems and typically professionals from multiple disciplines. Relational elements of treatment are critical in a multisystemic approach; there is a strong emphasis on strengthening relationships within and between systems. The process of intervention has numerous steps or phases. Although these steps are presented sequentially below, it is important to note that they unfold in a parallel, often recursive manner. For example, it is important to promote participant engagement from the outset, but it is critical to maintain the use of engagement strategies throughout the course and especially during periods of transition during which families are likely to become disengaged (e.g., shortly after hospitalization and reentry into the community; beginning of a new school year).

Step 1: Promote Engagement

Intervention effectiveness depends in part on the extent to which participants are actively engaged in the process. The participants in treatment include the child, parents, health providers, school professionals, and often other family members and professionals in the community. Engagement refers to participant attendance at sessions, active involvement in sessions, and adherence to recommendations or homework tasks after sessions.

Numerous strategies have been developed to promote family engagement in intervention. Telephone contacts with families have been demonstrated repeatedly to be effective in improving treatment initiation and maintenance. In particular, telephone contacts conducted by professional as opposed to administrative staff and phone conversations that affirm parents' help-seeking efforts and link parental concerns with the intervention process have been shown to be effective (McKay & Bannon, 2004).

An extensive body of research has demonstrated the effectiveness of motivational interviewing strategies in promoting engagement and preparing participants for the process of change (Miller & Rollnick, 2002). Motivational interviewing includes multiple components, such as expressing empathy for participants, prompting participants to describe their efforts to change, affirming efforts to change, not confronting participants when there is resistance, identifying barriers to change, and engaging in problem solving to address barriers (Dishion & Stormshak, 2007).

Another potentially useful strategy is enlisting "community partners" or parent advocates to facilitate engagement. Community partners are professionals or paraprofessionals who have expertise related to the health, mental health, and education of children, and who have deep knowledge of the cultural backgrounds of families receiving services. Community partners serve as cultural brokers who assist providers in making the process of intervention meaningful for families and ensuring that the needs of parents are articulated and addressed (Power, Dowrick, Ginsburg-Block, & Manz, 2004).

Although research on engagement typically has focused on children and parents, it is important for other participants in the treatment process to become invested and maintain their involvement throughout the process. Health providers and teachers can vary in their level of investment in the process of intervention, which may have an effect on treatment effectiveness. Strategies to enlist and maintain the investment of health and educational professionals may be needed to promote the process of change (Power et al., 2009)

Step 2: Strengthen Systems

Children's ability to cope successfully with illness depends in large measure on the extent to which major systems in their lives are adaptable and responsive to their needs. For families, one challenge is to maintain a strong parent–child relationship at the onset and throughout the course of the illness. If the parent–child relationship has been conflictual at the time of illness onset, the child is at risk for unsuccessful coping. In these cases, it is important to work on gradually strengthening this attachment. Another challenge for families following a period of heightened parental involvement during the initial stages of coping is to promote higher levels of child autonomy once the illness begins to stabilize and the child seeks to become reinvolved in school and community activities (Kazak et al., 2009). Some families need assistance in providing support to children in a manner that promotes individuation and successful coping in the community. Further, given the importance of family rituals in promoting adaptation to illness, clinicians may assist families in developing or maintaining routines throughout the process of coping (Fiese & Wamboldt, 2000).

The strength of the clinical system and health care team is clearly important to promote successful coping. Systems that are well organized and teams that are well coordinated and communicate effectively are able to provide children and families with an integrated, high quality patient care experience. Of course, every clinical system has areas in need of improvement. It is essential for professional teams to commit to a process of quality improvement to address systems issues that can enhance the quality of patient care. The Plan-Do-Study-Act (PDSA) methodology is often used to guide the process of quality improvement. *Plan* refers to identifying objectives, strategies to achieve each objective, and a metric to track change; *Do* involves implementation of the plan, starting on a small scale; *Study* is the ongoing monitoring of progress and periodic evaluation of outcomes; and *Act* involves data-based decisions to continue implementing strategies, modifying strategies, or terminating the change process (Moen, Nolan, & Provost, 1999). The PDSA methodology is now being commonly used to inform and guide the process of quality improvement in pediatric settings (e.g., Lynch-Jordan et al., 2010).

School factors also have a strong influence on adaptation to illness. These variables include responsiveness of the school to the culture of the community, principal support of teacher needs, and faculty support of one another. The nature of the classroom climate, in particular the quality of the teacher–student relationship, has been shown to have a strong effect on students' academic and social success (Pianta, 1999). Children coping with medical conditions often present unique challenges to teachers that may serve as barriers to an affirming and encouraging teacher–student relationship (Logan, Simons, & Kaczynski, 2009). It is necessary but often not sufficient to provide education to teachers about medical illness and school interventions to assist children. Teachers often require ongoing consultation to ensure a strong teacher–student relationship and to modify educational approaches so as to be responsive to student needs.

Step 3: Strengthen Connections Across Systems

Connecting systems and strengthening partnerships across systems is fundamental to a multisystemic approach to care. For children and youth coping with health conditions, the family, health system, and school are almost always involved in providing care and promoting successful adaptation. Each party in the relationship (family, health providers, school professionals) shares ownership and responsibility for promoting health. Within the context of a partnership framework, all parties have critical roles to serve and are responsible for resolving problems and overcoming barriers when they arise. Problems related to nonadherence are viewed as system breakdowns and not patient or family failures; the solution is to clarify roles and responsibilities and to identify resources to improve implementation of interventions across systems (Power, DuPaul, Shapiro, & Kazak, 2003).

The relationship between the family and health system is vital. The adoption of a family-centered approach to care fosters the empowerment of families to be full partners in the illness management process. The care team works to create a climate that promotes family trust and enables families to feel confident that they can get access to the information, resources, and support needed for their child (Seid, Opipari-Arrigan, & Sobo, 2009). In the context of primary care, the medical home model has been developed to promote strong relationships between the health team and families, as well as to coordinate communications and promote integration of care across systems and providers. Even in practices using this model, families, especially those of low income background or minority status, often face challenges in accessing services and becoming connected with providers. To address this need, interventions have been developed to foster strong relationships between primary care providers and families and to promote family engagement in services (see Wissow et al., 2008).

The quality of the connection between family and school can make a substantial difference to the child's educational experience. Strong relationships are those in which parents and teachers share ownership and responsibility for the child's education. Teachers recognize the critical value of parents in the educational process; they continually look for ways to assist parents in their efforts to promote the child's development and they regularly reach out to parents to invite them to become involved in the child's schooling (Christenson & Sheridan, 2001). Parents acknowledge the vital role that teachers serve in promoting their child's development; parents look for ways to affirm and build the relationship between the teacher and their child, understanding that the teacher–student relationship is essential for academic and social success in school. Within the context of a strong working alliance between family and school, parents and teachers are well positioned to engage in a problem-solving process to address challenges when they arise in the school setting (Sheridan & Kratochwill, 2008).

Although the relationship between the health system and school is often critical for educational success, this connection is typically poorly developed. Numerous factors serve as barriers to effective communication between health and school systems, including fiscal constraints that limit the amount of time physicians can devote to school communications; differences in the theoretical orientations of health and school professionals that may contribute to discrepant perspectives about the nature of children's problems and how to resolve them; laws protecting privacy that restrict the exchange of information across institutions; and the absence of a natural mechanism to coordinate communications between systems (Guevara et al., 2005; Leslie, Weckerly, Plemmons, Landsverk, & Eastman, 2004). A consequence of the lack of coordination between the health and school systems is that caregivers generally are placed in the untenable position of having to coordinate communications between health and school professionals.

Step 4: Strengthen Resources and Solve Problems

Once the foundation for change has been established by promoting participant engagement and strengthening systems and interconnections, the stage is set for problem solving. Effective problem solving involves not only strategies to reduce deficits but also approaches to promote strengths and protect against risks. We have found the conjoint behavioral consultation (CBC) model to be especially useful in solving problems in the context of a multisystemic approach to intervention (Sheridan & Kratochwill, 2008). Although this model was developed originally to guide problem solving in the context of a family–school partnership, it has been adapted for use across multiple systems, including the health system (Sheridan et al., 2009). The CBC model includes four major steps, which are described below.

Identify Strengths and Problems. A useful way to begin the process of problem solving is to identify and acknowledge strengths in the family, school, and health systems as well as the child. For example, it is useful for clinicians to affirm parents, teachers, and health providers for their commitment to the child, their persistent efforts to help the child, and their willingness to work together to resolve the child's difficulties. Also, it is important to acknowledge the strengths of the child, such as the student's concern about emerging problems, motivation to succeed, and previous efforts to overcome challenges. Within a context in which all parties are affirmed, the identification of problems can be productive and not discouraging. Clinicians facilitating the collaboration look for common ground among family, school, health providers, that is, problems of mutual concern to all stakeholders. Further, they seek to identify a problem for which there is a reasonable chance of succeeding at the outset. Finally, they assist in defining the problem in clear, specific terms that can be translated readily into measurable objectives.

Analyze the Problem and Design the Intervention. Earlier in this chapter, we described numerous assessment approaches (i.e., categorical, dimensional, functional behavioral, social-cognitive, and ecological) that are useful in analyzing problems, examining resources, and designing interventions. Given the limitations inherent in each approach, a combination of strategies is typically the best course of action. Consistent with a partnership model, it is important for all participants in the intervention process to contribute information about the problem and resources for addressing it, review assessment data, and use the data to inform treatment planning. The intervention plan emerges through a dialogic process in which there is careful consideration of evidence-based practices as well as participants' views about what is reasonable and appropriate.

Implement the Intervention. It is essential for there to be collaboration among all parties to define each other's roles in a straightforward manner so that participants understand the components of the intervention they are to implement. Given the multiple systems and participants involved in the process, it is challenging to coordinate communications to ensure that participants are clear about their roles and the steps to implement. At times, a participant in the process may be expected to serve a role that he or she is not ready to perform. In these cases, it is important to offer training and support to enable the person to perform capably. In addition, the success of intervention depends upon the integrity with which strategies are implemented. As described earlier in this chapter, integrity refers not only to the content of treatment but also to the quality by which it is implemented. An important step of intervention is to devise methods for monitoring the content and quality of implementation and provide ongoing feedback to participants to maintain a reasonably high level of integrity.

Evaluate the Intervention. The evaluation of an intervention involves all participants and includes an assessment of social validity, feasibility, and outcomes. Social validity refers to the perceived significance of the treatment goals, the acceptability of the methods of treatment, and the clinical utility of the effects. Feasibility involves an assessment of perceived benefits versus costs to determine whether it is worthwhile to maintain treatment. Examination of outcomes involves assessment of domains corresponding to the goals of treatment as delineated by the treatment team. Evaluation has both formative and summative elements. Formative evaluation uses progress monitoring strategies described previously, which enable the treatment team to make midcourse corrections as needed. Summative evaluation involves multimethod assessment of the domains of treatment and is used to inform the team whether to maintain or fade the intervention, discontinue the treatment, or shift to a more intensive level of care. Increasingly in school and health settings, evaluation is conducted in the context of a response to intervention paradigm whereby outcomes of treatment using a relatively nonintensive approach to care are used to determine whether intervention at a higher level of intensity is needed (Glover & DiPerna, 2007; Kazak et al., 2006). A case study illustrating interventions for children with health conditions is included in the attached CD.

Applications in Diverse Settings

Interventions to improve the educational functioning of children with health conditions can be applied in multiple contexts. These settings include hospitals, primary care practices, and schools.

Applications in the Hospital

A major purpose of hospitalization for children is to overcome illness and promote successful reintegration back into the community, which typically includes school. The process of preparing children for school reintegration begins as soon as the medical condition has been stabilized. Factors that can have an effect on adaptation back into the school setting include (a) effects of the illness on central nervous system functioning that may have an impact on attention, memory, learning, and social perception; (b) change in physical appearance that could result in child self-perceptions of unattractiveness and anxiety in social situations; (c) impairment in motor skills that could have an effect on the child's mobility, ability to exercise, and ability to be productive in the classroom; (d) symptoms of posttraumatic stress that may contribute to emotional distress and have an effect on attention and learning in school; and (e) the experience of pain that can have an effect on concentration and persistence, which may become exacerbated in school situations when children are separated from parents, face pressure to succeed on tests, and must cope with the challenges of interacting with many of their peers (Power & Werba, 2006).

Programs to assist hospitalized children with reintegration back into school have focused on skill building (e.g., cognitive retraining, coping skills training, social skills training), teacher education, and peer education. Although each of these approaches may have some beneficial effects, comprehensive programs that include multiple components have demonstrated the most promise (Prevatt, Heffer, & Lowe, 2000). These approaches consist of elements that are applied prior to reentry (i.e., child training, family support, teacher education); components that are implemented at the beginning of the transition back into school (i.e., family–school collaboration, teacher consultation, and peer education), and follow-up services to modify strategies and ensure effective adaption over the long term (Madan-Swain, Katz, & LaGory, 2004).

Critical to the successful reintegration of children into school is the strengthening of the family and school systems and the formation of strong partnerships among the family, school, and health care teams. Power and colleagues (2003) described several stages of a comprehensive school reintegration plan that emphasize the relational aspects of programming: Stage 1 involves strengthening the family during the initial stages of coping with illness and assisting them in their interactions with the health team. Stage 2 focuses on preparing the family to collaborate with the school and advocate for the child's educational needs. Stage 3 emphasizes the preparation of school professionals to understand the child and collaborate effectively with the family, and Stage 4 focuses on the formation of a strong partnership between family and school to build resources, promote the child's adaptation to school, and address the child's challenges in coping with the demands of school. The CBC model described previously is strongly recommended as a framework for establishing effective family–school partnerships to guide the process of reintegration.

Applications in Primary Care

The responsibility of caring for children with chronic health conditions has been shifting from hospital-based medical experts to primary care providers. The medical home model provides a framework for the care of children with chronic illnesses by emphasizing the importance of strong attachments between primary care providers and families and the critical role of health providers in orchestrating the services of multiple specialists who may be caring for the child with special needs (American Academy of Pediatrics, 2002). Although this model was originally designed to address the needs of children with chronic medical illnesses and those who are the victims of abuse or neglect, it has been adapted to encompass children with or at risk for developmental problems (e.g., intellectual disabilities, autism spectrum disorders, learning disabilities) and behavioral health concerns (e.g., ADHD, disruptive behavior disorders, anxiety, and depression).

Although the medical home model emphasizes collaboration across systems of care, most applications of this approach are limited with regard to coordinating efforts with schools. Unfortunately, even though primary care practices and schools share a similar mission of promoting child development and often serve the same children, the connections between these systems typically is poorly developed. As an effort to address this limitation, Power and colleagues (2010) developed an intervention, referred to as Partnering to Achieve School Success (PASS), to meet the needs of children with ADHD, although it can be adapted readily for children with other mental health and physical health conditions. This intervention has been developed in primary care settings, in particular urban practices serving primarily low-income families of diverse racial and ethnic backgrounds. Key components of PASS include: family engagement strategies, brief family therapy, family–school consultation using the CBC model, collaborative management of medication when indicated, and crisis intervention when needed (Power, Jones, Mautone, & Blum, 2010; for a further description of this program, see chapter 5).

The promotion of family engagement is strongly emphasized in the PASS program given that a relatively high percentage of the families served by this program have difficulty initiating and maintaining their involvement in care (Power, Hughes, et al., 2010). The primary strategy used to promote engagement is to include a community partner or family advocate on the treatment team. The community partner is a paraprofessional who resides in the local community, has substantial experience interacting with health and school systems, and has strong family advocacy skills. This individual works in close collaboration with the PASS clinician to connect with families and to overcome barriers that could preclude involvement in treatment.

Applications in the School

There are many ways in which school professionals can contribute to the management of chronic health conditions in a school setting. Perhaps the role that has been described most extensively in the literature is collaboration with prescribing physicians to evaluate the effectiveness of medication. Single-subject research methods generally are useful in making these determinations. Although the application of placebo-controlled, double-blind procedures are ideal when evaluating medication effects, it is often not feasible to use these methods in school practice. Nonetheless, it is often possible to keep teachers blind to medication condition, which can help to reduce methodological bias. School professionals, such as school psychologists and nurses, can easily gain access to a wealth of data that is valuable in making medication decisions. For example, school professionals can directly observe a child's behavior in classroom and playground settings using standardized observation methods. Also, they can readily obtain brief direct behavior ratings from teachers on a frequent basis to monitor progress over time. In addition, samples of children's performance on classroom assignments have been used successfully in monitoring medication effects (Phelps, Brown, & Power, 2002).

School professionals can serve a vital role in assisting students with the management of pain in school. Research suggests that educating teachers about the biopsychosocial model of pain is an important component of treatment. This framework enables teachers to appreciate biological contributions to the experience of pain so that they are less likely to minimize the child's experience of pain. Also, research suggests that the family–school relationship is important in the management of pain; families who approach the school in a cooperative manner appear to be more likely to obtain school accommodations for their child than those who make demands (Logan, Coakley, & Scharff, 2007). Further, there is an accumulation of evidence supporting the use of cognitive-behavioral strategies in the management of pain (Dahlquist & Nagel, 2009), and it is often feasible for school counselors and psychologists to apply these methods in a school setting.

Another role for school professionals is promoting adherence to medical regimens in school. Nonadherence to medical plans is highly prevalent across age ranges and settings, but the school setting may be especially problematic due to the absence of parents to provide supervision. Family–school collaboration is critical to enlist the assistance of school professionals, such as the nurse, counselor, and teachers, define each party's role in the intervention process, and monitor progress. A range of intervention strategies, including organizational techniques for the child, self-monitoring procedures, visual cues and verbal prompts, and reinforcement procedures have been shown to be effective, and it is often feasible to implement these strategies in the school setting (Power & Werba, 2006).

Conclusions

Chronic health conditions often have an effect on the functioning of children in school settings. The magnitude of school impairments may vary depending on the extent of central nervous system involvement, the effect on physical appearance, and the intensity, frequency, and duration of pain experienced. Although a major role of pediatric psychologists is to develop, implement, and evaluate interventions for children coping with chronic illnesses, the scope of their work typically does not extend into school settings. In contrast, school psychologists generally serve vital roles with regard to interventions for academic, social, and behavioral problems in school, but they typically have limited expertise in addressing the challenges presented by children with chronic health issues. Experts in pediatric school psychology are needed to link the educational and health systems to facilitate the development of effective and socially valid interventions to address the school impairments of children with chronic health conditions.

A wide range of empirical methods has been developed to guide decisions regarding the development, implementation, and evaluation of interventions. With regard to intervention design, multiple assessment paradigms, including categorical, dimensional, functional behavioral, social-cognitive, and ecological, have been demonstrated to be useful in designing interventions that have the potential to be effective, feasible, and acceptable to participants. Each is associated with multiple strengths and limitations, suggesting that a combination of approaches is generally indicated. With respect to implementation, the collection of information related to both the content and process of intervention delivery is critical to determining whether the intervention is being provided in a valid and meaningful manner. To evaluate intervention effectiveness, both formative, progress monitoring approaches as well as summative, outcome assessment methods are recommended.

Interventions to address the school impairments of children with chronic health conditions are inherently multisystemic in that they require strong linkages among the family, school, and health systems. In addition, interventions are strongly rooted in a partnership model espousing that all participants in the process (i.e., family, school professionals, health providers) have a strong and equal voice in designing, implementing, and evaluating interventions. This chapter outlines several steps in the multisystemic intervention process, including promoting participant engagement, strengthening system connections, strengthening interconnections across systems, and solving problems while building resources. The Conjoint Behavioral Consultation model developed by Sheridan and Kratochwill (2008) is highly useful in guiding the process of problem solving in the context of a multisystemic, partnership-based framework.

Interventions to assist children with chronic health conditions can be applied in multiple contexts, including hospital, primary care practice, and school setting. There is limited empirical research to guide the practice of pediatric school psychology at this time; practice models reflect an extension of theory and practice related to pediatric psychology and school psychology as separate disciplines. Research based on integrated, interdisciplinary models is needed to shape practice in the future.

Questions for Discussion

1. What are the limitations of the assessment methods you use, and how can these be addressed using alternative assessment methods?
2. What strategies have you used to promote the engagement of parents and teachers in the intervention work you do? Can you think of additional strategies you can use?
3. What are the limitations of a problem-focused approach to intervention? How can you incorporate approaches that build on strengths and promote resilience?
4. What are some of the challenges of providing pediatric intervention services in primary care and school settings, and what strategies could be developed to overcome these barriers?

References

Abidin, R. R., & Brunner, J. F. (1995). Development of a parenting alliance inventory. *Journal of Clinical Child Psychology, 24,* 31–40.

Achenbach, T. M., & Rescorla, L. A. (2001). *Manual for ASEBA school-age forms and profiles.* Burlington: University of Vermont, Research Center for Children, Youth, and Families.

Ambrosini, P. J. (2000). Historical development and present status of the Schedule for Affective Disorders and Schizophrenia for School-age Children (K-SADS). *Journal of the American Academy of Child and Adolescent Psychiatry, 39,* 49–58.

American Academy of Pediatrics. (2002). The medical home. *Pediatrics, 110,* 184–186.

Andersen, R. M. (1995). Revisiting the behavioral model and access to medical care: Does it matter? *Journal of Health and Social Behavior, 36,* 1–10.

Barakat, L. P., Lutz, M. J., Nicolaou, D. C., & Lash, L. A. (2005). Parental locus of control and family functioning in the quality of life of children with sickle cell disease. *Journal of Clinical Psychology in Medical Settings, 12,* 323–331.

Bernard, R. S., Cohen, L. L., & Moffett, K. (2009). A token economy for exercise adherence in pediatric cystic fibrosis: A single-subject analysis. *Journal of Pediatric Psychology, 34,* 354–365.

Chafouleas, S. M., Volpe, R. J., Gresham, F. M., & Cook, C. R. (2010). School-based behavioral assessment within problem-solving models: Current status and future directions. *School Psychology Review, 39,* 343–349.

Christenson, S. L., & Sheridan, S. M. (2001). *Schools and families: Creating essential connections for learning.* New York: Guilford.

Dahlquist, L. M., & Nagel, M. S. (2009). Chronic and recurrent pain. In M. Roberts & R. Steele (Eds.), *Handbook of pediatric psychology* (pp. 153–170). New York: Guilford.

Dane, A. V., & Schneider, B. H. (1998). Program integrity in primary and early secondary prevention: Are implementation effects out of control? *Clinical Psychology Review, 18,* 23–45.

DeCivita, M., & Dobkin, P. (2004). Pediatric adherence as a multidimensional and dynamic construct, involving a triadic partnership. *Journal of Pediatric Psychology, 29,* 157–170.

DeVellis, R. F., DeVellis, B. M., Blanchard, L. W., Klotz, M. L., Luchok, K., & Voyce, C. (1993). Development and validation of the Parent Health Locus of Control Scales. *Health Education Quarterly, 2,* 211–225.

Dishion, T. J., & Stormshak, E. A. (2007). *Intervening in children's lives: An ecological, family- centered approach to mental health care.* Washington, DC: American Psychological Association.

DuPaul, G. J., & Ervin, R. A. (1996). Functional assessment of behaviors related to attention-deficit/hyperactivity disorder: Linking assessment to intervention design. *Behavior Therapy, 27,* 601–622.

DuPaul, G. J., & Stoner, G. (2004). *ADHD in the schools: Assessment and intervention strategies.* New York: Guilford.

Durlak, J. A., & DuPre, E. P. (2008). Implementation matters: A review of research on the influence of implementation on program outcomes and the factors affecting implementation. *American Journal of Community Psychology, 41,* 327–350.

Eiraldi, R., Mazzuca, L., Clarke, A., & Power, T. (2006). Service utilization among ethnic minority children with ADHD: A model of help-seeking behavior. *Administration and Policy in Mental Health and Mental Health Services Research, 33,* 607–622.

Fiese, B., & Wamboldt, F. (2000). Family routines, rituals and asthma management: A proposal for family-based strategies to increase treatment adherence. *Families, Systems, and Health, 18,* 405–418.

Furman, W., & Giverson, R. (1995). Identifying the links between parents and their children's sibling relationships. In S. Shulman (Ed.), *Close relationships and socioemotional development* (pp. 95–108). Norwood, NJ: Ablex.

Glover, T. A., & DiPerna, J. C. (2007). Service delivery for response to intervention: Core components and directions for future research. *School Psychology Review, 36,* 526–540.

Gresham, F. M., Cook, C. R., Collins, T., Dart, E., Rasetshwane, K., Truelson, E., & Grant, S. (2010). Developing a change-sensitive brief behavior rating scale as a progress monitoring tool for social behavior: An example using the social skills rating system- teacher form. *School Psychology Review, 39,* 364–379.

Guevara, J. P., Feudtner, C., Romer, D., Power, T. J., Eiraldi, R. B., Nihtianova, S., … Schwarz, D. (2005). Fragmented care for inner-city minority children with attention-deficit/hyperactivity disorder. *Pediatrics, 116,* e512–e517.

Hall, M. A., Camacho, F., Dugan, E., & Balkrishnan, R. (2002). Trust in the medical profession: Conceptual and measurement issues. *Health Services Research, 37,* 1419–1421.

Janicke, D. M., & Finney, J. W. (2003). Children's primary health care services: Social-cognitive factors related to utilization. *Journal of Pediatric Psychology, 28,* 547–558.

Kazak, A., Kassam-Adams, N., Schneider, S., Zelikovsky, N., Alderfer, M., & Rourke, M. (2006). An integrative model of pediatric medical traumatic stress. *Journal of Pediatric Psychology, 31,* 343–355.

Kazak, A. E., Rourke, M. T., & Navsaria, N. (2009). Families and other systems in pediatric psychology. In M. Roberts & R. Steele (Eds.), *Handbook of pediatric psychology* (pp. 656–671). New York: Guilford.

Kohl, G. O., Lengua, L. J., McMahon, R. J., & Conduct Problems Prevention Research Group. (2000). Parent involvement in school: Conceptualizing multiple dimensions and their relations with family and demographic risk factors. *Journal of School Psychology, 38,* 501–524.

Krain, A. L., Kendall, P. C., & Power, T. J. (2005). The role of treatment acceptability in the initiation of treatment for ADHD. *Journal of Attention Disorders, 9,* 425–434.

La Greca, A. M., & Mackey, E. R. (2009). Adherence to pediatric treatment regimens. In M. Roberts & R. Steele (Eds.), *Handbook of pediatric psychology* (pp.130–152). New York: Guilford.

Leslie, L. K., Weckerly, J., Plemmons, D., Landsverk, J., & Eastman, S. (2004). Implementing the American Academy of Pediatrics attention-deficit/hyperactivity disorder diagnostic guidelines in primary care settings. *Pediatrics, 114,*129–140.

Logan, D. E., Coakley, R. M., & Scharff, L. (2007). Teachers' perceptions of and responses to adolescents with chronic pain syndromes. *Journal of Pediatric Psychology, 32,* 139–149.

Logan, D., Simons, L. E., & Kaczynski, K. J. (2009). School functioning in adolescents with chronic pain: The role of depressive symptoms in school impairment. *Journal of Pediatric Psychology, 34,* 882–892.

Lynch-Jordan, A. M., Kashikar-Zuck, S., Crosby, L. E., Lopez, W. L., Smolyansky, B. H., Parkins, I. S., ... Powers, S. W. (2010). Applying quality improvement methods to implement a measurement system for chronic pain-related disability. *Journal of Pediatric Psychology, 35,* 32–41.

Madan-Swain, A. Katz, E. R., & LaGory, J. (2004). School and social reintegration after a serious illness or injury. In R. T. Brown (Ed.), *Handbook of pediatric psychology in school settings* (pp. 637–655). Mahwah, NJ: Erlbaum.

McKay, M. M., & Bannon, W. M. (2004). Engaging families in child mental health services. *Child and Adolescent Psychiatric Clinics of North America, 13,* 905–921.

Miller, W. R., & Rollnick, S. (2002). *Motivational interviewing: Preparing people for change* (2nd ed.). New York: Guilford.

Moen, R. D., Nolan, T. W., & Provost, L. P. (1999). *Quality improvement through planned experimentation.* New York: McGraw-Hill.

Multimodal Treatment Study of Children with ADHD Cooperative Group. (1999). A 14-month randomized clinical trial of treatment strategies for attention-deficit/hyperactivity disorder. *Archives of General Psychiatry, 56,* 1073–1086.

Nastasi, B. K., Moore, R. B., & Varjas, K. M. (2004). *School-based mental health services: Creating comprehensive and culturally specific programs.* Washington, DC: American Psychological Association.

Perepletchikova, F., Treat, T. A., & Kazdin, A. E. (2007). Treatment integrity in psychotherapy research: Analysis of studies and examination of the associated factors. *Journal of Consulting and Clinical Psychology, 75,* 829–841.

Phelps, L., Brown, R. T., & Power, T. J. (2002). *Pediatric psychopharmacology: Facilitating collaborative processes.* Washington, DC: American Psychological Association.

Pianta, R. C. (1999). *Enhancing relationships between children and teachers.* Washington, DC: American Psychological Association.

Pianta, R. C. (2002). *Student–teacher relationship scale.* Odessa, FL: Psychological Assessment Resources.

Pianta, R. C., La Paro, K. M., & Hamre, B. K. (2008). *Classroom assessment scoring system.* Baltimore, MD: Brookes.

Power, T. J., Dowrick, P. W., Ginsburg-Block, M., & Manz, P. H. (2004). Partnership-based community-assisted early intervention for literacy: An application of the participatory intervention model. *Journal of Behavioral Education, 13,* 93–115.

Power, T. J., DuPaul, G. J., Shapiro, E. S., & Kazak, A. E. (2003). *Promoting children's health: Integrating school, family, and community.* New York: Guilford.

Power, T. J., & Eiraldi, R. E. (2000). Educational and psychiatric classification systems. In S. Shapiro & T. R. Kratochwill (Eds.), *Behavioral assessment in schools: Theory, research, and clinical foundations* (2nd ed., pp. 464–488). New York: Guilford.

Power, T. J., Eiraldi, R. B., Clarke, A. T., Mazzuca, L., & Krain, A. (2005). Improving mental health service utilization for children and adolescents. *School Psychology Quarterly, 20,* 187–205.

Power, T. J., Hughes, C. L., Helwig, J. R., Nissley-Tsiopinis, J., & Mautone, J. A. (2010). Getting to first base: Promoting engagement in family-school intervention for children with ADHD in urban, primary care practice. *School Mental Health, 2,* 52–61.

Power, T. J., Jones, H. A., Mautone, J. A., & Blum, N. J. (2010). Partnering to achieve school success: A collaborative care model of early intervention for attention and behavior problems in urban contexts. In B. Doll, W. Pfohl, & J. Yoon (Eds.), *Handbook of youth prevention science* (pp. 375–392). New York: Routledge.

Power, T. J., Karustis, J. L., & Habboushe, D. (2001). *Homework success for children with ADHD: A family-school intervention program.* New York: Guilford.

Power, T. J., Soffer, S. L., Mautone, J. A., Costigan, T. E., Jones, H. A., Clarke, A. T., & Marshall, S. A. (2009). An analysis of teacher investment in the context of a family-school intervention for children with ADHD. *School Mental Health, 1,* 107–117.

Power, T., & Werba, B. (2006). Interventions for health problems: A multisystemic cognitive-behavioral approach. In R. Mennuti, A. Freeman, & R. Christner (Eds.), *Cognitive-behavioral interventions in educational settings* (pp. 323–342). New York: Brunner-Routledge.

Prevatt, F. F., Heffer, R. W., & Lowe, P. A. (2000). A review of school integration programs for children with cancer. *Journal of School Psychology, 38,* 447–467.

Robins, P. M., Smith, S. M., Glutting, J. J., & Bishop, C. T. (2005). A randomized controlled trial of a cognitive-behavioral family intervention for pediatric recurrent abdominal pain. *Journal of Pediatric Psychology, 30,* 397–408.

Rofey, D. L, Szigethy, E. M., Noll, R. B., Dahl, R. E., Lobst, E., & Arslanian, S. A. (2008). Cognitive-behavioral therapy for physical and emotional disturbances in adolescents with polycystic ovary syndrome: A pilot study. *Journal of Pediatric Psychology, 34,* 156–163.

Schulte, A. C., Easton, J. E., & Parker, J. (2009). Advances in treatment integrity research: Multidisciplinary perspectives on the conceptualization, measurement, and enhancement of treatment integrity. *School Psychology Review, 38,* 460–475.

Seid, M., Opipari-Arrigan, L., & Sobo, E. J. (2009). Families' inter-
actions with the health care system. In M. Roberts & R. Steele
(Eds.), *Handbook of pediatric psychology* (pp. 703–718). New
York: Guilford.

Seid, M., Varni, J. W., Gidwani, P., Gelhard, L. R., & Slymen, D. (2010).
Problem-solving skills training in vulnerable families of children with persistent asthma: Report of a randomized trial on
health-related quality of life outcomes. *Journal of Pediatric Psychology, 35,* 1133–1143.

Sheridan, S. M., & Kratochwill, T. R. (2008). *Conjoint behavioral consultation: Promoting family-school connections and interventions* (2nd ed.). New York: Springer.

Sheridan, S. M., Swanger-Gagné, M., Welch, G. W., Kwon, K., & Garbacz, S. A. (2009). Fidelity measurement in consultation: Psychometric issues and preliminary examination. *School Psychology
Review, 38,* 476–495.

Sheridan, S. M., Warnes, E. D., Woods, K. E., Blevins, C. A., Magee,
K. L., & Ellis, C. (2009). An exploratory evaluation of conjoint
behavioral consultation to promote collaboration among family,
school, and pediatric systems: A role for pediatric school psychologists. *Journal of Educational and Psychological Consultation, 19,* 106–129.

Silverman, W. K., & Albano, A. M. (1996). *Anxiety Disorders Interview Schedule for Children for* DSM-IV: (*Child and Parent Versions),* San Antonio, TX: Psychological Corporation/Graywind.

Spanier, G. B. (1976). Measuring dyadic adjustment: New scales for
assessing the quality of marriage and similar dyads. *Journal of
Marriage and Family, 38,* 15–28.

Steege, M. W., & Watson, T. S. (2009). *Conducting school-based functional behavioral assessments* (2nd ed.). New York: Guilford.

Stehl, M. L., Kazak, A. E., Alderfer, M. A., Rodriguez, A., Hwang,
W.-T., Pai, A. L. H., ... Reilly, A. (2009). Conducting a randomized
clinical trial of a psychosocial intervention for parents/caregiv-
ers of children with cancer shortly after diagnosis. *Journal of
Pediatric Psychology, 34,* 803–816.

Volpe, R. J., & Gadow, K. D. (2010). Creating abbreviated rating scales
to monitor classroom inattention-overactivity, aggression, and
peer conflict: Reliability, validity, and treatment sensitivity.
School Psychology Review, 39, 350–363.

Wissow, L. S., Gadomski, A., Roter, D., Larson, S., Brown, J., Zachary,
C., ... Wang, M.-C. (2008). Improving child and parent mental
health in primary care: A cluster-randomized trial of communication skills training. *Pediatrics, 121,* 266–275. doi:10.1542/
peds.2007-0418.

Four

Conceptual Model for Health Promotion and Illness Prevention

Historically, psychosocial services for children and youth have been mobilized in response to a problem that needs to be understood and requires intervention. In school settings, children have been referred by teachers for psychoeducational testing when they are struggling academically or behaviorally and there is a question as to whether special education intervention is needed. In primary care settings, children with behavioral or emotional problems have been identified by primary care providers and when the need for intervention is apparent, they have been referred to mental health professionals. Similarly, in hospitals children have been referred to pediatric psychologists when there are health (e.g., pain, nonadherence to medical treatment) or mental health concerns that need attention.

Although an intervention orientation makes sense and has considerable merit, the approach has numerous limitations. First, withholding resources until there are identified problems fails to take advantage of opportunities to assist the child earlier in the process when signs of risk are beginning to emerge. Second, intervening when children are having difficulties, particularly serious problems, can be labor intensive and financially expensive. Much less effort or expense is involved if services are provided when children are healthy or when signs of risk are first emerging. Third, an intervention orientation directs all psychosocial resources to those who have problems. Such an approach fails to take advantage of what mental health providers can offer healthy children with regard to promoting adaptive lifestyles and patterns of behavior, which can serve a protective function and prevent problems later in development.

Another limitation is that from a developmental perspective if the population of children at a particular point is differentiated into those with problems and those without, more individuals in the nonproblem group will eventually acquire a serious health condition than those in the problem group (Rose, 1989). The reason for this is that the nonproblem group will include a relatively large proportion of children who are vulnerable by virtue of exposure to chronic stress, which predisposes them to acquiring serious disorders later in life. This broad perspective provides a strong argument for directing resources to children who are not currently manifesting problems, especially those who are at increased risk by virtue of psychosocial adversity (i.e., poverty or exposure to repeated stressful events; Shonkoff, Boyce, & McEwen, 2009).

This chapter describes important concepts and critical elements of programming related to health promotion and problem prevention (i.e., illness, disorder). The chapter discusses how a prevention orientation is rooted in the public health model and how epidemiology and developmental psychology (psychopathology) serve as foundations for prevention science. As described in this chapter, many of the key elements of effective prevention programming are similar to those for intervention programming (e.g., strengthening and linking systems, forming strong partnerships among key providers and family members, and implementing change strategies in a high quality manner).

Roots of Prevention Science

A prevention approach is rooted in the public health model, which incorporates a population-based approach. Prevention focuses on all children within a population, defined by one or more parameters. For example, the population might be very broad, such as all children who attend school in a particular state, county, or school district; or it might be quite specific, such as all children who attend ninth grade health classes in a particular high school, or all preschool-age children who receive care in a specific primary care practice. A key feature of a public health orientation is that it focuses on all children in a specified population, ranging from healthy (and without identified problems) to unhealthy (with problems). It is also possible to apply a public health model in the context of children who have an identified health problem, but who may vary with regard to their level of risk for mental health problems. For example, the population of families coping with children who have cancer varies substantially with regard to their risk for posttraumatic stress symptoms and associated impairments (Kazak et al., 2007).

A public health approach has numerous objectives: (a) promote the health of all individuals within a given population, (b) understand how risk arises and prevent the emergence of risk, and (c) understand how risk develops into a problem (illness, disorder) and intervene to reduce risk. The public health orientation in psychology has its roots in epidemiology and developmental psychology (psychopathology).

Epidemiology

The purpose of epidemiology is to understand the distribution of health-related behaviors in a population and factors contributing to health and illness, as well as to translate this knowledge into practices to promote health and prevent illness. Epidemiology typically includes the identification of demographic factors associated with health risk. For instance, numerous survey studies have identified disparities in the use of mental health services as a function of ethnic group status, health insurance status, gender, and age (Kataoka, Zhang, & Wells, 2002). This information is useful in directing research efforts to understand factors contributing to health disparities; for instance, determinants of the low rate of mental health service use among Latino children and their families. The search for these determinants has identified numerous barriers, including access issues (insurance, transportation, scheduling) and beliefs (trust, self-efficacy, acculturation) that prevent families from initiating and maintaining the use of services for their children (Cauce et al., 2002; Eiraldi, Mazzuca, Clarke, & Power, 2006). Explanatory models for health disparities can serve as the basis of a prevention approach to remove barriers and promote greater mental health service use by this population (Shonkoff et al., 2009).

Developmental Psychology (Psychopathology)

The purpose of developmental psychology is to understand how individuals adapt to a changing environment over time, acknowledging that individuals and context reciprocally influence each other (Sameroff, 1993). The constructs of risk, vulnerability, resources, and resilience in developmental psychology have been highly useful in informing approaches to prevention programming (Holmbeck, Zebracki, & McGoron, 2009). Risk occurs when a factor has a negative effect on development regardless of the presence or absence of adversity. An example of a risk factor might be a conflictual teacher–student relationship. Vulnerability refers to the increased likelihood that a factor will result in a poor outcome under conditions of high adversity. For example, children living in poverty may be especially vulnerable to the maladaptive effects of a low-quality teacher–student relationship. Resources or promotive factors are variables that can have a positive impact on individuals regardless of the presence or absence of adverse conditions. A useful resource for virtually all children is a collaborative family–school relationship. Finally, the term *resilience* refers to the presence of factors that increase the likelihood of a favorable outcome under adverse conditions. For example, a good friendship can promote the resilience of children who are victims of teasing in school.

Developmental psychopathology is a subset of developmental psychology that focuses on the emergence of risk and mental health disorder, which usually occurs during childhood or adolescence. Understanding the emergence of conditions such as depression and aggression has elucidated variables that increase risk and protective factors that promote resilience. This information has been highly useful in formulating theories of change that serve as the foundation for the development of prevention initiatives (Dodge, 2001).

Positive psychology is another outgrowth of developmental psychology that has been highly influential in shaping prevention science (Linley, Joseph, Harrington, & Wood, 2006). Positive psychology focuses on understanding individuals' competencies and strengths as well as factors that promote competence (Suldo & Shaffer, 2008). This orientation is highly useful in formulating population-based approaches to foster competence and develop preventive interventions to promote resilience among children experiencing heightened levels of adversity.

Levels of Prevention

Although the terminology used to refer to levels of prevention has changed over the years, virtually all experts in prevention agree that there are multiple levels. The term *universal prevention* refers to efforts to prevent problems or disorders that are targeted for the entire specified population. Recent conceptualizations of universal prevention generally include initiatives to promote health as well as those to prevent illness (Doll, Pfohl, & Yoon, 2010). The term *selective prevention* refers to initiatives for a subset of the population with increased risk for problems, although definitions vary with regard to whether individuals at this level manifest actual signs of risk or belong to subgroups (e.g., children living in poverty) known to be at heightened risk. *Targeted prevention* refers to efforts to intervene with a subgroup manifesting actual signs of risk, although the literature varies as to how much risk is needed to differentiate this level from selective prevention.

Comprehensive, Multitier Models

Levels of prevention have been incorporated into comprehensive, multitier models of service delivery (Sugai & Horner, 2006). Universal efforts are targeted for the entire population and it is presumed that the successful application of prevention initiatives at this level will minimize the proportion of children requiring selective and targeted approaches. Strategies used at the universal level generally can be implemented in an efficient and cost effective manner. Selective prevention efforts typically are focused on 5 to 20% of the population and require additional time and cost, but are still relatively efficient and cost effective. Targeted prevention generally focuses on 5 to 10% of the population and involves the use of strategies provided in small-group or individualized formats that entail greater resources and expenses. Varying multitier models of prevention and intervention have been proposed; models may differ in the number of levels and the definition of each level. However, virtually all of the models are similar with regard to their focus on altering the level of service intensity and resource allocation based upon the degree of risk or need.

Response to Intervention

A critical feature of most models of prevention is that response to intervention (or prevention efforts) at one level determines whether there is a need to move to a more intensive level of service. A response to intervention framework depends upon numerous factors, including selection of evidence-based practices, resource capacity, implementation quality, monitoring implementation and outcome, and sustainability (Glover & DiPerna, 2007).

Selection of Evidence-Based Practices. At each level of service delivery, it is important to select programs that have been demonstrated to be effective. It is often the case that the science base is limited with regard to the strength of evidence to support prevention efforts in a particular area (e.g., prevention of aggression among inner city girls). In these cases, it makes sense to select programs that demonstrate strong promise, such as the PRAISE program for preventing relational and overt aggression among inner city girls (Leff et al., 2010), or to select programs that incorporate components that have a strong basis in empirical research.

Resource Capacity.   The provision of evidence-based practices requires that there is sufficient support for providers to deliver services effectively. Relatively intensive training may be needed for staff to deliver the program successfully, which may require resources to underwrite the cost of involving experts to provide the training and staff to receive training. In addition, resources are required to provide ongoing oversight and supervision. Also, materials are typically required to support the training process and to guide implementation efforts. In some cases, partnerships with community-based agencies or universities may be indicated to enlist the personnel needed to successfully implement a prevention initiative (Tucker, 2002).

Promotion of Implementation Quality. The effectiveness of an evidence-based program depends in large measure on the quality with which it is implemented. Failure of an intervention to work often is not due to selection of the wrong intervention. Instead, failure may be due to insufficient quality of implementation, including the procedures and processes (including interpersonal dynamics) of the program (Sanetti & Kratochwill, 2009). For this reason, it is important to provide adequate training prior to implementation and careful oversight during the course of programming. Developing intervention strategies in partnership with participants (Kelleher, Riley-Tillman, & Power, 2008) and providing ongoing performance feedback (Noell et al., 2005) are two strategies that have been demonstrated to improve quality of implementation.

Monitoring Implementation and Outcomes. A hallmark of response to intervention is data-based decision making. Progress monitoring tools are needed to determine whether programs are being implemented with sufficient quality and what outcomes are being achieved (Glover & DiPerna, 2007). Multiple methods of assessing intervention integrity are recommended to capture the multidimensional elements of this construct, including dimensions pertaining to intervention procedures, competence in intervention delivery, and participant engagement (Sanetti & Kratochwill, 2009), and the limitations of each method of assessment (Sheridan, Swanger-Gagne, Welch, Kwon, & Garbacz, 2009). With regard to outcome assessment, the domains to be assessed need to be mapped to the goals of programming, as determined by key stakeholders, including the student, teachers, parents, and administrators. Typically, a multimethod, multidimensional approach to outcome assessment is needed, although it is critical to develop a feasible, efficient assessment plan to insure consistent use of these tools. Data from these measures are critical for making decisions about whether to continue the preventive intervention, whether the intensity of intervention can be increased or decreased, and what modifications are needed. See chapter 6 for a further discussion of issues related to program evaluation.

Role of Screening in Prevention

A commonly used prevention strategy is to engage in universal screening to determine which individuals in a given population are at risk and in need of more support. There are two primary forms of risk: risk of disorder/illness and risk of adversity or vulnerability. Risk of disorder typically is assessed using surveillance methods (e.g., interview questions) or brief rating scales. Risk of vulnerability is assessed by taking note of demographic factors associated with adversity (e.g., poverty as indicated by Medicaid status or eligibility for subsidized lunch in school), or administering a brief measure of adversity.

Screening for Risk of Disorder and Vulnerability

Screening measures have been developed to assess a range of disorders. For example, the Patient Health Questionnaire—9 Item (PHQ-9; Spitzer, Kroenke, & Williams, 1999) is a measure commonly used in health settings for the screening of adolescent depression. The Pediatric Symptom Checklist—17 Items (PSC-17; Gardner, et al., 1999) and the Strengths and Difficulties Questionnaire (SDQ; Goodman, 2001) have strong psychometric properties and are frequently used in primary care to screen for emotional and behavioral disorders. More recently, given the risks to children associated with depression among mothers, screening for maternal depression in the child's first year of life is being conducted in many pediatric primary care settings (Olson, Dietrich, Prazar, & Hurley, 2006).

Screening for vulnerability is less common but potentially just as important. One measure that has been well validated for this purpose is the Adverse Childhood Events (ACE) Scale (Dube et al., 2001). This self-report measure has been designed to assess vulnerability as a function of child maltreatment, substance abuse, domestic violence, parental mental health status, parental separation/divorce, and parental incarceration. Elevated scores on this measure have been associated with increased risk for substance abuse, depression, suicide attempts, poor adult health, and increased health care utilization (Chartier, Walker, & Naimark, 2010).

Although screening identifies a segment of the population likely to acquire a disorder, in the long run most cases of disorder are not detected by a symptom screening test (Rose, 1989). Longitudinal studies have repeatedly shown that individuals at perhaps the greatest risk are those who are repeatedly exposed to adverse psychosocial circumstances (Shonkoff et al., 2009). Thus, to increase the potential impact of prevention efforts, it is important to intervene at a broad level among those currently demonstrating signs of disorder as well as those who are not currently doing so but who do show evidence of vulnerability. Table 4.1 illustrates how the interaction of risk of disorder and level of vulnerability are associated with levels of prevention programming. Children who are at low risk of disorder and low in vulnerability can be provided with universal methods of prevention. Those who are low in risk for

Table 4.1   Levels of Prevention Programming as a Function of Risk of Disorder and Degree of Vulnerability

	Low Risk of Disorder	High Risk of Disorder
Low Vulnerability	Universal Prevention	Targeted Prevention—Moderate Intensity
High Vulnerability	Selective Prevention	Targeted Prevention—High Intensity

disorder but high in vulnerability can be targeted for selective prevention efforts. Children high in risk for disorder but low in vulnerability require targeted intervention, but a moderate level of intervention intensity may be sufficient. Finally, those who are at high risk of disorder and high in vulnerability need relatively intensive preventive intervention efforts.

Key Elements of Screening

Screening typically involves use of a questionnaire or rating scale. Screening is typically conducted in a setting that serves the general population, such as schools or primary care. Screening can be conducted by a wide range of professionals, such as teachers or school mental health professionals in schools, and physicians or nurses in primary care settings. As with any measure, it is important for the scale to be reliable and valid. In addition, the clinical utility of the measure for purposes of screening should be established. Clinical utility involves two key constructs: sensitivity and specificity. Sensitivity refers to the probability that children who have a disorder (or are at risk for a disorder) will screen positive for the disorder (i.e., exceed the established cut point) on the measure. Specificity is the probability that children who do not have a disorder will screen negative for the disorder (i.e., fail to exceed the established cut-point) on the measure. For purposes of screening, the following elements are especially important.

Capture Children Who Have the Disorder or Are at Risk. Effective screening involves capturing a very high percentage of children who actually have the disorder (i.e., high sensitivity). It is problematic to miss cases that have a disorder, because failure to identify such a child represents a lost opportunity to intervene, which in some cases could have serious consequences (e.g., failure to identify a child at risk for suicidal behavior). By the same token, it is usually not possible for a screening measure to capture all children with the disorder, because every measure has psychometric limitations and the cut-point required for a very high level of sensitivity may result in identifying an intolerable number of false positives.

Keep False Positives to a Minimum. For screening it is important to minimize the number of false positives (1–specificity); that is, to keep to a minimum the number of children identified as having a disorder (or being at risk) who do not actually have the disorder. Minimizing false positives helps to keep the time and costs involved in screening and assessment at a reasonable level. Also, maintaining a relatively low level of false positives will minimize the anxiety caused in families when there is evidence of risk of disorder.

Provide Screening Services in an Efficient Manner. In order for a universal screening program to work and be acceptable to providers, it is important for there to be an efficient process for screening children and communicating the results to families (Schonwald, Horan, & Huntington, 2009). One of the advantages of electronic health records (EHRs) is they can streamline the process of screening. Also, EHRs can incorporate decision and communication tools to assist providers in scoring and interpreting the findings of screening tests and communicating the results to families.

Offer Resources for Children Who Screen Positive. Providers generally are highly reluctant to engage in screening practices if resources are not available to treat children who screen positive for a disorder. It is essential to offer providers resources in the form of handouts for parents and contact information about how to obtain services to further evaluate potential problems and receive intervention services, if needed.

Prioritize Target Areas for Screening. It may be justifiable at any point to screen for multiple disorders. For example, during the preschool years, it is justifiable to screen for developmental problems, autism, behavioral disorders, parent–child conflict, and obesity. Although it may be feasible to use surveillance methods to screen for multiple conditions at a time, it is generally not feasible to use multiple rating scales to screen for a range of problems. As such, it is important for key stakeholders, such as parents, children, health professionals, school professionals, and community leaders, to set priorities for areas to be targeted for screening in each age (grade level) group.

Components of Effective Prevention Programming

Effective prevention programs are responsive to the goals and values of key stakeholders. Also, given that factors reducing risk and promoting resilience include both child and contextual variables, prevention programs need to include elements focused on promoting child skill acquisition as well as strengthening systems so that they are successful in fostering healthy development.

Forming Partnerships to Promote Prevention Efforts

A key to the success of prevention efforts (e.g., development of a suicide prevention program) is to form partnerships with multiple stakeholder groups from the outset to identify goals, priorities, and key guiding principles (Nastasi, Bernstein Moore, & Varjas, 2004). Conducting focus groups and interviews with participating groups at the outset can provide valuable data about goals and values (Ginsburg et al., 2002). Also, formation of a project advisory group, with representation from the full range of stakeholder groups, can be an effective strategy. The advisory group not only can provide direction during the initial stages, but offer guidance about necessary course corrections during the planning, implementation, and evaluation phases of the project.

The essence of partnership is the formation of a collaborative, nonhierarchical relationship among stakeholders involved in a project (Power et al., 2005). There is recognition from the outset and throughout every stage of the project that each partner has unique expertise and has a vital role in ensuring that the overall effort is a success. For example, parents have special knowledge of the child's talents and developmental course; teachers are experts in educating the child and have a unique perspective of how the child functions with peers; community members are knowledgeable about neighborhood resources and cultural values; health professionals have special expertise in medical and developmental factors contributing to the child's welfare; and consultants or researchers have unique expertise in program development and evaluation.

Promoting Change through Skill Development

A major focus of prevention efforts for children is to impart knowledge to them and develop their skills to improve their ability to cope with situations. For example, a critical element of successful nutrition education programs is improving children's knowledge about healthy foods, in particular the importance of eating fruits and vegetables (Blom-Hoffman, Kelleher, Power, & Leff, 2004). As another example, most aggression prevention programs include components to improve children's ability to recognize emotions, regulate emotions and behaviors, take the perspective of others, recognize and change attributions, set goals, and solve problems (Lochman & Wells, 2002). In addition, for youth residing in low income, urban settings, it has been postulated that a critical skill is the ability to distinguish controllable from uncontrollable stressors and utilize coping strategies that match appraisals of controllability (Clarke, 2006).

Prevention programs typically use a wide range of strategies to convey knowledge and promote skill building. An obvious strategy is to provide education to children using verbal instructions and audiovisual aids, which can be facilitated using computer-based technologies. Role modeling is another strategy commonly used to build skills. Role models may include adult instructors or peer models. Further, the use of self-modeling strategies aided by video technology has been shown to be highly effective (Dowrick, Kim-Rupnow, & Power, 2006). Effective prevention programs typically provide children with opportunities to practice newly learned skills with guidance and support provided by adults and peers. Also, the use of Internet-based technologies can be useful and often provide interactive exercises that facilitate learning and mastery.

Creating Family Contexts That Promote Health and Development

Improving children's knowledge and skills is only one component of effective prevention programming. The systems in which children develop need to be designed in such a way that they promote health and well-being.

The family clearly has the greatest influence on children with regard to promoting healthy development. The quality of the parent–child attachment is especially critical. It is noteworthy that educating caregivers about positive parenting was identified in Healthy People 2020 as a key strategy for promoting the health of youth in early and middle childhood (U.S. Department of Health and Human Services, 2010). The strength of the parent–child relationship is associated with children's ability to regulate their behavior and emotions at home as well as in school and other settings. Also, this attachment prepares children for successful interactions with adults and peers outside the home (Pianta, 1997).

Other critical family factors are the level of parental surveillance, with high levels of parental monitoring typically

associated with greater prosocial behavior. There are limits to
the effectiveness of parental supervision, however, especially
during the adolescent years when the importance of parental
monitoring needs to be balanced with respect and promotion
of youth autonomy. Also, the effective use of behavior management strategies has consistently been shown to promote
self-regulation among children (McMahon & Forehand, 2003;
Webster-Stratton, 2005). These strategies include clear delineation of family rules; firm, respectful statement of directives
for compliance; frequent use of positive reinforcement, including parental attention, praise, and privileges; introductive of
a token economy system to increase the effectiveness and efficiency of behavior management strategies; and strategic and
relatively infrequent use of punishment, including corrective
feedback and privilege withdrawal. In addition, establishing
consistent family routines has been shown to be effective in
fostering children's self-regulation and may help to reduce
parental stress and burden (Fiese & Wamboldt, 2000). Family
routines might include rituals related to waking up and getting ready for school, completing homework, eating meals as
a family, preparing for sports activities, and preparing for bed
and going to sleep. In adolescence, the ability of youth and
parents to communicate and negotiate with each other effectively are key to successful family relationships (Robin, 2006).

Creating Health-Promoting School Contexts

Children spend an appreciable amount of their time each
week in school, and therefore schools have the potential to be
highly influential in terms of children's health and development. Healthy schools are characterized by being connected
closely with the surrounding community and being highly
responsive to the values and priorities of community leaders.
In a similar vein, educators in healthy schools recognize the
critical importance of family involvement in education (Christenson & Sheridan, 2001). Families can be involved in their
children's education in multiple ways, including investment
in educational activities in the home setting (e.g., shared book
reading, discussion of current events as a family), meaningful participation in school activities (e.g., attending parent–
teacher association meetings, volunteering to be a classroom
or playground assistant, helping on field trips), and frequent
home–school communication (e.g., home–school notes,
parent–teacher conferences in person or over the phone).

School leadership is obviously a critically important factor in promoting healthy schools. Effective principals work to understand the challenges faced by teachers and advocate to ensure teachers have the resources and support needed to be effective. At the same time, they are responsible for holding teachers accountable while promoting their professional development. Also, in healthy schools structures are created for teachers to convene to share resources, provide support to each other, and solve problems through forums such as grade-level teacher assistance teams.

The classroom climate is especially important for fostering academic and social development. There are numerous factors related to classroom climate, including resources available, curriculum used, and the organization of space and materials. Perhaps the most critical factor pertains to the interactions between teachers and students in classrooms. Pianta, La Paro, and Hamre (2008) have developed a highly useful system for understanding and measuring the interactive features of class climate. They identified three dimensions of teacher–student interaction that are most important: emotional support, classroom organization, and instructional support. In addition, to the relationships between teachers and students, the interactions among students have a significant impact on a student's learning experience. Classrooms in which students feel safe, free of teasing and bullying from others, and affirmed by their peers promote successful academic performance and social development (Hughes & Barrois, 2010).

The time children spend in relatively unstructured settings, such as the playground and lunchroom, can have a major impact on their experience in school. Physical, verbal, and relational acts of aggression occur most commonly when students are in these settings. It has been demonstrated that well-organized playgrounds in which developmentally appropriate games are readily available to students foster cooperative social behavior and reduce the likelihood of aggression (Leff, Costigan, & Power, 2004). Further, close supervision of students in these settings and the provision of positive reinforcement for prosocial behavior are effective strategies for preventing aggression.

Increasingly, social networking sites accessed via the Internet have served as a forum for the expression of verbal and relational aggression. School professionals, including school psychologists and counselors, can serve an important role in developing programs to educate youth and families about strategies to prevent cyberbullying and mitigate its harmful effects on children.

Creating Health-Promoting Contexts in the Community

As children grow older, they spend more and more time outside the family and in the community. Neighborhoods vary widely with regard to the availability of settings and activities that can have a positive effect on youth, and the success of these programs in actively engaging youth. The hours after school appear to be especially important because the level of parental supervision may be relatively low during these times when caregivers are often at work.

The availability of developmentally appropriate after-school programs can be especially important to youth during this period of the day. After-school programs may be situated in schools, faith-based organizations, recreation centers, or neighborhood organizations. Effective programs often provide opportunities for academic support and enrichment, including homework assistance and tutoring. Programs typically provide youth with opportunities to engage in supervised recreational activities that promote fair, appropriate social interactions. Many programs offer students opportunities to become involved in service learning activities that may be effective in promoting leadership skills and character development. Characteristics of effective service learning programs include opportunities to develop skills in self-determination, including an internal locus of control and sense of self-efficacy, and opportunities to build strong relationships with others and with the community, including a sense of civic responsibility and efficacy in contributing to the betterment of the community (Lakin & Mahoney, 2006).

Forming Partnerships For Change

The ability of a system, such as family or school, to promote healthy development depends to a large extent upon the strength of the linkages between systems. For example, a student's success in school is influenced greatly by the extent of family involvement in education and the quality of the partnership between family and school. When the family places a strong priority on the child's education and demonstrates this consistently by setting aside time on a regular basis for literacy activities, carefully monitoring student performance during homework time, and limiting television and recreational computer time, the child is likely to be more highly motivated and engaged in school work (Christenson & Sheridan, 2001). Also, when teachers and parents are able to form a strong relationship, keep each other informed about the child's performance on a regular basis, affirm the child's success, and solve problems when they begin to arise, the student is likely to be successful in school with academics and peer interactions.

Another link that is vitally important for the developing child is the connection between the family and health systems. For a high percentage of children, primary care is the setting through which they receive most of their health care. The Medical Home model has been developed to optimize the primary care experience for individuals and their families, especially those with special health care needs (Sia, Tonniges, Osterhus, & Taba, 2004). This model emphasizes the critical importance of coordinating the efforts of providers from multiple disciplines who offer services to children by building strong connections among systems of care in the community. Community systems include schools, early intervention programs, community mental health centers, youth and family services, civic organizations, and faith-based organizations. Also, this model places strong emphasis on forming and maintaining strong relationships between the primary care provider and child/family.

An especially important linkage for promoting healthy development is the connection between school and primary care (Brown, 2004). The importance of this linkage is underscored by the fact that major providers of mental health services in this nation are primary care and school professionals. The services rendered by these professionals are quite different, yet complementary. For example, primary care providers focus on addressing child health issues and the most commonly used intervention strategies for mental health concerns are family education and psychotropic medication. In contrast, school professionals focus on the child's education and the most commonly used interventions are instructional and behavioral strategies.

School and primary care providers often have information that is important to share. For instance, school professionals can readily obtain information about attention and behavior that is important in assessing ADHD and other mental health disorders, and monitoring response to medication. Primary care providers may have information about the health of children and how to treat chronic conditions (e.g., asthma, diabetes) that is important for school professionals to know. Also, school and primary care providers serve complementary roles in a child's life and it is important to synchronize efforts to achieve optimal outcomes. Unfortunately, the efforts of school and primary care professionals typically are not well coordinated. A consequence is that families are often placed in the position of coordinating efforts, which is untenable for many families, especially those who are poor or those that have been exposed repeatedly to stressful experiences (Power & Blom-Hoffman, 2004).

Promoting Readiness for Change

Prevention programming involves skill building, systems change, and systems alignment, but it is also necessary to address the readiness of children, families, and other key participants to engage in preventive services. The stages of help seeking embedded within the behavior model of health service use, first developed by Andersen and Newman (1973), is a useful model for conceptualizing readiness for change. This multistage model was originally designed to address the challenges of providing health care to adult populations, but it has subsequently been adapted for pediatric populations of diverse socioeconomic status and racial/ethnic minority status (Eiraldi et al., 2006; see Table 3.1 in chapter 3). Although the model was intended to guide research and practice related to interventions for individuals with identified conditions, it can be adapted to a prevention framework.

In the context of prevention involving families, the first stage of help seeking is family recognition of the importance of health-promoting behaviors and the potential harm associated with certain patterns of behavior. Family education and effective communication between provider and family are useful to assist families in this stage of help seeking. The second stage is willingness on the part of the family to seek assistance in efforts to promote health and prevent a problem from arising. Numerous culturally determined factors have an effect on family beliefs to seek help, including acculturation, trust in health providers, and stigma. Motivational interviewing strategies may be helpful to families at this level. The third stage is selection of preventive services by the family. At this stage, collaborative problem solving strategies or shared decision making techniques can be useful. The fourth and final stage is family engagement in services and implementation of evidence-based strategies at a sufficient level to produce change. Numerous factors have an effect on the successful movement of families through these stages, including reduction of access barriers, formation of a trusting relationship with the provider, effective communication between provider and family, and use of culturally effective education and prevention strategies (Power, Eiraldi, Clarke, & Mazzuca, 2005).

Sustaining and Disseminating Prevention Programs

Although developing and implementing prevention programs can be highly challenging, sustaining these efforts can be even more daunting. Further, disseminating or transporting programs developed under well-resourced conditions to less resourced circumstances requires careful planning and ongoing support.

Sustainability

Prevention programs typically are instituted when there is a confluence of opinion among stakeholders that an initiative should be launched and resources are procured to begin the project. Resources often include a grant or contract that is publicly or privately funded. Programs generally fade out or end when resources are depleted. Typically, there is not enough momentum and institutional support to keep an initiative going without the external support.

Planning for the sustainability of a project should begin as soon as the program is initiated. Sustainability requires institutional commitment and administrative buy-in from the outset. Institutional commitment can be demonstrated in a range of ways, including in-kind financial support, allocation of space, and dedication of administrative time. A highly useful strategy is to advocate for a change in institutional policy to support the prevention program or practice (Grimes, Kurns, & Tilly, 2006). For example, a school could institute a policy that all children will be screened for behavioral and emotional problems upon entering first grade. Alternatively, a consortium of primary care practices can institute a policy that all children will be screened for autism at 2 and 4 years of age. Of course, the practice of screening needs to be linked with strategies of prevention and intervention for those identified as having a problem or being at risk. Further, advocating for policy change at a local, state, and federal level can set in motion a chain of events that leads to policy change at the institutional level.

In many schools passage of the Individuals with Disabilities Education Act of 2004 has been the impetus for introducing a prevention model that incorporates a response to intervention framework. This policy change has supported innovations in service delivery, such as Positive Behavior Support (PBS; Sugai & Horner, 2006), which is now being implemented in thousands of schools across the United States. The success of prevention initiatives such as PBS requires the alignment of organizational priorities and resources to support the change process and sustain the use of the model over time. By so doing, the innovation is not solely dependent on the leadership ability of school administrators, the commitment of a faculty of teachers, or the financial resources available to the district through federal, state, and local resources.

Dissemination

Prevention programs are often initiated as model demonstration projects. The intent is to resource the project sufficiently to develop the program, modify it as needed, evaluate preliminary outcomes, and determine what is needed to make the program successful. The conditions in which programs are developed, pilot tested, and evaluated often are quite different from typical practice parameters.

The successful dissemination of prevention programs to other contexts involves multiple steps (Grimes et al., 2006). First, it is important to secure administrative buy-in and ensure that a minimal infrastructure is in place to support the project (Sugai & Horner, 2006). Second, it is important to identify key staff and to secure their buy-in. Often it is useful to have an institutional champion or key opinion leader to serve as a role model and promote buy-in (Atkins, Graczyk, Frazier, & Abdul-Adil, 2003). Third, resources to support the initial training of key staff are needed. Training is required to convey the key components of the program and process dimensions (e.g., building therapeutic relationships, promoting child, family, and teacher engagement) that are critical for program success. Fourth, resources to support ongoing integrity monitoring and performance feedback in the context of supervision are required to ensure a reasonably high level of program implementation. Fifth, a plan to monitor progress and evaluate outcomes is needed to determine whether the program is successful.

Conclusions

A prevention orientation makes sense in that it can promote the health of all children, reduce chronic health conditions among youth and adults, and reduce the cost of health care. Prevention science is strongly rooted in epidemiology and developmental psychology. Most models of prevention incorporate a multitier framework involving increasingly more intensive and costly services in response to level of risk. A key aspect of multitier models is response to intervention, which relies on data-based decision making and involves providing increasing levels of support contingent upon response to services at less intensive levels. Effective prevention programming incorporates multiple strategies, such as partnering with key stakeholders throughout the process of planning and implementation, including skill building strategies for participants, creating family and school contexts that promote change, forming key partnerships among professionals across systems of care, and providing services in response to a family's and other participants' readiness for change. The ultimate indicator of the effectiveness of a prevention initiative is the success of efforts to sustain the program and disseminate the project to diverse contexts.

Questions for Discussion

1. How does the knowledge of risk and resilience factors help in the development of prevention programs?
2. In the context of a multitier intervention framework, what factors should a practitioner consider when the child's response to intervention at a particular tier has not been successful?
3. What are some of the challenges of using a community-based participatory approach to prevention programming and how can these obstacles be addressed?
4. What strategies can a consultant use to build institutional resources to sustain prevention program efforts?

Additional Teaching Aids

PowerPoint slides pertaining to health promotion and illness prevention are included in the attached CD.

References

Andersen, R. M., & Newman, J. F. (1973). Societal and individual determinants of medical care utilization in the United States. *Milbank Quarterly, 51*(1), 95–124.

Atkins, M. S., Graczyk, P. A., Frazier, S. L., & Abdul-Adil, J. (2003). Toward a new model for promoting urban children's mental health: Accessible, effective, and sustainable school-based mental health services. *School Psychology Review, 32*(4), 503–514.

Blom-Hoffman, J., Kelleher, C., Power, T. J., & Leff, S. S. (2004). Promoting healthy food consumption among young children: Evaluation of a multi-component nutrition education program. *Journal of School Psychology, 42*(1), 45–60. doi:10.1016/j.jsp.2003.08.004

Brown, R. T. (2004). Introduction: Changes in the provision of health care to children and adolescents. In R. T. Brown (Ed.), *Handbook of pediatric psychology in school settings* (pp. 1–19). Mahwah, NJ: Erlbaum.

Cauce, A. M., Domenech-Rodriguez, M., Paradise, M., Cochran, B. N., Shea, J. M., Srebnik, D., & Baydar, N. (2002). Cultural and contextual influences in mental health help seeking: A focus on ethnic minority youth. *Journal of Consulting and Clinical Psychology, 70*(1), 44–55.

Chartier, M. J., Walker, J. R., & Naimark, B. (2010). Separate and cumulative effects of adverse childhood experiences in predicting adult health and health care utilization. *Child Abuse and Neglect, 34*, 454–464.

Christenson, S. L., & Sheridan, S. M. (2001). *Schools and families: Creating essential connections for learning.* New York: Guillford.

Clarke, A. T. (2006). Coping with interpersonal stress and psychosocial health among children and adolescents: A meta-analysis. *Journal of Youth and Adolescence, 35*(1), 11–24.

Dodge, K. A. (2001). The science of youth violence prevention: Progressing from developmental epidemiology to efficacy to effectiveness to public policy. *American Journal of Preventive Medicine, 20*(1), 63–70.

Doll, B., Pfohl, W., & Yoon, J. (Eds.). (2010). *Handbook of youth prevention science.* New York: Routledge.

Dowrick, P. W., Kim-Rupnow, W. S., & Power, T. J. (2006). Video feedforward for reading. *Journal of Special Education, 39*(4), 194–207.

Dube, S. R., Anda, R. F., Felitti, V. J., Chapman, D. P., Williamson, D. F., & Giles, W. H. (2001). Childhood abuse, household dysfunction, and the risk of attempted suicide throughout the life span: Findings from the Adverse Childhood Experiences Study. *Journal of the American Medical Association, 286*, 3089–3096.

Eiraldi, R. B., Mazzuca, L. B., Clarke, A. T., & Power, T. J. (2006). Service utilization among ethnic minority children with ADHD: A model of help-seeking behavior. *Administration and Policy in Mental Health and Mental Health Services Research, 33*(5), 607–622.

Fiese, B., & Wamboldt, F. (2000). Family routines, rituals and asthma management: A proposal for family-based strategies to increase treatment adherence. *Families, Systems, and Health, 18*, 405–418.

Gardner, W., Murphy, M., Childs, G., Kelleher, K., Pagano, M., Jellinek, M., ... Chiapeta, L. (1999). The PSC-17: A brief pediatric symptom checklist with psychosocial problem subscales. A report from PROS and ASPN. *Ambulatory Child Health, 5*, 225–236.

Ginsburg, K. R., Alexander, P. M., Hunt, J., Sullivan, M., Zhao, H. Q., & Cnaan, A. (2002). Enhancing their likelihood for a positive future: The perspective of inner-city youth. *Pediatrics, 109*(6), 1136–1143.

Glover, T. A., & DiPerna, J. C. (2007). Service delivery for response to intervention: Core components and directions for future research. *School Psychology Review, 36*(4), 526–540.

Goodman, R. (2001). Psychometric properties of the strengths and difficulties questionnaire. *Journal of the American Academy of Child and Adolescent Psychiatry, 40*(11), 1337–1345.

Grimes, J., Kurns, S., & Tilly, W. D. I. (2006). Sustainability: An enduring commitment to success. *School Psychology Review, 35*(2), 224–244.

Holmbeck, G. N., Zebracki, K., & McGoron, K. (2009). Reseach design and statistical applications. In M. C. Roberts & R. G. Steele (Eds.), *Handbook of pediatric psychology* (4th ed., pp. 52–70). New York: Guilford.

Hughes, J. N., & Barrois, L. K. (2010). The developmental implications of classroom social relationships and strategies for improving them. In B. Doll, W. Pfohl & J. Yoon (Eds.), *Handbook of youth prevention science* (pp. 194–217). New York: Routledge.

Kataoka, S. H., Zhang, L., & Wells, K. B. (2002). Unmet need for mental health care among U.S. children: variation by ethnicity and insurance status. *American Journal of Psychiatry, 159*(9), 1548–1555.

Kazak, A. E., Rourke, M. T., Alderfer, M. A., Pai, A., Reilly, A. F., & Meadows, A. T. (2007). Evidence-based assessment, intervention and psychosocial care in pediatric oncology: A blueprint for comprehensive services across treatment. *Journal of Pediatric Psychology, 32*(9), 1099–1110.

Kelleher, C., Riley-Tillman, T. C., & Power, T. J. (2008). An initial comparison of collaborative and expert-driven consultation on treatment integrity. *Journal of Educational and Psychological Consultation, 18*(4), 294–324.

Lakin, R., & Mahoney, A. (2006). Empowering youth to change their world: Identifying key components of a community service program to promote positive development. *Journal of School Psychology, 44*(6), 513–531.

Leff, S. S., Costigan, T., & Power, T. J. (2004). Using participatory research to develop a playground-based prevention program. *Journal of School Psychology, 42*(1), 3–21.

Leff, S. S., Waasdorp, T. E., Paskewich, B., Gullan, R. L., Jawad, A. F., MacEvoy, J. P., ... Power, T. J. (2010). The Preventing Relational Aggression in Schools Everyday Program: A preliminary evaluation of acceptability and impact. *School Psychology Review, 39*(4), 569–587.

Linley, P. A., Joseph, S., Harrington, S., & Wood, A. M. (2006). Positive psychology: Past, present and (possible) future. *Journal of Positive Psychology, 1*, 3–16.

Lochman, J. E., & Wells, K. C. (2002). Contextual social-cognitive mediators and child outcome: A test of the theoretical model in the Coping Power program. *Development and Psychopathology, 14*(4), 945–967.

McMahon, R. J., & Forehand, R. L. (2003). *Helping the noncompliant child: Family-based treatment for oppositional behavior* (2nd ed.). New York: Guilford.

Nastasi, B. K., Bernstein Moore, R., & Varjas, K. M. (2004). *School-based mental health services: Creating comprehensive and culturally specific programs*. Washington, DC: American Psychological Association.

Noell, G. H., Witt, J. C., Slider, N. J., Connell, J. E., Gatti, S. L., Williams, K. L., ... Resetar, J. L. (2005). Treatment implementation following behavioral consultation in schools: A comparison of three follow-up strategies. *School Psychology Review, 34*(1), 87–106.

Olson, A. L., Dietrich, A. J., Prazar, G., & Hurley, J. (2006). Brief maternal depression screening at well-child visits. *Pediatrics, 118*(1), 207–216.

Pianta, R. C. (1997). Adult–child relationship processes and early schooling. *Early Education and Development, 8*, 11–26.

Pianta, R. C., La Paro, K. M., & Hamre, B. K. (2008). *Classroom assessment scoring system (CLASS) manual (K-3)*. Baltimore, MD: Brookes.

Power, T. J., & Blom-Hoffman, J. (2004). The school as a venue for managing and preventing health problems: Opportunities and challenges. In R. T. Brown (Ed.), *Handbook of pediatric psychology in school settings* (pp. 37–48). Mahwah, NJ: Erlbaum.

Power, T. J., Blom-Hoffman, J., Clarke, A. T., Riley-Tillman, T. C., Kelleher, C., & Manz, P. H. (2005). Reconceptualizing intervention integrity: A partnership-based framework for linking research with practice. *Psychology in the Schools, 42*(5), 495–507. doi: 10.1002/pits.20087

Power, T. J., Eiraldi, R. B., Clarke, A. T., & Mazzuca, L. B. (2005). Improving mental health service utilization for children and adolescents. *School Psychology Quarterly, 20*, 203–221.

Robin, A. L. (2006). Training families with adolescents with ADHD. In R. A. Barkley (Ed.), *Attention-deficit hyperactivity disorder: A handbook for diagnosis and treatment* (3rd ed., pp. 499–546). New York: Guilford.

Rose, G. (1989). High-risk and population strategies of prevention: Ethical considerations. *Annals of Medicine, 21*(6), 409–413.

Sameroff, A. J. (1993). Models of development and developmental risk. In C. H. Zeanah (Ed.), *Handbook of infant mental health* (pp. 3–13). New York: Guilford.

Sanetti, L. M. H., & Kratochwill, T. R. (2009). Toward developing a science of treatment integrity: Introduction to the special series. *School Psychology Review, 38*(4), 445–459.

Schonwald, A., Horan, K., & Huntington, N. (2009). Developmental screening: Is there enough time? *Clinical Pediatrics, 48*(6), 648–655.

Sheridan, S. M., Swanger-Gagne, M., Welch, G. W., Kwon, K., & Garbacz, S. A. (2009). Fidelity measurement in consultation: Psychometric issues and preliminary examination. *School Psychology Review, 38*(4), 476–495.

Shonkoff, J. P., Boyce, W. T., & McEwen, B. S. (2009). Neuroscience, molecular biology, and the childhood roots of health disparities: Building a new framework for health promotion and disease prevention. *Journal of the American Medical Association, 301*(21), 2252–2259.

Sia, C., Tonniges, T. F., Osterhus, E., & Taba, S. (2004). History of the medical home concept. *Pediatrics, 113*(5), 1473–1478.

Spitzer, R. L., Kroenke, K., & Williams, J. B. W. (1999). Validation and utility of a self-report version of PRIME-MD—The PHQ primary care study. *Journal of the American Medical Association, 282*(18), 1737–1744.

Sugai, G., & Horner, R. R. (2006). A promising approach for expanding and sustaining school-wide positive behavior support. *School Psychology Review, 35*(2), 245–259.

Suldo, S. M., & Shaffer, E. J. (2008). Looking beyond psychopathology: The dual-factor model of mental health in youth. *School Psychology Review, 37*, 52–68.

Tucker, C. M. (2002). Expanding pediatric psychology beyond hospital walls to meet the health care needs of ethnic minority children. *Journal of Pediatric Psychology, 27*(4), 315–323. doi: 10.1093/jpepsy/27.4.315

U.S. Department of Health and Human Services. (2010). Healthy People 2020: the road ahead Retrieved from http://healthypeople.gov/hp2020/default.asp

Webster-Stratton, C. (2005). *The incredible years: A trouble-shooting guide for parents of children aged 2–8 years.* Seattle, WA: Incredible Years.

Five

Research to Practice

Prevention Programs in Community Settings

with Stephen S. Leff and Jessica A. Hoffman

In the previous chapter, we presented a framework for conceptualizing prevention programming at multiple levels, including universal, selective, and targeted. In that chapter, we described numerous components of successful prevention programming, including forming partnerships with key stakeholders to develop programs, using evidence-based practices to promote skill acquisition, strengthening relationships in the family, fostering child development in school, creating a community context that promotes child competence, linking systems of care in the community, and promoting child and family readiness for change. This chapter applies research to practice and provides examples of prevention programs at multiple levels (universal, selective, targeted) that can be applied in diverse contexts, including school, primary care, and other community settings. The examples provided describe a wide range of prevention initiatives designed to promote health and prevent illness or disorders, including programs to promote successful peer relationships, health and wellness, and to prevent aggression and school failure. Each of the programs described in this chapter highlight multiple components of effective programming.

School-Based, Partnership-Oriented Prevention: The Playground, Lunchroom, and Youth Success (PLAYS) Program

Aggression and violence in schools is a widespread and pervasive problem that is especially prevalent in inner-city schools situated in low-income neighborhoods (Peskin, Tortolero, & Markham, 2006). The consequences of aggression and violence can be serious and may include injury; victimization of students, which can lead to the victim internalizing problems, and in turn expressing aggression toward others; mental health problems; and academic underachievement (Crick, 1996).

The PLAYS program (Leff, Costigan, & Power, 2004) is an example of a school-based initiative in urban schools that primarily serve children from low-income families. Although the program was designed for the entire student population, and therefore could be considered universal, it is perhaps more accurately classified as an exemplar of selective prevention in that the students were at risk by virtue of their psychosocial circumstances and increased likelihood of being exposed to adverse events on a chronic basis. The program reflects the conjoint efforts of a team of university researchers and school staff. A hallmark of this program is the use of partnership strategies to design and implement the initiative and to evaluate its success. The project also illustrates a data-based approach to monitor and promote high-quality intervention implementation.

The PLAYS program was developed in response to concerns expressed by members of the school community regarding the need to reduce aggression on the playground. Monitoring on the playground was conducted by paraprofessionals who generally were parents and grandparents of students attending the school. The school principal was concerned about the problem and supportive of developing an initiative to address the concerns. The physical education teacher had a key role because he was asked by the principal to provide training to the staff and redesign the playground to promote cooperative behavior among students.

The initial steps in program planning consisted of a series of meetings between the university-based consultants and paraprofessionals, some of which were attended by the principal. These meetings were designed to understand the nature of the concerns, identify factors that might be contributing to the problem, obtain background information about what strategies had been tried and were thought to be useful, and determine which strategies were perceived to be acceptable and feasible by the playground paraprofessionals. During the meetings, the aides described numerous concerns, including rough play often leading to aggression, failure of children to engage in cooperative play, and a lack of play among children of diverse ethnic/racial backgrounds (i.e., African American, Southeast Asian, and White). The aides indicated that they had tried numerous strategies in the past, including close supervision and efforts to involve students in organized games on the playground. They indicated that the physical education teacher had arranged for toys and games to be taken to the playground, and he demonstrated methods to the aides for successfully involving children in games.

Several observations conducted by the consultants confirmed that there were relatively high rates of aggression and victimization occurring on the playground. Further, playground aides generally were observed standing together in the corner of the playground closest to the door to the school, resulting in a lack of surveillance over large sections of the playground. Also, during the observations there were generally no games for the students and no attempt to get them involved in organized activities.

A review of the literature conducted by the consultants confirmed that the preventive interventions used in the past by the playground aides had the potential to be effective in promoting prosocial behavior and reducing aggression. Studies have shown that providing age-appropriate games that involve children in cooperative activities increases the occurrence of prosocial behaviors and decreases the incidence of aggressive actions (Bay-Hinitz, Peterson, & Quilitch, 1994; Murphy, Hutchison, & Bailey, 1983). In addition, research has demonstrated that the provision of active monitoring on the playground by supervisors who are trained to affirm cooperative, prosocial behavior decreases the incidence of aggressive and maladaptive playground behavior.

After collecting this information, the consultants engaged in a series of meetings with the aides to design a playground intervention. The principal and physical education teacher were highly supportive of this process and attended meetings when possible. The consultants used a partnership-based framework based on participatory action research (PAR) methods to develop the intervention (see Nastasi, Bernstein

Moore, & Varjas, 2004). The consultants involved the aides as full partners in the planning process, recognizing the aides' expertise with regard to understanding the playground and broader school context and understanding neighborhood culture, while acknowledging the consultants' own expertise pertaining to program design, evidence-based intervention, and program evaluation. The aides and consultants committed to a process of developing a plan together, collecting data to evaluate the plan, reviewing the data, and using the data to determine a future course of action.

The aides and consultants rapidly reached agreement that the intervention should include providing organized games and active supervision to the playground. Much of the time in the planning meetings was spent making arrangements for: (a) the games to be delivered to the playground each day; (b) the aides to interact with the children to set up the games; (c) the aides to develop a plan to ensure surveillance of the entire playground; (d) the aides to encourage cooperative play behavior; and (e) ways teachers could provide support for these efforts.

The consultants and school professionals collaborated and developed intervention strategies during the first year and conducted an evaluation of the program the following school year. The consultants designed an observation system to monitor student behavior and implementation of the intervention plan. To assist in the observation of behavior, the playground was divided into sections and observers focused on student behavior and playground assistant implementation of recommended strategies within each section for the designated observation period. The student behaviors observed were cooperative play (i.e., mutual play with peers that was not rough), rough-and-tumble play (i.e., mutual play among children that was active, vigorous, playful, and rough), intercultural exchanges (i.e., interactions between children of apparently different racial/ ethnic background), and aggressive behavior, which included acts of physical, relational, and verbal aggression. Rough-and-tumble play was a concern to the playground aides because this type of play often escalated into aggressive actions. The implementation variables were presence of organized games and presence of a playground supervisor within a designated section of the playground. The coding procedure is described in detail in Leff et al. (2004).

The intervention was implemented over the course of several weeks. During this time the consultants collected data about student behavior and intervention implementation by the playground aides. The findings pertaining to the impact of having organized games available was particularly striking. Children were engaged in cooperative play 78% of the time when organized games were observed in an area of the playground as opposed to 26% of the time when games were not present. Children were involved in rough-and-tumble play 13% of the time when organized games were present as opposed to 26% of the time when the games were not present. In addition, intercultural exchanges occurred significantly more often when active supervision was provided than when it was not (59 vs. 40%).

The consultants presented these findings to the school team and a discussion ensued about the meaning of the findings. The implications were obvious: Students were more likely to play in a cooperative, prosocial, respectful manner when organized games were accessible and active supervision was provided. The aides discussed a plan to improve intervention implementation and coordination of efforts among team members. Consistent with research on the importance of sharing performance feedback to sustain treatment integrity (Noell et al., 2005), the consultants continued to collect information about intervention implementation and student outcomes and presented these findings to the school team on a regular basis. Through this partnership, the consultants and paraprofessionals were able to design a useful and acceptable prevention program and work together to promote consistent implementation of strategies.

School-Based, Multisystemic Selective Prevention: Promotion of Fruit and Vegetable Consumption

Diets high in fruits and vegetables (F&Vs) are associated with reduced risk of cardiovascular disease, stroke, and cancer, and can help individuals achieve a healthy weight (Epstein et al., 2001). In the United States, almost all children eat fewer than the recommended number of servings of F&V (Guenther, Dodd, Reedy, & Krebs-Smith, 2006). Encouraging children to consume F&Vs is important because food preferences develop at a young age (Birch & Fisher, 1998) and eating behaviors tend to be stable over time (Kelder, Perry, Klepp, & Lytle, 1994). School lunches, which are required to include F&V, have the potential to increase the consumption of healthy foods and to shape healthy eating habits among children.

The F&V Promotion Program (F&VPP; Hoffman et al., 2011) is an exemplar of a school-based, multicomponent prevention initiative implemented across multiple settings for an extended time period (2.5 years). This program has been uniquely designed for young elementary-age students (kindergarten and first grade). The F&VPP is rooted in social learning theory and developmental-ecological psychology, and it includes school-wide, classroom, lunchroom, and home-based components (Blom-Hoffman, 2008). Like PLAYS, this program is universal in that it is implemented with all kindergarten and first grade students in the school, but it is more accurately conceptualized as a selective prevention program because of its intentional, targeted focus on students from low-income families who are attending urban schools and are at increased risk for obesity.

The F&VPP was designed to communicate the importance of F&V consumption across multiple contexts. Key stakeholders engaged in program delivery included teachers, lunch aides, principals, parents, and school coaches. As discussed in the previous chapter, the success of a program depends in large part on the development of strong partnerships with key stakeholders and planning that builds upon existing resources in the community (Nastasi et al., 2004). At the outset it is important to train providers to deliver program elements reliably and effectively, develop a plan to collect integrity data during program delivery, and arrange for ongoing discussions with stakeholders regarding their perceptions of program components. One key factor that contributed to the successful implementation of F&VPP is that several individuals had key roles in delivering the program. This explicit design feature ensured that no one individual was overly burdened and that key concepts were reinforced multiple times each day. Additionally, program developers made a conscious attempt to build redundancy into the model; if one element of the program was not implemented adequately, students were able to obtain that component from another source.

In F&VPP, consultants met with key stakeholders on a continual basis to monitor how program elements were being implemented, address problems that arose, and identify ways to adapt strategies so that they better fit the context in which they were being implemented. For example, the F&VPP uses a series of computer-based lessons in the classroom to deliver information about healthy eating behaviors to students. Computer-based instruction has multiple advantages, which include the need for only limited teacher training, implementation of procedures with a high degree of integrity, and high levels of student engagement in the gamelike activities. Although teachers were enthusiastic about using the computer-based program, some of them did not have sufficient training and technical support to actually use it. Subsequent discussions with grade-level teams of teachers and school administrators led to the conclusion that the computer class would be an ideal location for the computer-assisted instruction. Computer teachers interacted with all students in the schools and they were pleased to incorporate the F&VPP curricular materials, which featured cartoon characters on a CD-ROM, into their instruction.

Building resource capacity was also explicitly addressed when designing the home-based component of the F&VPP (Blom-Hoffman, Wilcox, Dunn, Leff, & Power, 2008). A review of school-based nutrition education programs revealed that a majority include a home component, which generally entails teachers sending information home to the family through the student. Although cost-effective, sending information home does not ensure that parents will read the materials. The home-based component of F&VPP involved the use of five interactive children's books. Teachers invited parents to become involved in the program by assigning students the homework task of reading the books together with a parent at home. The books, which included cartoon characters similar to those in the CD-ROM, highlighted information that students had learned in school and communicated to parents clear, straightforward messages about healthy eating habits. Each of the books included exercises for the students to complete as homework and return to the teacher. Evaluation data showed that on average 56% of books were returned to class by students; most of the books showed evidence that the homework was completed, and parents and children reported that the books were enjoyable to read and informative.

The major behavior change component of the F&VPP was delivered by lunch monitors in the cafeteria. In addition to hanging posters featuring the F&VPP cartoon characters near the cafeteria line to raise awareness of the F&V being served that day, lunch monitors were trained to "catch students eating F&V" by giving them stickers that featured the cartoon characters. The stickers were highly reinforcing to students, who used them to decorate their backpacks and binders. Most lunch monitors were enthusiastic about giving out the stickers and reported that it did not take much time and effort to administer. They did report some difficulty remembering to bring the stickers to the cafeteria, so a safe place had to be identified in each building to store them. Lunch monitors were engaged as intervention partners through ongoing meetings, small thank you gifts, and administrator recognition regarding the importance of their efforts in promoting healthy eating for students. Data from integrity monitoring indicated that lunch monitors were somewhat inconsistent in providing specific verbal feedback to students when administering stickers; however, when asked, almost 100% of students reported they received the stickers for eating their F&V at lunch.

Intervention implementation in this program was assessed using a multidimensional model that incorporates multiple methods. Integrity was monitored using direct observations in the cafeteria conducted by research staff, a review of permanent products (e.g., completion of homework assignments), teacher-completed logs of CD-ROM use, teacher reports of students' attention and engagement during instruction, and student questionnaires. In addition, student responsiveness to the program was monitored via teacher and student reports (Power, Blom-Hoffman, et al., 2005).

The effectiveness of the program was evaluated in a randomized clinical trial comparing children who received F&VPP to those who received education as usual. The results indicated clear and persistent improvements in student knowledge, as well as improvements in F&V consumption during lunch. However, the findings displayed evidence of a decay in the behavioral effects of the intervention over time, suggesting the need for even more intensive treatment and approaches that are infused throughout the school day, as well as in activities offered in the home and community (Hoffman et al., 2011). The results highlight the challenging nature of programmatic efforts based in urban settings to prevent overweight and obesity; intensive treatment across multiple settings and the persistence of efforts over many years is needed to promote and sustain gains in healthy eating habits.

Community-Based, Multitier, Selective Prevention: Promoting Infant Pediatric Care

Receiving adequate health care early in life is a protective factor in the promotion of children's health and development. Indicators of appropriate health care early in life are

attendance at scheduled well child visits (WCVs) and being
up to date with expected immunizations. Infants of racial/
ethnic minority background who are born into economically
disadvantaged families are at increased risk of not receiving
adequate pediatric care (Wooten, Luman, & Barker, 2007),
thereby placing them at risk for poor health outcomes. Several
prevention programs have been developed to reduce health
disparities in infant pediatric care (e.g., Olds et al., 2007). The
program developed by Hambidge and colleagues (Hambidge,
Phibbs, Chandramouli, Fairclough, & Steiner, 2009), referred
to in this chapter as the Promoting Infant Pediatric Care program (PIPC), is noteworthy in that it used a stepped or tiered
approach, which allocates higher intensity and more expensive resources to families demonstrating risk of not engaging
in infant child care. Also, this program incorporated well-
trained community partners or patient navigators in an effort
to provide high quality case management services in a culturally competent manner.

Participants in the PIPC program were healthy infants born
at a large urban medical center over the course of a 12-month
period. A high percentage of the children (90%) were eligible
for Medicaid, 74% were Hispanic, and 19% were Black. Clinicians were patient navigators who were well trained (masters'
degrees) and lived in the nearby community. The directors of
the program intentionally recruited navigators for their case
management skills, commitment to the urban population
being served, ability to engage with families and establish
strong working relationships, and cultural competence. The
initial encounter between the mother and patient navigator
was shortly after the child's birth in the hospital, over the telephone, or at a home visit.

The intervention included three tiers and incorporated a
response-to-intervention framework (see Figure 5.1); the determination about whether to advance to the next tier was based
upon the success of intervention at each step in addition to the
presence of factors associated with risk for nonengagement in
services (i.e., mother who was noninsured, did not intend to
breastfeed the infant, had a history of poor prenatal care, or
had a history of substance abuse or violence). The Tier 1 universal strategy consisted of a language-appropriate postcard
sent to the family to remind them of an upcoming WCV. The
Tier 2 selective prevention approach was a telephone reminder
before each WCV along with a postcard and another telephone
call after a missed WCV. The Tier 2 intervention procedure

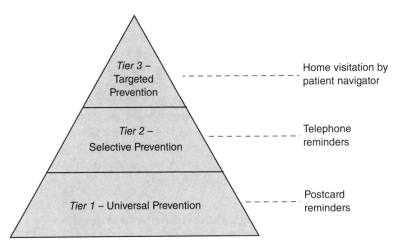

Figure 5.1   Tiered approach to prevention in promoting infant pediatric care program

was provided to all families who missed a WCV and to those who manifested one or more risk factors for nonengagement in pediatric services. Once a family received the Tier 2 intervention, this level was provided for the duration of the program (until the infant was 15 months of age), unless there was reason to advance to Tier 3. The targeted prevention strategy at Tier 3 was offered to those families who were still missing WCVs after Tier 2. The Tier 3 intervention consisted of intensive outreach and home visitation by the patient navigator. Once families advanced to Tier 3, they continued to receive this level of care for the duration of the program. During home visitation, the role of the patient navigators was to provide support, assess barriers to care, and assist families in resolving barriers (e.g., addressing transportation, insurance, and billing issues, making referrals for child care; and providing assistance with housing and food crisis issues when appropriate).

Results demonstrated that 7% of the families were successfully managed at Tier 1; 56% needed Tier 2 and not Tier 3; and 37% advanced to Tier 3. Families in the intervention program were compared to those who received usual care. At 15 months of age, 44% of infants in the intervention group and 33% in the control group were up-to-date with immunizations, and the intervention group had substantially fewer days without immunization coverage than the control group (109 versus 192 days). In addition, at 15 months, 65% of infants in intervention and 47% of those in control had at least five WCVs (Hambidge et al., 2009). The presence of maternal risk factors previously noted (e.g., noninsured, history of substance abuse or violence, inadequate prenatal care) was associated with poorer outcomes with regard to immunization rates and attendance at WCVs. The fact that relatively few families responded at Tier 1 suggests that the intervention procedure used at this level (postcard reminder) needs to be adapted or intensified in a manner that is feasible to implement in a cost-effective manner, so that Tier 1 can be effective for a higher percentage of families. Despite this limitation, this study is an exemplar of a multitier prevention initiative and a program that successfully incorporated community partners.

School-Based, Developmentally Appropriate, and Culturally Sensitive, Targeted Prevention: Friend-to-Friend (F2F) Program

Nearly one in three school-age children is involved either as a peer aggressor or victim. Peer aggression and bullying occur frequently in schools across the country, and these behaviors are associated with students' problem-solving deficits, psychosocial adjustment difficulties, feelings of being unsafe at school, and lower levels of academic achievement (Leff, Waasdorp, & Crick, 2010). Further, peer bullying is of especial concern for urban minority youth who are exposed to many acute and chronic stressors within their homes and neighborhoods (Wandersman & Nation, 1998). Despite these challenges for urban youth, prior prevention programs have been limited in that they: (a) focus only on the aggressor/bully without addressing broader classroom and school climate issues, limiting generalization of learned skills across settings (Swearer & Espelage, 2011); (b) focus solely on physical forms of bullying and fail to account for relational forms such as starting rumors and threatening to withdraw friendship (Crick & Grotpeter, 1995); (c) fail to address the unstructured school settings (e.g., playground and lunchroom), where most bullying occurs for elementary age children (Leff et al., 2004); and (d) fail to adapt efficacious programs through partnering with key stakeholders within urban settings, resulting in programs that may not be developmentally appropriate or culturally sensitive for minority youth (Bauer, Lozano, & Rivara, 2007).

   In response to the limitations of existing aggression prevention programs, the Friend to Friend (F2F) program was developed through an extensive partnership process. The result is an engaging and meaningful program that helps aggressive girls in urban settings to learn to recognize and control their anger while promoting their friendship-making skills across both structured and unstructured school settings. F2F is an example of a targeted school-based prevention program. It has been developed specifically for third to fifth grade urban, predominately African American aggressive girls. This 20-session, pull-out program is conducted twice per week for 10 weeks during the lunch-recess period by a research interventionist who partners with a classroom teacher or teacher's assistant. The program incorporates social information processing (SIP) intervention strategies; this helps at-risk girls to learn to think and act like social *detectives* in order to identify different types of conflict situations, recognize when they are becoming angry, develop strategies to stay calm so that they can objectively evaluate social situations, and generate and enact positive responses. F2F teaches participants how to apply these new detective skills in commonly occurring conflict-laden situations that happen at school, including how to more effectively handle rumors and to more successfully enter groups and activities on the playground during lunch and recess.

Once group participants have completed approximately 10 to 12 of the group sessions, they then serve as cofacilitators, along with interventionists, for eight classroom sessions. The classroom sessions mirror the content of the group intervention, and are designed to allow girls in the F2F program to practice teaching their new detective strategies to their classmates and to change the way in which these at-risk girls may be viewed by their classmates and teachers (e.g., having a reputation for being aggressive). In addition, the classroom component of F2F helps to address a need articulated by teachers that boys in their classrooms also exhibit relationally aggressive behaviors that are of concern, and is consistent with the public health orientation of providing universal prevention services to all youth.

An innovative feature of F2F is that the program was designed through strategic partnership with third and fourth grade students, teachers, and community members in order to ensure that both the content of the intervention and the delivery method are developmentally appropriate, culturally responsive, and engaging for the urban, predominately African American girls (see Leff et al., 2007). For example, the intervention team partnered extensively with six, third and fourth grade girls to design culturally specific cartoons, video illustrations, and role-plays as the primary teaching modalities. The girls indicated that these types of presentation modalities would be engaging, relevant, and fun for girls of their age and background. In addition, the interventionists worked extensively with two teachers from different urban elementary schools to ensure that the curriculum and key concepts were presented clearly and succinctly, and that strategies employed were consistent with classroom behavior management techniques used by teachers.

The F2F Program is grounded in three theoretical paradigms, a social information processing (SIP) model (e.g., Crick & Dodge, 1994), Bronfenbrenner's ecological and systems paradigm (1986), and social learning theory (Dishion, Capaldi, Spracklen, & Li, 1995). F2F teaches participants how to process a series of problem-solving steps following the SIP model, similar to best practice programs that have been found to be effective with urban physically aggressive boys (Brain Power Program, Hudley & Graham, 1993; Coping Power Program, Lochman & Wells, 2004). As such, F2F teaches girls to recognize signs of physiological arousal, retrains them at each SIP step, and helps them learn to apply these problem-solving strategies to commonly occurring social situations. Bronfenbrenner's ecological/systems theory (1986) is based on the premise that one's behavior is determined by interactions within and between key systems in the child's life (i.e., family, school, peer group, and broader community). Whereas the SIP paradigm focuses on improving problem-solving skills, an ecological/systems orientation emphasizes the importance of changing the social environment in which the child is embedded. Having F2F participants serve as role models and teach their classmates the problem-solving strategies helps simultaneously to teach SIP skills and change the way in which they are viewed by their peers and teachers, impacting the broader classroom and school ecology. Finally, a range of behavioral techniques are utilized in F2F to help reinforce the learning of new strategies through role plays and shaping of new behaviors, with a particular focus on the unstructured school settings such as the playground and lunchroom (Dishion et al., 1995).

In a study of the effectiveness of the F2F Program, 361 third through fifth graders from two elementary schools completed baseline measures to identify which youth were in need of this relational aggression intervention. The resulting 32 girls (along with several prosocial role models) were randomly assigned to the intervention or were placed in a control condition in which they were referred to the school counselor as needed. A preliminary evaluation of F2F indicated that it was well received by teachers, parents, children, and other school personnel, and that it resulted in increased likeability by peers, improved problem-solving, and decreased relational and physical aggression for youth in F2F as compared to those in the control condition (Leff et al., 2009).

The F2F Program is an example of a targeted, school-based prevention program developed through extensive partner-ships between intervention developers, youth, teachers, and community members. Further, partnering in the design and implementation of the program helped to ensure pro-gram buy-in and applicability. In addition, the program was designed to promote a healthy school context in which youth can feel safe and free to learn, both academically and socially.

Targeted Prevention in Primary Care: Partnering to Achieve School Success (PASS)

Children with attention, learning, and behavior problems are at risk for school failure, which often results in student disen-gagement from school, school dropout, and a host of adverse health and mental health consequences (Barkley, 2006; DuPaul & Stoner, 2003). Early identification and intervention for these students is critical to alter the pathway leading to failure, social alienation, and unhealthy patterns of behav-ior. Strengthening families, promoting family involvement in education, and connecting families and schools are essential elements of programs designed to promote child development and prevent school failure for this at risk population (Chris-tenson & Reschly, 2009).

The PASS program addresses the needs of students at risk for school failure and early dropout by virtue of the presence of attention, learning, and behavior problems. Most of the students in this program meet criteria for attention-deficit/ hyperactivity disorder (ADHD), but this is not a requirement. Hallmarks of this program are that it is based in a primary care setting and uses a colocation model whereby a mental health clinician provides services in primary care and collaborates on an ongoing basis with the child's primary care provider (PCP; Cassano, Lefler, Tresco, Mautone, & Power, 2011). The services provided are multisystemic in nature, and include strategies to promote child development at home and school by connecting the family, school, and primary care systems.

The PASS program was designed specifically to address the challenges encountered by children and families residing in low-income neighborhoods. These families typically face significant barriers to care (e.g., insurance, scheduling, transportation, child care), and may have beliefs that pose challenges in the provision of health and mental health services (e.g., lack of trust in providers, low sense of self-efficacy in being able to obtain help and apply recommended strategies; Power, Eiraldi, Clarke, Mazzuca, & Krain, 2005). These barriers often result in low rates of engagement in services, including failure to initiate intervention and low rates of attendance (McKay & Bannon, 2004).

Referrals to the program are made by PCPs working in an urban-based practice. Eligibility criteria include enrollment in grades K-6, presence of attention or behavior problems related to ADHD, and evidence that the problems were not so serious that an alternative service was needed. About 70% of the children are eligible for Medicaid and approximately 90% are African American. Contacting families by telephone to schedule an initial session has proven to be a significant challenge. This role typically is assumed by the clinician assigned to the case, who is enrolled in a doctoral program in clinical or school psychology. The clinician is trained to engage families by making repeated phone calls and by using motivational interviewing strategies (i.e., listen empathically, indicate how the service can address specific concerns, identify barriers to care, and engage in problem solving to address barriers) when families are successfully contacted.

During the initial cohort of families offered this program, 80 referrals were made by PCPs and 66 children were eligible for services. Clinicians were able to make contact with 54 (82%) of the eligible families, and 48 (89%) of these families were interested in services and were scheduled to attend an intake session. Altogether, 43 of the families (65% of those who were eligible) attended an initial, face-to-face intake session. Factors that predicted family attendance at an initial session were clinician success rates in contacting families by telephone and number of parent-initiated phone calls. Also, length of the phone conversation between clinician and family appeared to have an important mediating effect, suggesting that even when there was difficulty making contact by phone, a sustained, meaningful phone conversation served the purpose of facilitating family engagement in the service (Power et al., 2010).

The PASS program is based upon a participatory model that tailors strategies and sequences components in a manner that is highly responsive to the goals and preferences of families (Power, Soffer, Cassano, Tresco, & Mautone, 2011). The PASS program has several components (see Table 5.1). A critical component is the use of family engagement strategies throughout the course of the program (McKay & Bannon, 2004). When possible, a community partner has been enlisted to join the clinical team in providing this service. The community partner is a resident of the local community who is knowledgeable about the cultural backgrounds of the families and skilled in offering support to them. The role of the community partner is to promote family engagement over the telephone and during sessions, assist families in voicing their questions and

Table 5.1 Components of the Partnering to Achieve School Success (PASS) Program

Component	Description
Promotion of Family Engagement	Strategies to promote family engagement in treatment, including assignment of trained clinicians to make telephone contact, use of motivational interviewing strategies to use during those phone contacts, assistance to families in overcoming barriers to care, and inclusion of a community partner to serve as family advocate (McKay & Bannon, 2004).
Brief Family Behavioral Therapy	Strategies to build the parent–child relationship, foster increased parental involvement in education, and improve child behavior regulation skills using direct commands, positive reinforcement procedures, and appropriate use of punishment (Power, Karustis, & Habboushe, 2001; Webster-Stratton, 2005).
Family–School Consultation	Strategies to build the family–school relationship and guide parents and teachers in a problem solving process using Conjoint Behavioral Consultation methods (Sheridan & Kratochwill, 2008).
Collaborative Medication Management	Family education regarding the potential effects and side effects of medication. Assessment of the acceptability of medication to the family (Krain et al., 2005). Collaboration between the primary care provider and PASS clinician to evaluate the effects of medication using parent and teacher rating scales (Phelps et al., 2002), when medication is indicated and acceptable to families.
Crisis Intervention	Strategies to address family crises when they arise. Crises might include child abuse, family violence, parental health condition, severe marital conflict, loss of work, or neighborhood violence. PASS clinician provides assistance in stabilizing the family and obtaining additional community resources.

concerns, provide education about community and school resources, and help families to advocate for their children in the school and community.

A second component is brief parent training, which is provided when families identify a problem at home as a primary concern. Parent training incorporates elements of well-established programs (e.g., McMahon & Forehand, 2003; Webster-Stratton, 2005) as well as strategies that focus on how parents can support their children's education, such as by structuring the homework routine and using goal setting and contingency management strategies during homework (Power, Karustis, & Habboushe, 2001). A third component is family-school consultation, which is offered when school concerns are raised. Family-school consultation follows the conjoint behavioral consultation model (CBC; Sheridan & Kratochwill, 2008). The primary objectives of CBC are to strengthen the family–school partnership and to engage parents and teachers in a collaborative problem solving process to address school concerns, including problem identification, problem analysis, strategy implementation, and evaluation of progress. In the context of this partnership, daily report cards are frequently used. Daily report cards require teachers to rate the child's performance on targeted behaviors that have been mutually identified by the parent and teacher, one or more times per day. Daily reports typically are sent home for parents to review, and parents are trained in how to establish realistic goals for performance and administer appropriate, meaningful rewards when goals are reached (Kelley, 1990).

A fourth component of the program is collaborative management with the child's PCP. Given that services are provided in the context of colocation, opportunities for collaboration are available at multiple points. Collaboration typically involves sharing of progress notes and phone conversations, when appropriate, although at times it is possible to have sessions attended jointly by the clinician and PCP. The focus of this component is typically on medication management, although other health-related issues are also addressed (i.e., adherence to asthma treatment, follow-through on referrals to address developmental issues; management of obesity). Many families are skeptical about the use of medication to address their children's attention and behavior problems, and this view is common among ethnic minority families, including African Americans (Krain, Kendall, & Power, 2005). The clinician assesses family beliefs about the acceptability of interventions and provides education and guidance to parents in sorting out decisions about which services to pursue.

A final component is crisis intervention. Given that families residing in low-income neighborhoods are at heightened risk of experiencing trauma related to violence, abuse, illness, and disruptions in the family, it is important to offer crisis intervention services when indicated. In general when a crisis arises, it is possible to continue providing other components of the program, but occasionally it is necessary to suspend other aspects of the service until the crisis has abated.

Surveys administered to parents and providers have affirmed that they view the program as acceptable, practical, and helpful. Although attendance at sessions has varied considerably, most families have been able to get an appreciable amount of service (i.e., mean of 4.6 sessions), addressing both family and school problems. Observations of family sessions have revealed that critical treatment components have been provided with a high level of integrity. In addition, there is evidence that the intervention is effective in reducing perceived barriers to treatment, and that intervention effectiveness is related to the extent of engagement in treatment (Power, Lavin, Mautone, & Blum, 2010; Power & Mautone, 2011). The findings highlight the critical importance of efforts to promote family engagement from the point of initial referral through the entire process of intervention.

Conclusions

This chapter describes numerous examples of community-based programs designed to promote children's health and prevent illness or disorders. The programs described illustrate initiatives offered in school and primary care settings, as well as through home visitation. Each of the programs highlights the critical importance of partnership with key stakeholders at multiple stages of the process, from program inception through development, implementation, and evaluation. The process of partnership provides a mechanism for virtually ensuring that the program is community responsive. Most of the programs successfully involved community partners (that is, well-trained neighborhood residents) as key agents of intervention. A partnership between community professionals or paraprofessionals and expert consultants can be an effective strategy for delivering evidence-based practices in a manner that is developmentally appropriate and culturally competent.

This partnership can also provide valuable feedback about adaptations that are necessary to enable the program to be effective with a diverse range of children.

Successful prevention programs typically are firmly rooted in theory and empirical research. The Friend-to-Friend (F2F) program is an illustration of a program with strong grounding in developmental research, specifically social information processing and developmental-ecological theory. Prevention programs often incorporate multitier models that use a response to intervention framework, such as the Promoting Infant Pediatric Care (PIPC) program, which promote cost effectiveness by allocating more costly and labor intensive services to those who need them. Also, effective programs often provide components of intervention across multiple contexts. The Fruit and Vegetable Promotion Program (F&VPP) illustrates how consistent messages conveyed to children through multiple sources across contexts can contribute to the effectiveness of prevention efforts. Similarly, the Partnering to Achieve School Success (PASS) program illustrates the advantages of a multisystemic approach; this initiative focuses on promoting development within multiple systems and linking efforts across systems.

This chapter focuses primarily on applications in urban, low income settings. Partnership-based consultation methods can also be applied to tailor the programs for use in alternative contexts, such as rural and suburban settings. A particular challenge in urban settings, and many rural settings, is promoting family engagement. The PASS program has a major focus on engagement and provides an illustration of approaches to promote family engagement. High quality implementation of intervention strategies is critically important for program success. Developing and implementing strategies in partnership with interventionists may help to promote effective implementation. In addition, continuous performance feedback, which was illustrated in the Playground, Lunchroom, and Youth Success (PLAYS) program, is an evidence-based approach that has been shown to improve the sustainability of intervention implementation.

Questions for Discussion

1. What are the characteristics of effective community partners and how can they assist in the implementation of prevention programs?

2. What are some barriers to involving families in prevention efforts and what strategies can be used to overcome these barriers?
3. How can participatory methods be used to improve the feasibility of prevention initiatives?
4. What strategies could be used to promote and sustain the engagement of adolescent youth in community-based prevention initiatives?

References

Barkley, R. A. (2006). *Attention deficit hyperactivity disorder: A handbook for diagnosis and treatment* (3rd ed.). New York: Guilford.
Bauer, N. S., Lozano, P., & Rivara, F. P. (2007). The effectiveness of the Olweus bullying prevention program in public middle schools: A controlled trial. *Journal of Adolescent Health, 40*(3), 266–274.
Bay-Hinitz, A. K., Peterson, R. F., & Quilitch, H. R. (1994). Cooperative games: A way to modify aggressive and cooperative behaviors in young children. *Journal of Applied Behavior Analysis, 27*(3), 435–446.
Birch, L. L., & Fisher, J. O. (1998). Development of eating behaviors among children and adolescents. *Pediatrics, 101,* 539–549.
Blom-Hoffman, J. (2008). School-based promotion of fruit and vegetable consumption in multiculturally diverse, urban schools. *Psychology in the Schools, 45*(1), 16–27.
Blom-Hoffman, J., Wilcox, K. R., Dunn, L., Leff, S. S., & Power, T. J. (2008). Family involvement in school-base health promotion: Bringing nutrition information home. *School Psychology Review, 37*(4), 567–577.
Bronfenbrenner, U. (1986). Ecology of the family as a context for human development: Research perspectives. *Developmental Psychology, 22*(6), 723–742. doi: 10.1037/0012-1649.22.6.723
Cassano, M. C., Lefler, E. K., Tresco, K. E., Mautone, J. A., & Power, T. J. (2011). Children with disruptive behavior: Effective family and educational interventions. *Consultant for Pediatricians, 10,* 75–80.
Christenson, S. L., & Reschly, A. L. (Eds.). (2009). *Handbook of school–family partnerships.* New York: Routledge.
Crick, N. R. (1996). The role of overt aggression, relational aggression, and prosocial behavior in the prediction of children's future social adjustment. *Child Development, 67,* 2317–2327.
Crick, N. R., & Dodge, K. A. (1994). A review and reformulation of social information-processing mechanisms in children's social adjustment. *Psychological Bulletin, 115*(1), 74–101.
Crick, N. R., & Grotpeter, J. K. (1995). Relational aggression, gender, and social-psychological adjustment. *Child Development, 66*(3), 710–722.

Dishion, T. J., Capaldi, D., Spracklen, K. M., & Li, F. (1995). Peer ecology of male adolescent drug use. *Development and Psychopathology, 7*(4), 803–824.

DuPaul, G. J., & Stoner, G. (2003). *ADHD in the schools: Assessment and intervention strategies* (2nd ed.). New York: Guilford.

Epstein, L. H., Gordy, C. C., Raynor, H. A., Beddome, M., Kilanowski, C. K., & Paluch, R. (2001). Increasing fruit and vegetable intake and decreasing fat and sugar intake in families at risk for childhood obesity. *Obesity Research, 9*(3), 171–178.

Guenther, P. M., Dodd, K. W., Reedy, J., & Krebs-Smith, S. M. (2006). Most Americans eat much less than recommended amounts of fruits and vegetables. *Journal of the American Dietetic Association, 106,* 1371–1379.

Hambidge, S. J., Phibbs, S. L., Chandramouli, V., Fairclough, D., & Steiner, J. F. (2009). A stepped intervention increases well-child care and immunization rates in a disadvantaged population. *Pediatrics, 124*(2), 455–464.

Hoffman, J. A., Thompson, D. R., Franko, D. L., Power, T. J., Leff, S. S., & Stallings, V. A. (2011). Decaying behavioral effects in a randomized multi-year fruit and vegetable intake intervention. *Preventive Medicine, 52,* 370–375.

Hudley, C., & Graham, S. (1993). An attributional intervention to reduce peer-directed aggression among African-American boys. *Child Development, 64*(1), 124–138.

Kelder, S. H., Perry, C. L., Klepp, K.-I., & Lytle, L. L. (1994). Longitudinal tracking of adolescent smoking, physical activity, and food choice behaviors. *American Journal of Public Health, 84*(7), 1121–1126.

Kelley, M. L. (1990). *School-home notes: Promoting children's classroom success.* New York: Guilford.

Krain, A. L., Kendall, P. C., & Power, T. J. (2005). The role of treatment acceptability in the initiation of treatment for ADHD. *Journal of Attention Disorders, 9*(2), 425–434.

Leff, S. S., Angelucci, J., Goldstein, A. B., Cardaciotto, L., Paskewich, B., & Grossman, M. (2007). Using a participatory action research model to create a school-based intervention program for relationally aggressive girls: The Friend to Friend Program. In J. Zins, M. Elias, & C. Maher (Eds.), *Bullying, victimization, and peer harassment: A handbook of prevention and intervention* (pp. 199–218). New York: Haworth Press.

Leff, S. S., Costigan, T., & Power, T. J. (2004). Using participatory research to develop a playground-based prevention program. *Journal of School Psychology, 42*(1), 3–21. doi: 10.1016/j.jsp.2003.08.005

Leff, S. S., Gullan, R. L., Paskewich, B. S., Abdul-Kabir, S., Jawad, A. F., Grossman, M., … Power, T. J. (2009). An initial evaluation of a culturally adapted social problem-solving and relational aggression prevention program for urban African-American relationally aggressive girls. *Journal of Prevention and Intervention in the Community, 37*(4), 260–274.

Leff, S. S., Waasdorp, T. E., & Crick, N. R. (2010). A review of existing relational aggression programs: Strengths, limitations, and future directions. *School Psychology Review, 39*(4), 508–535.

Lochman, J. E., & Wells, K. C. (2004). The Coping Power Program for preadolescent aggressive boys and their parents: Outcome effects at the 1-year follow-up. *Journal of Consulting and Clinical Psychology, 72*(4), 571–578.

McKay, M. M., & Bannon, W. M. (2004). Engaging families in child mental health services. Child and *Adolescent Psychiatric Clinics of North America, 13*(4), 905.

McMahon, R. J., & Forehand, R. L. (2003). *Helping the noncompliant child: Family-based treatment for oppositional behavior* (2nd ed.). New York: Guilford.

Murphy, H. A., Hutchison, J. M., & Bailey, J. S. (1983). Behavioral school psychology goes outdoors: The effect of organized games on playground aggression. *Journal of Applied Behavior Analysis, 16*(1), 29–35.

Nastasi, B. K., Bernstein Moore, R., & Varjas, K. M. (2004). *School-based mental health services: Creating comprehensive and culturally specific programs.* Washington, DC: American Psychological Association.

Noell, G. H., Witt, J. C., Slider, N. J., Connell, J. E., Gatti, S. L., Williams, K. L., … Duhon, G. J. (2005). Treatment implementation following behavioral consultation in schools: A comparison of three follow-up strategies. *School Psychology Review, 34*(1), 87–106.

Olds, D. L., Kitzman, H., Hanks, C., Cole, R., Anson, E., Sidora-Arcoleo, K., … Bondy, J. (2007). Effects of nurse home visiting on maternal and child functioning: Age-9 follow-up of a randomized trial. *Pediatrics, 120*(4), e832–e845.

Peskin, M. F., Tortolero, S. R., & Markham, C. M. (2006). Bullying and victimization among Black and Hispanic adolescents. *Adolescence, 41*(163), 467–484.

Power, T. J., Blom-Hoffman, J., Clarke, A. T., Riley-Tillman, T. C., Kelleher, C., & Manz, P. H. (2005). Reconceptualizing intervention integrity: A partnership-based framework for linking research with practice. *Psychology in the Schools, 42*(5), 495–507.

Power, T. J., Eiraldi, R. B., Clarke, A. T., Mazzuca, L. B., & Krain, A. (2005). Improving mental health service utilization for children and adolescents. *School Psychology Quarterly, 20*, 203–221.

Power, T. J., Hughes, C. L., Helwig, J. R., Nissley-Tsiopinis, J., Mautone, J. A., & Lavin, H. J. (2010). Getting to first base: Promoting engagement in family–school intervention for children with ADHD in urban, primary care practice. *School Mental Health, 2*(2), 52–61.

Power, T. J., Karustis, J. L., & Habboushe, D. (2001). *Homework success for children with ADHD: A family-school intervention program.* New York: Guilford.

Power, T. J., Lavin, H. J., Mautone, J. A., & Blum, N. J. (2010). Partnering to achieve school success: A collaborative care model of early intervention for attention and behavior problems in urban contexts. In B. Doll, W. Pfohl, & J. Yoon (Eds.), *Handbook of youth prevention science* (pp. 375–392). New York: Routledge.

Power, T. J., & Mautone, J. A. (2011, February). Linking schools and primary care in urban settings: Contributions of pediatric school psychology. In K. Bradley-Klug (Chair), *Contemporary issues in pediatric school psychology training and practice.* Symposium presented at the Annual Meeting of the National Association of School Psychologists, San Francisco, CA.

Power, T. J., Soffer, S. L., Cassano, M. C., Tresco, K. E., & Mautone, J. A. (2011). Integrating pharmacological and psychosocial interventions for ADHD: An evidence-based, participatory approach. In S. Evans & B. Hoza (Eds.), *Treating attention-deficit/hyperactivity disorder* (pp. 13–19). New York: Civic Research Institute.

Sheridan, S. M., & Kratochwill, T. R. (2008). *Conjoint behavioral consultation: Promoting family-school connections and interventions* (2nd ed.). New York: Springer Science + Business Media.

Swearer, S. M., & Espelage, D. L. (2011). Expanding the social-ecological framework of bullying among youth. In D. L. Espelage & S. M. Swearer (Eds.), *Bullying in North American schools* (2nd ed., pp. 3–10). New York: Routledge.

Wandersman, A., & Nation, M. (1998). Urban neighborhoods and mental health: Psychological contributions to understanding toxicity, resilience, and interventions. *American Psychologist, 53*(6), 647–656.

Webster-Stratton, C. (2005). *The incredible years: A trouble-shooting guide for parents of children aged 2–8 years.* Seattle, WA: Incredible Years.

Wooten, K. G., Luman, E. T., & Barker, L. E. (2007). Socioeconomic factors and persistent racial disparities in childhood vaccination. *American Journal of Health Behavior, 31*(4), 434–445.

Six

Program Development
and Evaluation

The ability to develop and evaluate programs is vitally important to the skill set of pediatric school psychologists. Because these professionals are invested in change at the population level as well as the individual level, it is essential that they have skills in developing and evaluating programs that can change behavior for a broad class of individuals. This chapter describes critical steps in program development, as well as types of program evaluation and methods commonly used to evaluate programs. Efforts to develop and evaluate programs are facilitated by effective measurement strategies and may be supported by grant activities. Chapter 7 provides a description of measurement development approaches and chapter 8 presents strategies to obtain grants to support programmatic activities.

Hallmarks of Program Development

There are several distinguishing features of program development described in this section. Although program development and evaluation are presented in separate sections, these processes are highly interconnected. In fact, effective program development involves an ongoing, recursive process of program evaluation.

Population as Unit of Analysis

Historically, the practice of child-serving psychology has had a primary focus on providing services to one child and family at a time. Although an individualized service delivery framework clearly has advantages, it is limited in that: (a) it tends to be reactive in that services typically are not provided until problems arise; (b) it does not address systematically social, cultural, and economic issues that have an effect on child development in systems and interactions between systems; and (c) it is not efficient and cost effective because it targets one person at a time and directs services to individuals when they have complex problems requiring labor-intensive services.

In contrast to a service delivery approach, a programmatic orientation focuses on a population as the unit of analysis (Doll & Cummings, 2008). A population encompasses a relatively large class of individuals with specified characteristics. Examples include children in the community who have asthma; students in a region of the state who have autism spectrum disorder; and children in a network of primary care practices who are at risk for behavioral health conditions.

Response to Identified Need

Program development is a systematic, goal-directed response to needs identified by stakeholders at multiple levels. Strong programs clearly respond to a need or gap in service identified by research or policy statements issued at a national or state level, such as those published by the Institute of Medicine, American Academy of Pediatrics, American Academy of Child and Adolescent Psychiatry, or American Psychological Association. Also, these initiatives directly address local needs identified by leaders in the community. The potential public health significance of a proposed project and its likelihood of being supported by the community and funded by sponsors are directly related to the extent to which the initiative addresses priorities established by leaders at multiple levels.

Importance of Community Partnership

Programs are likely to be successful when members of the community who have a stake in the project are involved at the outset and throughout every stage of the process (Nastasi, Moore, & Varjas, 2004). A key is to identify major stakeholders at the initial stages of conceptualizing the program. As an example, for school-based health promotion initiatives, this might entail involving parents, youth, school administrators, nurses, regular and special education teachers, physical education teachers, food service personnel, primary care providers, food store owners or managers, as well as community and faith leaders. The involvement of these stakeholders ensures that important perspectives are considered, and it promotes buy-in from individuals who are critical for the success of the initiative.

Investment in an Iterative Process

Program development is an iterative process that involves multiple steps. Initial development entails creating the program in collaboration with multiple stakeholders and reviewing the framework and implementation steps in a recursive manner with collaborators (Leff, Costigan, & Power, 2004). Next, the program needs to be field tested several times. In this phase, it is critical to collect acceptability and feasibility information using qualitative and quantitative methods to identify which aspects of the program are working and which need to be modified. Once major stakeholders have affirmed that the program is acceptable and feasible, a preliminary test of effectiveness can be conducted to ascertain whether the program seems to be working and is ready for larger-scale testing.

Commitment to Sustainability

Programs typically are developed when there is a groundswell of interest and a supply of resources available to promote the initiative. All too often programs are discontinued because motivation fades or there is a lack of resources to sustain the effort. Planning for sustainability is a critical aspect of program development and needs to be a priority from the outset to ensure that initiatives are continued when there are fluctuations in staffing, resources, and institutional or political will.

Steps to Program Development

Program development is a multistep process. This section describes key steps in the process from initial conceptualization through program planning and pilot testing.

Identification of Target Population and Need

At the outset it is important to identify the population and problem to be addressed, which should reflect perspectives of community representatives. In general, the best way to identify community priorities is to attend established meetings that involve key leaders from the community, such as school district board of education meetings, home–school association meetings at the local school, or parent advisory group meetings of local community agencies.

In collaboration with community leaders, it is critical to delineate parameters of the population and the problem to be addressed. This typically includes specifying the age range and setting of the population and the problems targeted for prevention or intervention. For example, for universal prevention programs designed to promote health and prevent obesity, the population could be elementary school students in schools situated in a particular section of the inner city, or the population could be children 5 years or younger served in primary care practices situated in rural counties within a state. For targeted prevention programs or intervention programs designed for youth with or at risk for depression, the population could be middle school students who screen positive on a brief measure of risk for depression, or perhaps children between the ages of 11 and 15 served in a primary care pediatric practice who screen positive for depression or suicide risk.

Enlistment of Key Stakeholders and Initiation of Partnership Process

A key to the success of programmatic efforts is to enlist key stakeholders from the very beginning of the project. Individuals representing all of the groups who have a stake in the project should be included. Stakeholders have vital roles on the project. They are not merely advisors or consultants to the project; in contrast, they are full members of the team who are involved in equitable partnerships with program experts, who might be university professors, researchers based in medical schools, or practicing pediatric school psychologists. The principles of community-based participatory research serve as a useful guide in establishing the role of community partners and informing the process of partnership (see Table 6.1).

Assessment of Need

Once the program team has been assembled, it is important to justify why the specified population of children has a need for special programming (Kern, Evans, & Lewis, 2011). The documentation of need typically includes estimates of the prevalence of targeted and related conditions at a national,

Table 6.1   Community-based participatory research principles

Collaborative, equitable partnerships among all stakeholders are essential in all phases of the project.
A balance between research and action is critical to ensure that the project is beneficial for all stakeholders.
The identity of the targeted community needs to be understood, valued, and promoted.
Programming is designed to strengthen assets and build the resources of the community.
Partnership involves co-learning and capacity building among all project participants.
The process of program development and evaluation necessitates commitment to a long-term process.
Programmatic efforts respond to public health priorities at the local level and incorporate an understanding of risk and protective factors related to the targeted problem.
Dissemination activities involve the efforts of all program stakeholders.
Programmatic efforts focus on the development of systems through an iterative process.

Note: These principles are derived from Israel, B. A., Schulz, A. J., Parker, E. A., Becker, A. B., Allen, A. J., and Guzman, J. R. Critical issues in developing and following community-based participatory research principles. In M. Minkler, N. Wallerstein (eds.), *Community-Based Participatory Research for Health.* San Francisco: Jossey-Bass, 2003, pp. 56–73.

state, and local level. Research reviews and advocacy group position papers are a useful source of information to justify need at a national and state level (see Perrin, Bloom, & Gortmaker, 2007 for an example related to the prevention of pediatric chronic health conditions, in particular obesity, asthma, and attention-deficit/hyperactivity disorder [ADHD]). Policy statements issued by government task forces (e.g., U.S. Prevention Services Task Force) and professional associations (e.g., American Academy of Pediatrics) are also helpful. Further, local data bases, such as those maintained by a school district, department of health, or department of human services, can be useful in documenting need at the local level. In addition, focus groups, interviews, and surveys conducted with key stakeholder groups are vital in making the case and clearly illustrating program need (e.g., see Ginsburg, Alexander, Hunt, Sullivan, Zhao, & Cnaan, 2002; Guevara et al., 2005).

Another important strategy for justifying need is to summarize the research on the natural course of the targeted conditions to highlight the human suffering and costs to society associated with the problem. Describing how the targeted condition fits within a life course model and increases the likelihood of serious health impairments later in development is useful in demonstrating the public health significance of the project (see Braveman & Barclay, 2009). In addition, the program justification should summarize research on programs that have been successful in addressing the identified needs and how the proposed program builds on these efforts (see Leff, Power, Manz, Costigan, & Nabors, 2001 for an example related to the prevention of various forms of aggression in schools).

Delineation of Program Goals

Early in the process of program development, it is critical to clearly specify project goals and objectives. Goals indicate the expected end points to be achieved by the project, and objectives refer to short-term outcomes that will contribute to the attainment of a goal. The identification of goals and objectives reflects a balance between the aspirations of the project team and information derived from research and past experience about what is feasible to accomplish. Projects may fail to achieve stakeholder buy-in if the goals do not reflect the aspirations and priorities of the community. By the same token, projects may fail to win the support of potential sponsors if the goals are viewed as lofty or unattainable. In addition, goals and objectives need to be stated in terms that clearly specify the outcomes to be achieved. At this stage, the process of evaluation begins, because program goals need to be closely linked with outcome variables that will be measured during the course of the project.

Development of Prevention and Intervention Strategies

Epidemiological and developmental research pertaining to the targeted problem is a critical foundation for program development (see chapter 4). This literature delineates factors exacerbating risk as well as factors promoting resilience and competence. For many problems, a theory of change has been delineated that specifies proximal variables (i.e., outcomes closely associated with change strategies, such as a reduction in risk or an improvement in competence), distal variables (i.e., outcomes that are more remotely associated with change strategies), and an explanation of how change strategies, proximal outcomes, and distal outcomes are related to one another. When a theory of change has not been previously specified by researchers, it is recommended that the program team collaborate to develop a theory of change and solicit input from multiple experts to review this model. For an example of a theory of change, chapter 7 provides an illustration of the model for Family–School Success, an intervention program for children with ADHD that links family and school (Mautone, Lefler, & Power, 2011).

Although research is essential for informing the development of change strategies, stakeholder input is essential to ensure that the interventions are developmentally appropriate, culturally relevant, and feasible to implement. Stakeholders should be involved throughout the process in selecting intervention options, adapting strategies, and refining them for use with the target population (see Evans, Green, & Serpell, 2005 for a description of how community development teams can be invaluable in the process of program development). Research suggests that intervention strategies are more likely to be implemented in a high quality and consistent manner when stakeholders actively participate in the adaptation of intervention strategies as opposed to when they are less actively involved and receive training based upon traditional, hierarchical methods of education (Kelleher, Riley-Tillman, & Power, 2008).

Adaptation and Refinement of Program

Programs designed by committees rarely work well in the real world, even when the committees include stakeholders from key segments of the community. An essential stage of program development is the recursive testing of the program with the intended population in the targeted settings (Kern et al., 2011). It is essential to collect data from multiple sources during the course of pilot testing. Variables to assess include acceptability, feasibility, integrity, and participant engagement (see chapter 8 related to measure development for a further description of assessment methods). Data sources can include participant self-reports of acceptability and feasibility, observations of the content and quality of practitioner implementation, records of participant attendance, permanent products completed by program participants, observations of participant responsiveness during program sessions, and participant reports of therapeutic alliance or the strength of the relationship between participant and practitioner. During pilot testing, it is useful to collect and review this information on a session by session basis to inform participants about adaptations to the intervention. In addition, it is helpful to conduct interviews with program participants after each session to obtain their input with regard to aspects (both content and process) that were beneficial and those that were not helpful. A case illustration related to program development is included in the attached CD.

Overview of Program Evaluation

Throughout this text we have discussed strategies for prevention and intervention related to youth with health issues; developing the most appropriate strategies and implementing them is just part of the process. An important component, and one that is often overlooked in the applied setting (Godber, 2008), is the inclusion of a structured process for evaluating the effectiveness of these strategies. Program evaluation is a method used to systematically investigate a particular program. Defined as "a study designed and conducted to assist some audiences to assess an object's merit or worth" (Stufflebeam, 2001, p. 11), program evaluation can be used on a small scale to assess the effectiveness of a classroom-based intervention for students with chronic health conditions or on a large scale to evaluate the ongoing development of a systems level strategy to encourage interdisciplinary collaboration. Results of a program evaluation are used to modify and improve the program under investigation, and ultimately to verify that the program is working and should be continued or alternatively, that it is not working and changes are needed or it should be discontinued.

There are a number of ways a program evaluation may be conducted. The method chosen is driven by the goals and objectives of the program and the specific questions under consideration. Typically, program evaluations are developed to investigate one or more of the following program components: the process, the outcome(s), or the overall impact (Isaac & Michael, 1981). If the process of the intervention is of interest, then formative evaluations are conducted, which involve ongoing data collection throughout the implementation of an intervention. A focus on outcomes or overall impact requires the use of summative assessments to determine if the intervention produces the expected or anticipated results. In many cases, both formative and summative data are collected to allow for analyses of process and outcomes, as well as the overall significance or impact of those outcomes.

Historically, program evaluation has consisted of enlisting an external expert who independently conducts the evaluation and shares findings with stakeholders. The feedback may be used to make program improvements, and the quality of the evaluation is often judged by whether or not the outcomes are consistent with the stakeholders' preconceived expectations and beliefs. More recently, program evaluation has been conceptualized within the context of participatory evaluation and action research (Weiss, 1998). As described throughout this book, a participatory approach incorporates stakeholders in the development of the program evaluation plan. Thus, strategies and methods for evaluation are not imposed from outside the system, but mutually determined by key stakeholders. Individuals work together to identify the issue or concern in question, develop a plan for evaluating the identified concern, collect data to analyze the identified problem, and then analyze the data and use the information to make changes. Action research is an iterative, cyclical process that allows for continuous data collection and revision leading to program improvement over time.

The following is an example of program evaluation within a participatory action research framework. In this example program evaluation was conducted in the context of a primary care pediatric practice in which patients frequently experienced excessive wait times. The pediatric psychologist working in the practice identified key stakeholders, who included the pediatricians, nurses, office manager and staff, and representative parents. This group identified program goals and initiated data collection to determine factors contributing to the wait time (e.g., patients were late for appointments, appointments were scheduled too close together with no break time in between, exam rooms were not available at scheduled times). Strategies such as reminder calls to families, raffle tickets for families arriving on time, 15-minute catch-up breaks for providers every 2 hours, and an accountability system for staff to efficiently clean exam rooms were developed and implemented over a period of 2 months. Wait time data were collected and compared to baseline data. In addition, a survey was administered to parents. At the end of the 2-month period, data were evaluated to determine how well the intervention was working and whether additional strategies were needed to achieve the goal of reducing wait times. The process of working collaboratively to evaluate a program can result in improved stakeholder investment in the program, higher levels of accountability, and enhanced skills in monitoring progress and modifying program effectiveness.

Approaches to Conducting a Program Evaluation

The following section presents the most common approaches to conducting program evaluations as they relate to youth with pediatric health issues. The approaches presented include feasibility, quality improvement, outcome, and cost-analysis studies. Each will be described and an example grounded in the empirical literature will be presented to illustrate the practical application of the type of evaluation.

In order to determine the best program evaluation approach to employ, one must first identify the goals of the evaluation. In other words, why is there a need for the evaluation, and what outcomes should be assessed? The needs for evaluation may involve questions about costs and benefits due to anticipated budget cuts, concerns about the quality of treatment implementation, consideration of ways to decrease the complexity of a program and improve efficiency, and determination of whether the program is resulting in the intended outcomes. Once the purpose of the evaluation is identified, the type of study or approach that best meets the purpose can be determined. Table 6.2 provides guidance in matching the evaluation purpose with the recommended approach.

Feasibility Studies

Feasibility studies are employed when the goals of the evaluation are to determine if the program is practical to implement, acceptable to participants, and engaging to participants. A program evaluation conducted by St. Leger and Campbell

Table 6.2 Aligning the Purpose of Program Evaluation with the Most Appropriate Approach

Purpose of Program Evaluation	Program Evaluation Approach
To investigate if the program is practical to implement, acceptable to participants, and engaging to participants	Feasibility Study
To conduct an ongoing evaluation of program effects on important process variables for the purposes of program improvement	Quality Improvement Study
To evaluate changes in targeted variables in response to a program	Outcome Study
To investigate the cost–benefit relationship of a program	Cost Analysis Study

(2008) serves as an example of a feasibility study. These authors evaluated the feasibility of the Back on Track Program, a technology-based intervention designed for youth who may be hospitalized or home bound due to long-term treatment for chronic health conditions and subsequent recuperation. The goals of the program are to offer support to students with regard to keeping up with academic requirements, relating effectively with peers, and enhancing systems-level collaboration. A participatory action research approach was used, as described previously in this chapter, to inform the evaluation, and program staff members were integrally involved in the evaluation process along with the key stakeholders. After 6 months of implementation, a formative evaluation was conducted through interviews with key hospital staff, school teachers, students, and parents. Data from these interviews resulted in revisions to the program, such as making sure all stakeholders had a shared understanding of the purpose of the program and how it was to be used; troubleshooting issues related to access, funding, and flexibility in the use of the technology incorporated in the intervention program; allowing for variability in student use of the program in response to barriers; and responding to the needs and preferences of families and students regarding the amount of program involvement during the transition back to school. In summary, this evaluation allowed for the developers of this program to be responsive to the needs of all involved for the overall purpose of promoting positive outcomes for youth with chronic health conditions.

Quality Improvement Studies

Quality improvement studies are used to determine if the program is having the intended effect on important process variables for the purpose of program improvement. A study by Lynch-Jordan and colleagues (2010) illustrates the use of quality improvement methods in the context of a pain management clinic based in a hospital setting. At the outset, the team selected a measurement tool to assess pain status throughout the course of treatment. Given practical concerns about adding an additional burden to a busy clinical service, the tool needed to be functional yet brief, and easy to administer, score, and interpret. The Functional Disability Inventory (FDI; Walker & Greene, 1991) met these criteria and was incorporated into the clinical protocol. The Plan-Do-Study-Act (PDSA) methodology was used for assessing process improvement (Langley, Nolan, Nolan, Norman, & Provost, 1996), and the feasibility of using the FDI in the context of this clinic was evaluated. Initial evaluation data indicated a number of barriers to using the FDI, and included limited access to the instrument during clinic visits, lack of guidelines for introducing the instrument to the patient, and inconsistent implementation of the instrument in the clinic. To facilitate use of the measure, a script was given to clinicians to help them explain the measure; copies of the FDI were placed in the clinic rooms; and electronic access to the measure was developed. Self-administration by the patient was implemented as an optional strategy in order to address the issue of the clinician forgetting to administer the instrument. Further analyses indicated that these strategies served to decrease the initial barriers and facilitated the incorporation of FDI into the day-to-day operation of the clinic. This recursive approach of program evaluation exemplifies a key feature of a quality improvement study.

Outcome Studies

Outcome studies are designed to evaluate changes in targeted variables in response to intervention. A study that evaluated the effectiveness of the STARBRIGHT *Fitting Cystic Fibrosis Into Your Life Everyday* CD-ROM (Davis, Quittner, Stack, & Yang, 2004) serves as an example of this type of program evaluation. The purpose of this program is to educate youth (ages 7–17 years) with cystic fibrosis (CF) about the disease, and provide them with strategies for coping with illness-related issues such as hospitalizations, treatment adherence, and pain management. Using an experimental design, all youth in the study were administered a baseline knowledge questionnaire and completed a measure of coping skills. Twenty-five youth with CF then viewed the CD-ROM while the 22 youth in the wait-list control group received treatment at a later date. All participants completed the baseline measures post treatment along with a measure of consumer satisfaction. Results demonstrated that knowledge of CF and ability to generate competent coping strategies increased as a result of viewing the CD-ROM. Youth reported that they enjoyed the program and offered recommendations to include additional topics such as dating, dying, and death. The participants also indicated that this program could be used to educate family members, peers, and classmates. In summary, results from the evaluation demonstrated that the program achieved the intended goals and provided suggestions for incorporating additional topics in the program as well as investigating the use of the intervention with additional target populations.

Cost Analysis Studies

Cost analysis studies are designed to investigate the cost–benefit relationship of a program. An investigation by Ellis and colleagues (2005) illustrates the benefits of program evaluation to determine the impact of a program in reducing medical costs. As background, adolescents with Type 1 diabetes who have poor metabolic control often require hospital services due to diabetic ketoacidosis (DKA). Poor adherence to treatment is a primary contributor to DKA and often leads to medical care that is very expensive. The purpose of this study was to determine if a specialized intervention program resulted in a reduction in hospitalization and a collateral reduction in overall cost of care for study participants. Thirty-one adolescents with Type 1 diabetes, identified as having poor metabolic control, and their families were recruited for this study. Participants were randomly assigned to either an intervention or control group. The intervention group received 6 months of multisystemic therapy (MST) consisting of intensive family psychotherapy delivered in the home. In addition to MST, these participants also received standard medical care. Participants in the control group received only standard medical care. Data were collected on the number of emergency room visits and hospital admissions per participant, as well as the diagnosis rendered and the associated charges and costs. These data were obtained for each participant for the 9 months prior to the study to provide baseline information, and subsequently were collected during the 9 months of study enrollment. Metabolic control data also were collected for each participant throughout the study. Results demonstrated that the number of hospital admissions significantly decreased for the MST group, likely due to improved metabolic control, as compared to the control group whose hospitalizations actually increased over the course of the study. Consequently, the charges and direct hospital costs significantly decreased for participants in the intervention group as compared to those in the control group. The authors concluded that for their study sample, MST resulted in improved health outcomes and decreased associated health care costs for adolescents with Type 1 diabetes.

Design of Program Evaluation Studies

Once the purpose and approach to the evaluation have been determined, the next step is to identify the study design that will most effectively address the purpose. The designs presented below are those most commonly used in program evaluation studies. Each will be described and discussed with respect to the strengths and limitations of the particular design as it pertains to program evaluation. Although scientific rigor is important, the application of certain research designs in some settings can be complex, cost prohibitive, and simply unrealistic to implement. When designing a program evaluation, a balance between the preferred design and the reality of available resources and feasibility issues must be achieved. This section provides only a brief overview of useful research designs; for an in-depth description of a wide range of designs, see Kazdin (2002).

Single Subject Designs

Single subject or small "n" designs are most appropriate when the focus of the program evaluation is to conduct a preliminary examination with a limited number of participants or units of individuals (i.e., classrooms, schools). A hallmark of single subject designs is the collection of data on a continuous basis across phases of evaluation. For example, to determine the feasibility and acceptability of a classroom-based physical activity program on the academic engagement of children with ADHD, the program may be implemented on a small scale in two special education classes in order to inform the development of the program prior to large scale study. Several single subject designs are appropriate for program evaluation. A-B or case study designs are the most simplistic and involve a baseline phase (A) followed by an intervention phase (B). These designs are used frequently in schools to evaluate a student's response to intervention (Brown-Chidsey, Steege, & Mace, 2008). Although relatively easy to implement in an applied setting, A-B designs are often criticized for their lack of experimental control. Multiple baseline designs, which involve replication of the intervention or program across participants or settings, afford a substantial level of experimental control. Reversal designs (A-B-A or A-B-A-B designs) incorporate a return to baseline phase and also offer a high level of experimental control. However, in some cases it is not feasible or acceptable to stakeholders to withdraw a program once it has been implemented.

Quasi-Experimental Designs

A quasi-experimental design is one in which the evaluator attempts to model an experimental design knowing that not all variables can be controlled due to the limitations of the setting. These types of designs are used when random assignment to a group is not feasible. A reasonable level of experimental control can be achieved if participants in groups are similar on important demographic and baseline variables (Kazdin, 2002). Many studies implemented in applied settings, such as schools, incorporate quasi-experimental designs to investigate program outcomes. An example of such a design might focus on the use of a particular instructional style for reading in one fourth grade classroom while another fourth grade classroom receives the standard form of instruction typically used in the school. Although students are not randomly assigned to classrooms, equivalence of the groups can be demonstrated by comparing them on variables such as gender, socioeconomic status, and baseline reading ability. The performance of the students on reading outcome measures in the two classrooms can then be compared to evaluate the effectiveness of the alternative instructional style.

Experimental Designs

A true experimental design includes at least one treatment and one control group to which participants are randomly assigned. The effects of a particular program are evaluated by comparing outcomes between the treatment and control groups. A wait-list control study, such as the one described earlier in this chapter that evaluated the impact of the STAR-BRIGHT CD-ROM (Davis et al., 2004), exemplifies the use of an experimental design. Comparison groups that provide an active treatment and control for the nonspecific effects of treatment (e.g., opportunities to receive education and support from a therapist) offer an even greater level of methodological control. Although recognized as a design with high levels of scientific rigor, in many applied settings it is not feasible or even ethical to apply an experimental treatment to only one group of participants in the targeted sample.

Methods of Collecting Data

A variety of methods may be used to collect the data needed to inform a program evaluation. These methods include direct observations, self- and informant reports, interviews and focus groups, direct assessment using standardized testing measures, and the collection of naturalistic data. To increase the likelihood that the measurement plan will be viewed as acceptable, it is important to identify metrics that are currently being used in a particular setting, take advantage of existing resources, and obtain buy-in from team members to use additional measures.

Direct Observations

Direct observation of students in the school context can provide highly useful information about how chronic conditions may be having an effect on social, behavioral, and academic functioning. Naturalistic observations consist of recording all behaviors as they occur, as well as environmental events that precede or follow the observed behavior. In contrast, systematic observations utilize standardized coding methods and focus on clearly specified target behaviors. The Behavioral Observation of Students in Schools (BOSS; Shapiro, 2011), for example, is a systematic observational tool used to measure levels of engagement and off-task behavior in the classroom. In one case study, the BOSS was used to systematically monitor the effects of a stimulant medication on the classroom behavior of a student with attention-deficit/hyperactivity disorder (ADHD; Volpe, Heick, & Guerasko-Moore, 2005).

Self- and Informant Reports

Self-report scales are commonly used in pediatric school psychology to assess child functioning and general health literacy. For instance, Adams, Streisand, Zawacki, and Joseph (2002) developed a questionnaire called Living with a Chronic Illness (LCI) to assess the social functioning of children and adolescents ages 9 to 18 living with chronic illness. The LCI consists of a youth self-report form as well as a parent form. Questionnaire items address topics such as restriction of physical activity, interruption of daily activities, changes in physical appearance, and modifications in lifestyle (Adams et al., 2002). Another measure known as the Children's

Health Locus of Control scale (CHLC; Parcel & Meyer, 1978) is designed to evaluate children's locus of control (e.g., internal, external) regarding issues related to their health and chronic illness. Similarly, the Coping Strategies Inventory (CSI; Tobin, Holroyd, & Reynolds, 1989) evaluates children's coping behaviors and thought patterns in response to medical distress.

Informant reports, such as parent rating scales, are highly useful sources of information for evaluating health-related outcomes of students. One example is the Child Vulnerability Scale (Forsyth, Horwitz, Leventhal, Burger, & Leaf, 1996), which measures parents' perceptions of their children's vulnerability to health problems via an 8-item, 4-point Likert scale (0 = Definitely False; 3 = Definitely True). Also, the Child Behavior Checklist (CBCL; Achenbach & Edelbrock, 1991) has been completed by caregivers to assess behavioral disorders among children with chronic illness (Wallander & Thompson, 1995). Among children perinatally infected with HIV, for instance, the CBCL was completed by parents to measure significant differences in psychological functioning between children infected with HIV and a healthy control group (Bachanas et al., 2001). In addition, Warren, Henry, Lightowler, Bradshaw, and Perwaiz (2003) administered the Food Frequency Questionnaire (Hammond, Nelson, Chinn, & Rona, 1993) and the Baecke Activity Questionnaire (Baecke, Burema, & Frijters, 1982) to assess children's dietary patterns and physical activity levels in response to an obesity prevention program.

Interviews and Focus Groups

Although self- and informant reports allow for the collection of quantitative data, interviews and focus groups gather valuable qualitative information for use in program evaluation. For example, questionnaires can be used in an interview format to assess students' knowledge and perceptions of their chronic condition, the sources from which they learn about the condition, experiences of symptoms, treatments they are receiving, social relationships, and quality of life. The language utilized in interview questions can be modified to coincide with the developmental level of the child (e.g., preschool-age children, adolescents, etc.). Interviews can also be used to gain insight into the school experiences of children with chronic health conditions. Bessell (2001) developed a School Experience Interview to supplement information gained from standardized instruments concerning pediatric cancer survivors' social adjustment, quality of life, and school experiences. The interview provided qualitative data regarding students' perceived helpfulness and understanding of teachers, academic performance, peer interaction and acceptance, homebound instruction, and importance of attending school (Bessell, 2001).

Direct Assessment

Direct assessment measures include standardized tests to assess children's cognitive functioning and academic achievement. These measures permit the evaluation of students in relation to a large sample of children, typically derived at national level, of similar age or academic grade level. Although standardized norm-referenced measures have many advantages, often it is important to assess children in relation to local standards of performance established for a school. For this reason, curriculum-based measurement (CBM) procedures have been developed. CBM provides ongoing assessment of academic functioning in one or more subject areas (e.g., reading, math operations, spelling) in relation to locally established standards (e.g., expected reading performance at the end of the school year). Rates of progress on CBM measures across phases of intervention (e.g., baseline versus specialized reading program) can be examined to determine whether an intervention is resulting in significant improvement in academic skill performance (Shinn, 2010).

Naturalistic Data

Naturalistic data, such as report cards, office discipline referrals, and attendance records, are cost-effective tools for evaluating student outcomes. School attendance, for instance, can serve as an indicator of functional impairment for students with chronic illness (Breuner, Smith, & Womack, 2004). Similarly, low rates of school truancy are indicative of health and well-being among students (Weitzman & Siegel, 1992). In one study that determined risk factors for school absenteeism among adolescent students who experienced chronic headaches, school attendance and absenteeism were assessed by computing the average number of school days missed due to illness during the previous 6 months as estimated by students and their parents (Breuner et al., 2004). In another study, school absenteeism was assessed and used as baseline data before implementing a school-based program to improve health services for students suffering from asthma (Moonie, Sterling, Figgs, & Castro, 2006). To determine the relationship between absenteeism and asthma severity, participants rated the severity of their symptoms and explained reasons for absenteeism during the school year. In this study, children with asthma were absent more frequently than their healthy peers.

Grade point averages and standardized test scores also may be informative indicators of student health. For example, students with persistent asthma maintained trends of performing worse on the Missouri Assessment Program (MAP) standardized test compared to healthy peers (Moonie, Sterling, Figgs, & Castro, 2008).

Mixed Methods Approaches

To address the purposes of program evaluation, it is usually beneficial to collect data using both quantitative and qualitative approaches. Collecting formative and summative data through the combined use of interviews, rating scales, direct assessment, and observations may allow one to more comprehensively evaluate a program. However, the decision to follow a mixed methods approach must be part of the larger plan related the overall intent of the evaluation. Simply collecting a plethora of data using a number of different approaches may be time consuming and resource intensive, and may not enhance the program evaluation.

Conclusion

The role of the pediatric school psychologist has expanded beyond the traditional emphasis on individualized direct service delivery to include a focus on programming that targets populations of individuals and has an impact on health care at the systems level. To be effective in this expanded role, practitioners need to develop knowledge and skills in program development, including the ability to identify needs, develop partnerships and engage stakeholders, collaboratively determine goals, and implement strategies systematically to address issues of concern. As stated in this chapter, the process doesn't end with program development. A key to effective programming is the incorporation of a systematic evaluation component. Program evaluation informs the process of program development and modification, and enables one to determine if the identified needs, goals, and intended outcomes have been addressed by the selected strategies. Decisions regarding the design and measurement methods to be used as part of the evaluation are based upon numerous factors including the evaluation questions, setting, and time and resources available. A participatory action research approach is proposed as a framework to guide the pediatric school psychologist through the program development and evaluation process.

Discussion Questions

1. Discuss how the steps of program development can be shaped by community-based participatory research principles. Given your experience, what steps do you anticipate being the most challenging and what strategies could you use to minimize these challenges?
2. What approaches to program evaluation are relevant in the work you do? What research design(s) is feasible for you to use and what data can you collect to address program evaluation questions?
3. You have been asked to design a program evaluation for a rural school district that has implemented an interactive, Web-based professional development program for teachers that allows them to access information about various chronic health conditions for the purpose of instructional planning. The district administrators are planning the budget for the next school year and want to know if the program is a good investment in terms of making a difference in the lives of children with chronic health conditions.
   a. Given the scenario above, how would you go about designing a program evaluation? What questions would you ask? What additional information might be important to know?
   b. Would you collect formative data, summative data, or both? Why?
   c. Describe the specific types of data you would collect and how you would go about collecting these data. Be sure to consider issues of feasibility and practicality in your response.

Additional Teaching Aids

PowerPoint slides pertaining to leadership development that contain information about program development and evaluation are included in the attached CD.

References

Achenbach, T., & Edelbrock, C. (1991). *Manual for the Child Behavior Checklist 4–18 and 1991 profile.* Burlington: University of Vermont, Department of Psychiatry.

Adams, C. D., Streisand, R. M., Zawacki, T., & Joseph, K. E. (2002). Living with a chronic illness: A measure of social functioning for children and adolescents. *Journal of Pediatric Psychology, 27*(7), 593–605.

Bachanas, P. J., Kullgren, K. A., Schwartz, K. S., Lanier, B., McDaniel, J. S., & Smith, J. (2001). Predictors of psychological adjustment in school-age children infected with HIV. *Journal of Pediatric Psychology, 26*(6), 343–352.

Baecke, J. Burema, H., & Frijters, J. (1982). A short questionnaire for the measurement of habitual physical activity in epidemiological studies. *American Journal of Clinical Nutrition, 36,* 936–942.

Bessell, A. (2001). Surviving cancer: Social adjustment, quality of life, and school experiences. *The Council for Exceptional Children, 67*(3), 345–359.

Braveman, P., & Barclay, C. (2009). Health disparities beginning in childhood: A life-course perspective. *Pediatrics, 124,* S163–S175.

Breuner, C. C., Smith, M. S., & Womack, W. M. (2004). Factors related to school absenteeism in adolescents with recurrent headache. *Journal of Head and Face Pain, 44*(3), 217–222.

Brown-Chidsey, R., Steege, M. W., & Mace, F. C. (2008). Best practices in evaluating the effectiveness of interventions using case study data. In A. Thomas & J. Grimes (Eds.), *Best practices in school psychology* (Vol. 5, pp. 2177–2191). Bethesda, MD: National Association of School Psychologists.

Davis, M. A., Quittner, A. L., Stack, C. M., & Yang, M. C. K. (2004). Controlled evaluation of the STARBRIGHT CD-ROM program for children and adolescents with cystic fibrosis. *Journal of Pediatric Psychology, 29,* 259–267.

Doll, B., & Cummings, J. A. (2008). *Transforming school mental health services: Population-based approaches to promoting the competency and wellness of children.* Thousand Oaks, CA: Corwin Press.

Ellis, D. A., Naar-King, S., Frey, M., Templin, T., Rowland, M., & Cakan, N. (2005). Multisystemic treatment of poorly controlled type 1 diabetes: Effects on medical resource utilization. *Journal of Pediatric Psychology, 30,* 656–666.

Evans, S. W., Green, A. L., & Serpell, Z. N. (2005). Community participation in the treatment development process using community development teams. *Journal of Clinical Child and Adolescent Psychology, 34,* 765–771.

Forsyth, B. W. C., Horwitz, S. C., Leventhal, J. M., Burger, J., & Leaf, P. J. (1996). The child vulnerability scale: An instrument to measure parental perceptions of child vulnerability. *Journal of Pediatric Psychology, 21,* 89–101.

Ginsburg, K. R., Alexander, P. M., Hunt, J., Sullivan, M., Zhao, H., & Cnaan, A. (2002). Enhancing the likelihood for a positive future: The perspective of inner-city youth. *Pediatrics, 109* 1136–1143.

Godber, Y. (2008). Best practices in program evaluation. In A. Thomas & J. Grimes (Eds.), Best practices in school psychology (Vol. 5, pp. 2193–2205). Bethesda, MD: National Association of School Psychologists.

Guevara, J., Fuedtner, C., Romer, D., Power, T., Eiraldi, R., Nihtianova, S., ... Schwarz, D. (2005). Fragmented care for inner-city minority children with attention-deficit/hyperactivity disorder. *Pediatrics, 116,* e512–e517.

Hammond, J., Nelson, M., Chinn, S., & Rona, R. J. (1993). Validation of a food frequency questionnaire for assessing dietary-intake in a study of coronary heart-disease risk factors in children. *European Journal of Clinical Nutrition, 47,* 242–250.

Isaac, S., & Michael, W. B. (1981). *Handbook in research and evaluation* (2nd ed.). San Diego, CA: EdITS.

Kazdin, A. E. (2002). *Research design in clinical psychology* (4th ed.). Upper Saddle River, NJ: Pearson Education.

Kelleher, C., Riley-Tillman, T. C., & Power, T. J. (2008). An initial comparison of collaborative and expert driven consultation on treatment integrity. *Journal of Educational and Psychological Consultation, 18,* 294–324.

Kern, L., Evans, S. W., & Lewis, T. K. (2011). Description of an iterative process for intervention development. *Education and Treatment of Children, 34,* 593–617.

Langley, G. L., Nolan, K. M., Nolan, T. W., Norman, C. L., & Provost, L. P. (1996). *The improvement guide: A practical approach to enhancing organizational performance.* San Francisco, CA: Jossey-Bass.

Leff, S. S., Costigan, T., & Power, T. J. (2004). Using participatory research to develop a playground-based prevention program. *Journal of School Psychology, 42*(1), 3–21.

Leff, S. S., Power, T. J., Manz, P. H., Costigan, T. E., & Nabors, L. A. (2001). School-based violence prevention programs for young children: Current status and future directions. *School Psychology Review, 30,* 343–360.

Lynch-Jordan, A. M., Kashikar-Zuck, S., Crosby, L. E., Lopez, W. L., Smolyansky, B. H., Parkins, I. S., ... Powers, S. W. (2010). Applying quality improvement methods to implement a measurement system for chronic pain-related disability. *Journal of Pediatric Psychology, 35,* 32–41.

Mautone, J. A., Lefler, E. K., & Power, T. J. (2011). Promoting family and school success for children with ADHD: Strengthening relationships while building skills. *Theory into Practice, 50,* 43–51.

Moonie, S. A., Sterling, D. A., Figgs, L., & Castro, M. (2006). Asthma status and severity affects missed school days. *Journal of School Health, 76*(1), 18–24.

Moonie, S. A., Sterling, D. A., Figgs, L., & Castro, M. (2008). The relationship between school absence, academic performance, and asthma status. Journal of School Health, 78(3), 140–148.

Nastasi, B. K., Moore, R. B., & Varjas, K. M. (2004). *School-based mental health services: Creating comprehensive and culturally specific programs.* Washington, DC: American Psychological Association.

Parcel, G., & Meyer, M. (1978). Development of an instrument to measure children's health locus of control. *Health Education Monographs, 6,* 149–159.

Perrin, J. M., Bloom, S. R., & Gortmaker, S. L. (2007). The increase of childhood chronic conditions in the United States. *Journal of the American Medical Association, 297,* 2755–2759.

Shapiro, E. S. (2011). *Academic skills problems workbook* (4th ed.). New York: Guildford.

Shinn, M. R. (2010). Building a scientifically based data system for progress monitoring and universal screening across three tiers, including RTI using curriculum-based measurement. In M. R. Shinn & H. M. Walker (Eds.), *Interventions for achievement and behavior problems in a three-tier model including RTI* (pp. 259–292). Bethesda, MD: National Association of School Psychologists.

St. Leger, P., & Campbell, L. (2007). Evaluation of a school-linked program for children with cancer. *Health Education, 108,* 117–129.

Stufflebeam, D. L. (2001). *Evaluation models.* San Francisco, CA: Jossey-Bass.

Tobin, D. L., Holroyd, K. A., & Reynolds, R. V. (1989). The hierarchical factor structure of the coping strategies inventory. *Coping Theory & Research, 13,* 343–361.

Volpe, R. J., Heick, P. F., & Guerasko-Moore, D. (2005). An agile behavioral model for monitoring the effects of stimulant medication in school settings. *Psychology in the Schools, 42*(5), 509–523.

Walker, L. S., & Greene, J. W. (1991). The functional disability inventory: Measuring a neglected dimension of child health status. *Journal of Pediatric Psychology,16,* 39–58.

Wallander, J., & Thompson, R. (1995). *Psychosocial adjustment in children with chronic physical conditions.* New York: Guilford.

Warren, J. M., Henry, C. J. K., Lightowler, H. J., Bradshaw, S. M., & Perwaiz, S. (2003). Evaluation of a pilot school programme aimed at the prevention of obesity in children. *Health Promotion International, 18*(4), 287–296.

Weiss, C. H. (1998). Have we learned anything new about the use of evaluation? *American Journal of Evaluation, 19,* 21–33.

Weitzman, M., & Siegel, D. M. (1992). What we have not learned from what we know about excessive school absence and school dropout. *Journal of Developmental & Behavioral Pediatrics, 13,* 55–57.

Seven

Measurement Development and Evaluation

with Katherine Bevans and George DuPaul

Measurement is an essential component of program development and evaluation. Measurement serves a vital function in screening and determining eligibility for a program, assessing implementation of the program, tracking progress, evaluating outcomes and impact, and determining how a program was (or was not) effective. Measures have been developed to assess a broad range of constructs and assist practitioners and researchers with multiple functions in program development, implementation, and evaluation. When an existing measure is available to assist with an assessment function, it is wise to select this instrument because measurement development can be time consuming and costly. Unfortunately, existing measures often are not available for specific functions (e.g., progress monitoring, integrity monitoring) or important constructs (e.g., family–school relationship, school-primary care provider relationship). In these cases, it is often essential to develop, pilot test, and validate an instrument for use in a project.

This chapter presents the multiple functions of measurement and illustrates how vital measurement is to the success of a project. The steps of classical measurement development are described and guidelines for identifying, developing, pilot testing, and validating a new measure are outlined. In addition, the chapter includes a description of advances in measurement that have important implications for research and practice in pediatric school psychology, specifically item response theory and generalizability theory.

Roles of Measurement

Measures can be used to support many important assessment activities including screening; classification/diagnosis; treatment planning; progress monitoring; assessing integrity; and evaluating outcomes and impact. In addition, assessment activities can help to evaluate mechanisms of action associated with intervention and prevention programs.

Screening

The purpose of screening is to identify those children or adolescents who require further, more comprehensive assessment of a particular area of functioning or emotional/behavioral concern. When conducted in a systematic fashion using reliable and valid measures, screening can save valuable time and resources by targeting multimethod assessment activities for those students in greatest need.

There are at least two types of screening activities that can be conducted: universal screening of all individuals in a population (e.g., school, classroom, primary care practice) and individual screening following a referral. In the former case, all individuals in a targeted population are screened for specific academic, emotional, or behavioral difficulties. For example, *Systematic Screening for Behavior Disorders* (Walker & Severson, 1988) can be used on a class wide basis to identify students who may be exhibiting significant symptoms of externalizing or internalizing disorders. Students pass through several gates in the screening process based on teacher nomination, teacher ratings, and direct observations of behavior. Alternatively, screening measures may be used following a referral of an individual child for evaluation of specific difficulties. For example, when a student is referred for evaluation of possible academic problems, the student's teacher may be asked to complete a brief rating scale assessing academic performance in relation to their classmates (Bennett, Power, Eiraldi, Leff, & Blum, 2009). If the student scores below classmates in one or more academic skill areas, then additional assessment may be warranted.

Classification

Historically, a primary role for measurement has been to assess individuals for the purpose of classification or diagnosis.

Typically, multiple measures such as interviews, rating scales or questionnaires, direct observation, and direct assessments or tests are used for this purpose (Mash & Barkley, 2009). For some measures, a norm-referenced approach is taken wherein individual scores are compared with scores obtained by a relevant standardization sample (e.g., sample that is representative of the population of children in a given geographical location). In these cases, scores that exceed those obtained by a proportion of the standardization sample are used to make classification or diagnostic decisions. For other measures, a criterion-referenced approach is taken wherein scores are compared to a specific criterion of performance. For example, a classification decision regarding learning disability may be warranted for children who obtain scores on a curriculum-based measurement probe of reading fluency that is below a grade level benchmark (Shapiro, 2010). It is important to note that most classification and diagnostic decisions are made on the basis of combined information from multiple measures rather than scores on an individual test or assessment measure.

Treatment Planning

Assessment data are critical for developing intervention plans and are central in the problem analysis phase of behavioral consultation (Sheridan & Kratochwill, 2008). For example, the design of behavior modification strategies is greatly aided by the collection of functional assessment data (Steege & Watson, 2009). In school, teacher interviews and direct observations can be conducted to identify antecedent and consequent events that reliably precede and follow student target behavior, respectively. These data are used to identify the function (e.g., avoid/escape, obtain teacher attention, obtain peer attention) of the target behavior to guide the development of an intervention that allows the student to obtain the same function by engaging in appropriate rather than challenging behavior.

Progress Monitoring

Once an intervention is designed and implemented, it is important to collect data on an ongoing or periodic basis to determine the response to intervention and inform whether treatment should continue as designed, be modified in some fashion, or be discontinued. Typically, this is accomplished by systematically administering progress monitoring measures that are relatively brief, psychometrically sound, and not subject to practice effects (Shapiro, 2010). For academic interventions, for example, interventionists may collect curriculum-based measurement (CBM) probes several times per week both prior to and following intervention in order to assess change in level and slope of acquisition of academic skills. If the slope of CBM data is increased following intervention and is consistent with the desired level of change (i.e., goal line), then intervention continues as originally designed. If slope change is absent or lower than desired, then modifications to the intervention are made.

Integrity Monitoring

Intervention implementation involves a complex set of activities (e.g., clinician delivering accurate information/support to teacher or parent, teacher (parent) understanding treatment content and process, and teacher (parent) delivering treatment strategies to children accurately), all of which presumably must be completed with integrity in order for treatment to be fully successful (Leff, Hoffman, & Gullan, 2009). Data typically are collected through self-report, direct observation, or collection of permanent products to determine the degree to which various aspects of the intervention process have occurred. These data are also used to provide feedback to individuals involved in treatment so that fidelity can be enhanced when it falls below accepted levels (e.g., 80% adherence).

Outcome Evaluation

A primary indicator of treatment success is the degree to which desired change in target behavior or academic skill area is attained within a prescribed period of time. Thus, one or more measures are collected prior to and following a period of treatment implementation to gauge whether stated goals for change have been met (Power, DuPaul, Shapiro, & Kazak, 2003). Outcome evaluation differs from progress monitoring in that data for the latter are collected on an ongoing basis and typically involve repeated administration of brief measures. Alternatively, outcome evaluation measures are summative, more comprehensive, and are administered on only a few occasions (e.g., before treatment, after treatment, and at follow-up).

Impact Evaluation

Assessment data can be gathered to evaluate the impact of treatment strategies or prevention programs, particularly in terms of long-term, meaningful outcomes. For example, effects of programs can be examined on important health or educational indicators such as graduation rates, proportion of students scoring above prescribed levels of competence on high-stakes testing, prevalence of vaccination in primary care, or rates of visits to hospital emergency departments.

Evaluation of Mechanisms of Action

Outcome and impact evaluation measures indicate whether treatment has been effective and has made a significant impact on child functioning; however, how and why an intervention worked can only be determined if possible mechanisms of action are assessed (Breitborde, Srihari, Pollard, Addington, & Woods, 2010). Moderators are variables that impact the relationship between intervention and outcome. For example, age could be a moderator in that an intervention is more effective for younger than older children. Mediators are variables that intervene between treatment delivery and outcome that account for some or all of the variance in outcome. For instance, parent understanding of behavioral principles could mediate the effects of parent education in a homework support program on increases in child completion of assigned homework.

Steps of Classical Measurement Development

Measurement development based on classical theory involves multiple steps, which are described below. Measurement development, like program development, is an iterative process that uses information obtained in one step to inform decisions and modifications later in the process.

Identify the Constructs to be Measured

The process of measurement selection and development begins with a precise delineation of constructs to be measured. For screening and classification, this involves the identification of targeted diagnostic entities, such as anxiety, depression, traumatic stress, attention and hyperactivity, or aggressive behavior. For outcome evaluation, a theory of change is highly useful in identifying key variables for measurement. A theory of change depicts key outcome variables and moderating or mediating variables that may explain how a program is able to achieve desired outcomes.

As an example, Mautone, Lefler, and Power (2011) have proposed that their Family-School Success intervention for children with attention-deficit/hyperactivity disorder (ADHD) is effective in that it targets: (a) improvement in parenting practices, resulting in increased behavior regulation at home, which in turn leads to improved behavior regulation and academic engagement in school; (b) improvement in family involvement in education, which prepares the child to be more engaged in school; and (c) improvement in the family–school relationship, which enables the parents and teachers to engage in effective problem solving to improve behavior regulation and academic engagement in school (see Figure 7.1). The measurement plan for this program is designed to assess each of these key constructs, including parenting practices, family involvement in education, quality of the family–school relationship, behavior regulation at home and school, and academic engagement.

Examine Existing Measures

Once key constructs have been delineated, it is important to identify measures available to assess these variables. If there are existing measures, it is important to determine whether they have been shown to be reliable and valid for the purposes and populations similar to your project. For example, a measure designed for the screening of behavioral health problems

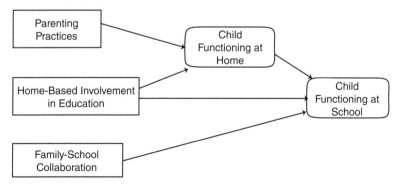

Figure 7.1   Proposed theory of change for the family-school success intervention for children with ADHD.

in primary care may have been shown to have strong psychometric properties across a broad range of pediatric practices, but that does not mean that it is appropriate and valid for use in practices serving specific populations, such as low-income families residing primarily in urban settings (Kostanecka et al., 2008). Further evaluation is needed to confirm the reliability and validity with the specific populations for which a measure is intended to be used.

Every method of assessment is associated with multiple limitations (Power et al., 2003). For example, child self-reports conducted with young children may not be accurate because they are based on an inadequate understanding of the construct being measured. Informant reports are subject to the biases of the individual providing the ratings. Behavioral observations are limited in that they typically include only a few samples of child behavior across a narrow range of settings and time periods. Permanent products are limited in that they do not reflect the processes involved in generating the products. For this reason it is generally important to select multiple methods of assessment, especially regarding constructs that are central to the assessment model. Thus, it is important to examine whether existing measures are available to conduct a multimethod assessment of key constructs.

Justify the Need for a New Measure

Developing a new measure is laborious and costly. Spending the time to create a new measure can slow down the process of developing a program and providing services to children and their families. By the same token, if measures of key constructs do not exist or have questionable psychometric properties, efforts directed at program development may be wasted because it is not possible to conduct a valid evaluation of outcomes.

From the outset, it is important to clearly delineate the measurement gaps that exist and the plan to address these limitations. For example, the Psychosocial Assessment Tool was developed in response to the need for measures of psychosocial risk among children with pediatric conditions for the purpose of determining the level of prevention and intervention services needed (Kazak et al., 2001). As a general rule, it is recommended that investigators and program leaders devote the minimum amount of resources needed to produce an adequate and valid set of measurement tools, so that they do not detract from the overall goal of the project; that is, to develop an effective program and provide needed services.

Understand the Theoretical and Empirical Foundation of the Construct

When developing a measure, it is important to understand the theory underlying the construct and empirical support for the variable. For example, child psychopathology research strongly supports the theory that ADHD is a multidimensional entity consisting of at least two constructs: inattention and hyperactivity-impulsivity. Numerous empirical investigations support this theoretical model (e.g., DuPaul et al., 1997). As a result, virtually all measures developed to assess this disorder include items that reflect both of these dimensions.

Nonetheless, investigators have identified a problem with the two-dimensional formulation of ADHD in that it does not account for a subgroup of individuals who have a particular type of inattention and a pattern of hypoactivity; this subgroup has been characterized by many as having a sluggish cognitive tempo (SCT). In response to this gap and emerging theory on dimensions of attention, researchers have developed measures of SCT (e.g., Penny, Waschbusch, Klein, Eskes, & Corkum, 2009). Empirical research and theory development are needed to clearly define the construct, identify multiple dimensions that may comprise the construct, and suggest a range of behaviors related to each dimension. This information is necessary in planning the phases of scale development and informing the process of item development.

Account for Stakeholder Perceptions

Like program development, measurement development can be improved by understanding the perspectives of the stakeholders involved in the process. The use of participatory methods of research can be highly useful in this process. As an example, Power and colleagues (2007) involved parents and teachers in the development of parent- and teacher-report measures to assess children's homework performance. Focus groups with parents helped the investigators understand that it was important to assess at least three dimensions: (a) child behaviors during homework, (b) family involvement in homework, and (c) teacher involvement in homework. Focus groups with teachers revealed that it was important to assess: (a) student behavior related to homework, and (b) family involvement with homework. This information along with a review of the theoretical and empirical literature related to homework and its assessment resulted in the development of separate parent and teacher versions of the Homework Performance Questionnaire (Power et al., 2007).

Generate Items and Identify a Suitable Scale

Numerous sources of information are useful in generating items to assess a measurement construct. First, research related to the nature of the construct, distinguishing features, and related characteristics provide useful guidelines. Second, empirical findings pertaining to related constructs can be informative. For example, factor analyses of similar constructs will identify items that have a strong fit (high factor loadings) with the variable. Also, symptom utility estimates, when available, indicate which items are strongest with regard to differentiating children who fit and do not fit a construct (Power, Costigan, Leff, Eiraldi, & Landau, 2001). Adaptation of these empirically supported items is a useful strategy in generating an item pool (Kostanecka et al., 2008). Third, the input of relevant stakeholders (e.g., parents, youth, school professionals, health providers) regarding key characteristics of the construct is helpful in generating items.

Determination of a suitable scale for the proposed items is another important consideration. Likert scales are feasible to use and are preferred by many researchers and practitioners. Anchor points on these scales generally refer to varying frequencies in behavior (e.g., never, sometimes, often, almost always) or levels of impairment. When possible, it is useful to provide a clear definition of anchor points (e.g., almost always = 90% or more) using terms that are clear and understandable to respondents.

Field Test Items

Once an item pool has been generated and the measure has been created in draft form, it is important to conduct pilot tests of the instrument with small samples that are similar to the proposed measure respondents. During the initial pilot test, which could consist of 5 to 10 participants, it is helpful to administer each item separately as part of an interview, so that respondents can provide feedback regarding the meaning of the item, its relevance, clarity of wording, and the ease of response using the proposed scale. Respondents typically are asked to suggest a change in item wording, if needed, to clarify its meaning. It is often useful to audiotape the interview to capture all of the information revealed by the respondents. Subsequently, it is useful to conduct a pilot test with a somewhat larger sample (e.g., 10 to 25 participants) to assess variability of participant responses to each item and the acceptability of the measure. Afterwards, it is useful to conduct an item analysis to determine whether there is a reasonable amount of variability in participant responses.

Leff and colleagues (2006) provided a useful illustration of how to engage in an iterative process for purposes of pilot testing a measure. The measure they developed used a cartoon format to assess hostile attribution bias in relationally aggressive situations among elementary-age girls attending urban schools. Students were asked about the relevance of the situations and appropriateness of the depictions of characters portrayed in the cartoons. Many of the students provided useful feedback about the facial expressions, hair styles, and clothing of the cartoon characters and contextual features portrayed in the illustrations. Based on feedback provided by the youth through multiple iterations of pilot testing, the investigators were able to develop items that were perceived as culturally sensitive, developmentally appropriate, and acceptable. In addition, students were asked to identify whether they perceived the actions depicted in the vignettes to be intentional or unintentional. Items were analyzed to ensure that there was variability among respondents with regard to their perceptions of the intentionality of the aggressor portrayed in each item.

Determine the Factor Structure of the Measure

Once the measure has been pilot tested, it is important to determine the dimensions assessed by the instrument. A wide range of factor analytic methods have been developed to identify the dimensional structure of measures. In general, there are two types: exploratory factor analysis (EFA) and confirmatory factor analysis (CFA). EFA is typically used during the relatively early stages of measure development, especially when the measure is not strongly based upon a conceptual model and there is limited information about the factor structure of the instrument. Two commonly used methods of extraction with EFA are principal components analysis and common factor analysis. Although each approach has its advantages, common factor analysis is often appropriate because it is designed to identify the latent structure of a scale and may produce more accurate estimates of population parameters (Wegener & Fabrigar, 2000). Also, several options are available for rotating factors (e.g., varimax and oblimin). A useful strategy is to use two or more approaches to extraction and rotation; identifying similar solutions across methods provides assurance that an adequate solution has been found (Kline, 1994). For example, in a study examining the factor structure of the Homework Problem Checklist, a two-factor solution was identified using EFA: factor I referred to inattention and avoidance of homework, and factor II consisted of items pertaining to poor organization and performance. This factor structure was replicated using both maximum likelihood and principal components methods of extraction and both varimax and oblimin techniques for rotation (Power, Werba, Watkins, Angelucci, & Eiraldi, 2006).

Several methods are useful in determining the optimal number of factors to retain when conducting an EFA (Velicer, Eaton, & Fava, 2000). Some of the most commonly used methods are: (a) minimum average partials, (b) parallel analysis, (c) scree test, (d) number of items loading on a factor (acceptable loadings typically are in the .3 to .4 range, and minimum number of items is typically four), and (e) items that theoretically relate to the construct purportedly assessed by the factor (see Power et al., 2006). For further reading about EFA, refer to Child (2006).

The other major type of factor analysis is CFA, which is used in the more advanced stages of scale development when there is considerable theoretical and empirical information available to hypothesize the dimensional structure of a measure. CFA tests the extent to which a measure used with a specific population fits the hypothesized factor structure. Typically, multiple models are tested to determine which meet criteria for acceptable fit and which, if any, model is superior. Two commonly used fit statistics are the comparative fit index (CFI) and root mean square error approximation (RMSEA). Acceptable levels of model fit are generally indicated when CFI is greater than .95 and RMSEA is less than .06 (Hu & Bentler, 1999). As examples, CFA has been used to evaluate the factor structure of two commonly used measures of behavioral health, assessed in the context of primary care practices: Strengths and Difficulties Questionnaire (Dickey & Blumberg,

2004) and the Pediatric Symptom Checklist—17-Item Version (Kostanecka et al., 2008). For further reading about CFA, refer to Brown (2006).

Assess Reliability

Reliability refers to the consistency with which an instrument measures a construct. A measure has little value if it is not able to assess a construct in a consistent manner. There are many types of reliability used to evaluate the psychometric soundness of a measure. One type of reliability is internal consistency. A statistic commonly used to evaluate the internal consistency of a scale is the alpha coefficient, which refers to the extent to which items on a factor are interrelated with one another. Researchers typically consider .70 or greater to reflect an acceptable level of internal consistency (e.g., Power et al., 2007). Another type is test–retest reliability, which reflects the stability of assessment over a relatively brief period of time (e.g., 1 to 4 weeks). Test developers strive for test–retest reliability greater than or equal to .80, with indices greater than .90 reflecting high levels of stability.

When rating scales are used and multiple informants provide responses, researchers and practitioners are often interested in knowing the extent of interrater agreement (e.g., agreement between a parent and teacher or between a parent and child). Interrater agreement typically is much lower than other forms of reliability, often in the .3 to .5 range (Achenbach, McConaughy, & Howell, 1987). One reason for this is that informants may observe individuals in different contexts and behavior may change across contexts. Also, informants may vary in their thresholds for viewing a behavior as a problem; in other words, one informant may view a behavior as more tolerable than another informant.

Another form of reliability is interobserver agreement, which is important to examine when developing an observational measure. This form of reliability provides an index of the extent to which two or more independent observers code behaviors in a consistent manner. Percent agreement is often used as an index of agreement, but this statistic is biased when behaviors have a low or high base rate. A better choice is to calculate a kappa coefficient, which controls for chance agreements that occur with low or high base rate behaviors (e.g., Leff, Costigan, & Power, 2004).

Evaluate Validity

Validity refers to the extent to which a measure accurately assesses the construct it is purported to assess. There are several forms of validity. One type is construct validity, which refers to the conceptual model assessed by an instrument or the dimensional structure of the measure. Factor analysis, described previously, is highly useful in examining construct validity. A second type is discriminant validity, which is an examination of how well a measure is able to discriminate groups falling into separate categories or diagnostic groups. For example, in examining the discriminant validity of the ADHD Rating Scale–IV, researchers investigated how well the Inattention and Hyperactivity-Impulsivity factors distinguished three groups: those with ADHD, Inattentive Type; those with ADHD, Combined Type; and those in a clinic-referred control group (DuPaul et al., 1998).

Another type is criterion-related validity, which refers to how well a measure compares to other well-established methods for assessing the construct. Extending the example of the ADHD Rating Scale–IV, researchers examined how well the factors of this measure correlated with similar factors on the well-established Conners Ratings scales (Conners, 1989). Also, they correlated factor scores with direct observations of off-task and fidgety behavior, as well as accuracy on independent class work assignments (DuPaul et al., 1998).

Establishing predictive validity is also important in evaluating the psychometric properties of measures, especially instruments designed for the purposes of screening and diagnostic evaluation. Predictive validity refers to the extent to which a measure is able to accurately predict the presence or absence of a condition. Predictive validity is often evaluated using discriminant function analysis (Eiraldi, Power, Karustis, & Goldstein, 2000) or logistic regression analysis (Power et al., 1998). As indicated in chapter 4, sensitivity and specificity are important to examine in evaluating predictive validity; these terms refer to the extent to which a measure is able to accurately identify those cases known to have a condition (sensitivity) and cases that do not have a condition (specificity). Sensitivity and specificity vary as a function of the cutpoint selected on a measure. Receiver operating characteristics analysis (ROC; see Chen, Faraone, Biederman, & Tsuang, 1994) is a highly useful method for identifying the overall ability of a measure to accurately identify cases known to have and not to have a condition, which simultaneously takes into account both sensitivity and specificity.

Predictive power analyses are also highly useful in examining the ability of a measure to accurately predict the presence and absence of a disorder. Positive predictive power (PPP) reflects the probability that an individual has a disorder given the presence of a score above a certain cut-point. Negative predictive power (NPP) reflects the probability that an individual does not have a disorder given the presence of a score below a selected cut-point on a measure. Given that PPP and NPP are highly sensitive to base rates of cases above and below cut-points in the population, it is important to use a kappa statistic to correct for chance agreement (see Frick et al., 1994; Power et al., 1998). Differentiating sensitivity, specificity, PPP, and NPP can be confusing. Table 7.1 provides an illustration and formulae for computing each of these statistics that helps to distinguish these statistics.

Incremental validity is another aspect of validity that is often useful to evaluate; the term refers to the extent to which a measure is able to add to the prediction of a diagnostic entity. This form of validity is important to examine when there are one or more existing measures of a construct and the question is whether a new method is able to add to the ability to predict (Haynes & Lench, 2003). For instance, an investigator may want to determine whether lab-based measures of executive functioning are able to improve the ability to predict a dysfunction in executive processing over and above teacher reports of this multidimensional construct. Of course, such an analysis requires that there is a valid way (i.e., gold standard) for establishing the presence or absence of a condition; in this case, a dysfunction in executive processing.

For measures used in progress monitoring and outcome evaluation, it is important to examine treatment sensitivity, which is the ability of an instrument to detect improvements in performance in response to intervention. In the context of progress monitoring when multiple data points are available during the course of intervention, treatment sensitivity is often evaluated by comparing rates of change (slope) between baseline and treatment phases (Fuchs & Fuchs, 2000).

Recent Advances: Item Response Theory

Classical test theory (CTT) methods such as those described above have many advantages, most notably that they depend

Table 7.1   Formulae for Determining Sensitivity, Specificity, Positive Predictive Power, and Negative Predictive Power

	Diagnosis Present	Diagnosis Absent	
Score Above Cut- Point	A	B	G
Score Below Cut- Point	C	D	H
	E	F	

E = A + C; F = B + D; G = A + B; H = C + D
Sensitivity = A/E
Specificity = D/F
Positive Predictive Power (PPP) = A/G
Negative Predictive Power (NPP) = D/H
Adapted from Laurent, Landau, and Stark (1993) with permission of the National Association of School Psychologists.

on few a priori assumptions and produce results that are relatively easy to interpret. An underlying assumption of CTT is that respondents' observed scores are an estimate of their true scores plus or minus some unobservable measurement error. In some circumstances, however, this assumption is an oversimplification because true scores may reflect both respondent characteristics and content of the assessment tool (Hambleton & Jones, 1993; van der Linden & Hambleton, 1997). Therefore, CTT methods cannot be used to determine whether variability in scores is attributable to respondents' actual state or the properties of the instrument. As a result, it is difficult to compare the outcomes of respondents based on results of different assessment instruments. Also, CTT methods assume (often erroneously) that the reliability of a measure remains constant for all respondents regardless of their level on the construct being assessed and that the relationships among items and between items and the underlying traits they are purported to measure are linear in nature (van der Linden & Hambleton, 1997).

Item response theory (IRT) underlies a set of generalized linear models and associated statistical procedures that connect observed survey responses to a respondent's location on an unmeasured underlying ("latent") trait. A unique aspect of IRT is that it facilitates the differentiation of respondent and item characteristics through the property of *parameter invariance* (Hambleton & Jones, 1993). A cornerstone of all IRT models is the joint measurement of people and items, specifically a respondent's "ability" (level of the underlying trait) and item "difficulty" (how much of the trait a person must have to endorse the item) are placed on the same continuum and assessed using the same metric. Figure 7.2 is a graphical depiction of a common respondent "ability" and item "difficulty" continuum. The vertical scale represents the relative degree of physical discomfort as measured by the Healthy Pathways Child-Report scale (Bevans, Riley, & Forrest, 2010). Higher numbers (theta) indicate less discomfort and number signs (#) show the distribution of children along the physical discomfort continuum. Item labels are shown at the item's difficulty level along the physical discomfort continuum. The joint estimation of child and item parameters is useful for determining the degree to which scales are composed of

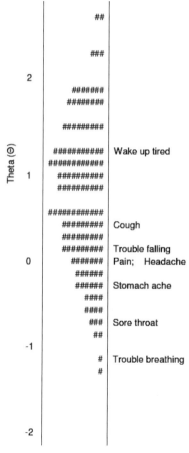

Note: # = 13 children

Figure 7.2　Item-person map for the Healthy Pathways Child Report Physical Discomfort scale.

items that adequately measure the full range of an underlying latent construct and have appropriate separation among items as indicated by minimal floor/ceiling effects, gaps in coverage (e.g., when there are no or too few items that provide information about respondents along the full range of the outcome continuum), and item redundancy (e.g., when too many items provide information about respondents at a specific point on the outcome continuum). The figure suggests that the physical discomfort scale can be improved by adding items to fill the gaps in coverage; for example, between "wake up tired," a relatively common symptom, and "cough," a symptom that is experienced by slightly over half of children. The scale can also be improved by adding items that assess the extreme positive end of the continuum (high symptoms) to better discriminate among children who experience high levels of physical discomfort.

In addition, IRT provides a framework for conceptualizing and investigating item bias as evidenced by differential item functioning (DIF) for members of salient subgroups. Examination of DIF is a method for studying measurement equivalence across groups. An item exhibits DIF if the item response differs across groups (e.g., age, race), controlling for an estimate of the construct being measured (e.g., physical discomfort). Because it is defined conditionally based upon the underlying variable measured, DIF is not the same as an unconditional difference between groups. Instead, the research question posed in DIF analyses is whether, after controlling for the underlying construct, the response to an item is related to group membership (Teresi & Fleishman, 2007). It is important to minimize DIF to obtain unbiased information about children's outcomes and experiences.

Finally, IRT supports the development of computerized adaptive test (CAT) versions of instruments that "match" the most appropriate set of items to each respondent based on his or her individual level of the outcome (Bjorner, Chang, Thissen, & Reeve, 2007). In CAT assessment, the sequence of items administered depends on an individual's response to previously administered items. Based on the respondent's prior performance, items that provide the most information about her or his unique level of a trait are administered. In this way, a smaller number of items can be administered without sacrificing measurement precision. As a result, it is possible to develop short instruments that afford precise measurement, thus contributing to the efficiency of the measurement process.

Increasingly, measures used to assess child outcomes are developed and validated using a combination of CTT-based and IRT-based approaches. For example, in 2004 the National Institutes of Health launched a program of research called the Patient Reported Outcome Measurement Information System (PROMIS®; Cella et al., 2007). The goal of PROMIS is to provide clinicians and researchers access to efficient, precise, valid, and responsive adult- and child-reported measures of health (see www.nihpromis.org for more information). PROMIS measures are rapidly proliferating throughout clinical and behavioral research, epidemiology and population surveillance, and clinical practice.

PROMIS uses a domain-specific measurement approach. Domains are defined as clinically coherent and empirically unidimensional health attributes. Pools of items that assess these attributes are developed and refined using rigorous qualitative methods (DeWalt, Rothrock, Yount, & Stone, 2007). Thereafter, they are subjected to psychometric testing using a combination of CTT and IRT methods (Reeve et al., 2007). Analyses are conducted to confirm assumptions about dimensionality of the items hypothesized to be within a single item bank, to test for differential item functioning (DIF) across sociodemographic groups, and to calibrate the items to support development of fixed-length, short forms and computerized adaptive test (CAT) versions of the instruments.

Recent Advances: Generalizability Theory

Although generalizability (G) theory is considered a recent advancement and an alternative to classical test theory, it was developed in the early 1970s (Cronbach, Gleser, Nanda, & Rajaratnam, 1972). In contrast to classical test theory, which was designed to differentiate "true score" variance from random error, G theory is able to identify sources of error variance, which is highly useful in developing strategies to reduce overall error variance and improve true score variance (Hintze, Owen, Shapiro, & Daly, 2000). Common sources of variance in assessment are described in Table 7.2. In essence, G theory is a method for evaluating and improving measurement reliability. It is especially useful in examining the reliability of measures used repeatedly, which is common when monitoring progress in the context of a prevention or intervention program, or examining change in the context of a quality improvement project.

Table 7.2   Common Sources of Variance in Assessment, which can be Examined Using Generalizability Theory

Source of Variance	Description
Person	Variance due to differences among individuals, which is considered "true score" variance
Setting	Variance due to differences across environmental context, such as class subject or peer group activity
Observer or Rater	Variance due to differences among observers or raters of a set of behaviors
Alternate Forms	Variance due to differences among sets of assessment forms or materials
Number of sessions	Variance due to differences across number of assessment sessions
Interactions	Variance due to interactions among two or more sources of variance

In the context of evaluating reliability when using direct observation methods in a school setting, variance can be attributed to multiple factors, including students, observers, class subject or setting (e.g., math versus language arts), and number of observation sessions (Hintze & Matthews, 2004). On-task behavior is commonly observed in a school setting because of its relationship to academic engaged time, which is associated with academic achievement. True score variance in this example is variance due to differences in on-task behavior among students in the sample. Error can be differentiated into the multiple sources of variance, including observer, class setting, and number of sessions. Using repeated measures analysis, it is possible to differentiate specific sources of variability in addition to interactions among sources (e.g., variance between class subjects over time or number of sessions). In addition, G theory provides an estimate of consistency of behavior under two conditions: (a) when making nomothetic, between-subject comparisons ($G_{absolute}$), and (b) when evaluating idiographic, within-subject comparisons ($G_{relative}$).

G theory is well suited to conducting follow-up (decision) studies to explore methods to improve reliability. For example, a relatively high level of variance due to informants would suggest the need for improved training of observers and ongoing checks of observer accuracy. A high level of variance due to number of sessions can often be addressed by adding observation sessions. Variability across school subjects may be difficult to change, and may be due to multiple factors such as differential student ability across subjects or differential teaching practices. Nonetheless, this information can be highly useful for intervention planning.

G theory has been applied in numerous other cases. For example, it has been used to evaluate the reliability of reading performance when assessed using multiple passages and assessment sessions, known as curriculum-based measurement. In this case, an important source of error variance is number of passages (brief reading sessions) included in the assessment. Subsequent decision studies have been used to identify the optimal number of reading sessions to conduct an assessment that is reliable for making nomothetic and idiographic decisions (Hintze et al., 2000).

As another example, G studies have been used to evaluate the reliability of using brief teacher ratings of student behavior. Important sources of variability using this method are variance due to rater and number of rating occasions. Decision studies have been conducted to explore methods for reducing error variance by adding number of rating occasions to the assessment procedure (Briesch, Chafouleas, & Riley-Tillman, 2010).

Conclusions

Measurement is an essential component of program development and evaluation and serves multiple roles, including screening, diagnostic assessment, treatment planning, integrity monitoring, progress monitoring, outcome and impact evaluation, and examination of mechanisms of action. Scale development involves multiple steps and can be labor intensive. Successful scale development requires conceptual clarity about the construct being measured, a deep understanding of the theoretical and empirical research related to the construct, and stakeholder input regarding key aspects of the construct and potential items to assess these. Establishing reliability is a critical step in measurement development; generalizability theory can be highly useful in examining reliability, isolating sources of variability, and identifying areas in which modifications may be needed. There are multiple strategies to evaluate the validity of a measure. When evaluating self-report and informant report measures, exploratory and confirmatory factor analyses are useful in identifying dimensions being evaluated by the scale. For measures used in screening and diagnostic assessment, it is important to establish predictive validity and clinical utility, including an examination of sensitivity, specificity, positive predictive power, and negative predictive power. For measures used in progress monitoring and outcome assessment, it is a critical to establish treatment sensitivity. Item response theory is a relatively recent advance that can improve the precision, developmental appropriateness, cultural sensitivity, and efficiency of measurement tools. Generalizability is another advancement that can be useful in improving measurement precision.

Discussion Questions

1. For the projects in which you are participating, how is measurement being used? What are the current gaps in measurement, and how can they be addressed?
2. What are the strengths and limitations of the measures being used in your intervention and prevention work? Which construct(s) are being measured inadequately and require measure development?
3. Evaluate your training in measurement development. What are the gaps in your training and how can these be addressed? Who can serve as mentors and consultants to you?
4. How can item response theory and generalizability theory be useful to you in your work?

Additional Teaching Aids

PowerPoint slides pertaining to leadership development that contain information about measure development are included in the attached CD.

References

Achenbach, T. M., McConaughy, S. H., & Howell, C. T. (1987). Child/adolescent behavioral and emotional problems: Implications of cross-informant correlations for situational specificity. *Psychological Bulletin, 101*, 213–232.

Bennett, A. E., Power, T. J., Eiraldi, R. B., Leff, S. S., & Blum, N. J. (2009). Identifying learning problems in children being evaluated for ADHD: Validity of the Academic Performance Questionnaire. *Pediatrics, 124*, e633–e639.

Bevans, K. B., Riley, A. W., & Forrest, C. B. (2010). Development of the Healthy Pathways Child-Report scales. *Quality of Life Research, 19*(8), 1195–1214.

Bjorner, J. B., Chang, C.-H., Thissen, D., & Reeve, B. B. (2007). Developing tailored instruments: Item banking and computerized adaptive assessment. *Quality of Life Research, 16*, 95–108.

Breitborde, N. J. K., Srihari, V. H., Pollard, J. M., Addington, D. N., & Woods, S. W. (2010). Mediators and moderators in early intervention research. *Early Intervention in Psychiatry, 4*(2), 143–152.

Briesch, A. M., Chafouleas, S. M., & Riley-Tillman, T. C. (2010). Generalizability and dependability of behavior assessment methods to estimate academic engagement: A comparison of systematic direct observation and direct behavior rating. *School Psychology Review, 39*(3), 408–421.

Brown, T. A. (2006). *Confirmatory factor analysis for applied research.* New York: Guilford.

Cella, D., Yount, S., Rothrock, N., Gershon, R., Cook, K., Reeve, B., … Rose, M. (2007). The Patient–Reported Outcomes Measurement Information System (PROMIS): Progress of an NIH Roadmap cooperative group during its first two years. *Medical Care, 45*, S3–S11.

Chen, W. J., Faraone, S. V., Biederman, J., & Tsuang, M. T. (1994). Diagnostic accuracy of the Child Behavior Checklist scales for attention-deficit hyperactivity disorder: A receiver-operating characteristic analysis. *Journal of Consulting and Clinical Psychology, 62*(5), 1017–1025.

Child, D. (2006). *The essentials of factor analysis* (3rd ed.). New York: Continuum.

Conners, C. K. (1989). *Conners Rating Scales manual.* North Tonawanda, NY: Multi-Health Systems.

Cronbach, L. J., Gleser, G. C., Nanda, H., & Rajaratnam, N. (1972). *The dependability of behavioral measurements.* New York: Wiley.

DeWalt, D. A., Rothrock, N., Yount, S., & Stone, A. A. (2007). Evaluation of item candidates: The PROMIS qualitative item review. *Medical Care, 45*, S12–S21.

Dickey, W. C., & Blumberg, S. J. (2004). Revisiting the factor structure of the Strengths and Difficulties Questionnaire: United States, 2001. *Journal of the American Academy of Child and Adolescent Psychiatry, 43*(9), 1159–1167.

DuPaul, G. J., Power, T. J., Anastopoulos, A. D., Reid, R., McGoey, K., & Ikeda, M. (1997). Teacher ratings of attention-deficit/hyperactivity disorder: Factor structure and normative data. *Psychological Assessment, 9,* 436–444.

DuPaul, G. J., Power, T. J., McGoey, K. E., Ikeda, M. J., & Anastopoulos, A. D. (1998). Reliability and validity of parent and teacher ratings of attention-deficit/hyperactivity disorder symptoms. *Journal of Psychoeducational Assessment, 16*(1), 55–68.

Eiraldi, R. B., Power, T. J., Karustis, J. L., & Goldstein, S. G. (2000). Assessing ADHD and comorbid disorders in children: The Child Behavior Checklist and the Devereux Scales of Mental Disorders. *Journal of Clinical Child Psychology, 29*(1), 3–16.

Frick, P. J., Lahey, B. B., Applegate, B., Kerdyck, L., Ollendick, T., Hynd, G. W., ... Waldman, I. (1994). DSM-IV field trials for the disruptive behavior disorders: Symptom utility estimates. *Journal of the American Academy of Child & Adolescent Psychiatry, 33*(4), 529–539.

Fuchs, L. S., & Fuchs, D. (2000). *Analogue assessment of academic skills: Curriculum-based measurement and performance assessment.* New York: Guilford.

Hambleton, R. K., & Jones, R. W. (1993). Comparison of classical test theory and item response theory and their applications to test development. *Educational Measurement: Issues and Practice, 12*(3), 38–47.

Haynes, S. N., & Lench, H. C. (2003). Incremental validity of new clinical assessment measures. *Psychological Assessment, 15*(4), 456–466.

Hintze, J. M., & Matthews, W. J. (2004). The generalizability of systematic direct observations across time and setting: A preliminary investigation of the psychometrics of behavioral observation. *School Psychology Review, 33*(2), 258–270.

Hintze, J. M., Owen, S. V., Shapiro, E. S., & Daly, E. J. (2000). Generalizability of oral reading fluency measures: Application of G theory to curriculum–based measurement. *School Psychology Quarterly, 15*, 52–68.

Hu, L.–t., & Bentler, P. M. (1999). Cutoff criteria for fit indexes in covariance structure analysis: Conventional criteria versus new alternatives. *Structural Equation Modeling, 6*(1), 1–55.

Kazak, A., Prusak, A., McSherry, M., Simms, S., Beele, D., Rourke, M., ... Lange, B. (2001). The Psychosocial Assessment Tool (PAT): Pilot data on a brief screening instrument for identifying high risk families in pediatric oncology. *Families, Systems and Health, 19*(3), 303–317.

Kline, P. (1994). *An easy guide to factor analysis.* New York: Routledge.

Kostanecka, A., Power, T. J., Clarke, A., Watkins, M., Hausman, C. L., & Blum, N. J. (2008). Behavioral health screening in urban primary care settings: Construct validity of the PSC-17. *Journal of Developmental and Behavioral Pediatrics, 29*(2), 124–128.

Laurent, J., Landau, S., & Stark, K. D. (1993). Conditional probabilities in the diagnosis of depressive and anxiety disorders In children. *School Psychology Review, 22*, 98–114.

Leff, S. S., Costigan, T., & Power, T. J. (2004). Using participatory research to develop a playground–based prevention program. *Journal of School Psychology, 42*(1), 3–21.

Leff, S. S., Crick, N. R., Angelucci, J., Haye, K., Jawad, A. F., Grossman, M., & Power, T. J. (2006). Social cognition in context: Validating a cartoon–based attributional measure for urban girls. *Child Development, 77*(5), 1351–1358.

Leff, S. S., Hoffman, J. A., & Gullan, R. L. (2009). Intervention integrity: New paradigms and applications. *School Mental Health, 1*(3), 103–106.

Mash, E. J., & Barkley, R. A. (Eds.). (2009). *Assessment of childhood disorders* (4th ed.). New York: Guilford.

Mautone, J. A., Lefler, E. K., & Power, T. J. (2011). Promoting family and school success for children with ADHD: Strengthening relationships while building skills. *Theory into Practice, 50*(1), 43–51.

Penny, A. M., Waschbusch, D. A., Klein, R. M., Eskes, G., & Corkum, P. (2009). Developing a measure of sluggish cognitive tempo for children: Content validity, factor structure, and reliability. *Psychological Assessment, 21*(3), 380–389.

Power, T. J., Andrews, T. J., Eiraldi, R. B., Doherty, B. J., Ikeda, M. J., DuPaul, G. J., & Landau, S. (1998). Evaluating attention deficit hyperactivity disorder using multiple informants: The incremental utility of combining teacher with parent reports. *Psychological Assessment, 10*(3), 250–260.

Power, T. J., Costigan, T. E., Leff, S. S., Eiraldi, R. B., & Landau, S. (2001). Assessing ADHD across settings: Contributions of behavioral assessment to categorical decision making. *Journal of Clinical Child Psychology, 30*(3), 399–412.

Power, T. J., Dombrowski, S. C., Watkins, M. W., Mautone, J. A., & Eagle, J. W. (2007). Assessing children's homework performance: Development of multi-dimensional, multi-informant rating scales. *Journal of School Psychology, 45*(3), 333–348.

Power, T. J., DuPaul, G. J., Shapiro, E. S., & Kazak, A. E. (2003). *Promoting children's health: Integrating school, family, and community.* New York: Guilford.

Power, T. J., Werba, B. E., Watkins, M. W., Angelucci, J. G., & Eiraldi, R. B. (2006). Patterns of parent–reported homework problems among ADHD-referred and non-referred children. *School Psychology Quarterly, 21*(1), 13–33.

Reeve, B. B., Hays, R. D., Bjorner, J. B., Cook, K. F., Crane, P. K., Teresi, J. A., ... Cella, D. (2007). Psychometric evaluation and calibration of health-related quality of life item banks: plans for the Patient-Reported Outcomes Measurement Information System (PROMIS). *Medical Care, 45*(5 Suppl. 1), S22–S31.

Shapiro, E. S. (2010). *Academic skills problems: Direct assessment and intervention* (4th ed.). New York: Guilford.

Sheridan, S. M., & Kratochwill, T. R. (2008). *Conjoint behavioral consultation: Promoting family–school connections and interventions* (2nd ed.). New York: Springer.

Steege, M. W., & Watson, T. S. (2009). *Conducting school-based functional behavioral assessments: A practitioner's guide* (2nd ed.). New York: Guilford.

Teresi, J. A., & Fleishman, J. A. (2007). Differential item functioning and health assessment. *Quality of Life Research, 16*, 33–42.

van der Linden, W. J., & Hambleton, R. K. (1997). Item response theory: Brief history, common models, and extensions. In W. J. van der Linden & R. K. Hambleton (Eds.), *Handbook of modern item response theory* (pp. 1–28). New York: Springer.

Velicer, W. F., Eaton, C. A., & Fava, J. L. (2000). Construct explication through factor or component analysis: A review and evaluation of alternative procedures for determining the number of factors or components. In R. D. Goffin & E. Helmes (Eds.), *Problems and solutions in human assessment: Honoring Douglas N. Jackson at seventy* (pp. 41–71). Boston, MA: Kluwer Academic/Plenum.

Walker, H. M., & Severson, H. (1988). *Systematic screening for behavioral disorders assessment system.* Longmont, CO: Sopris West.

Wegener, D. T., & Fabrigar, L. R. (2000). Analysis and design for non-experimental data. In H. T. Reis & C. M. Judd (Eds.), *Handbook of research methods in social and personality psychology* (pp. 412–450). New York: Cambridge University Press.

Eight

Grant Writing Strategies

Developing and implementing programs that benefit children and their families requires considerable resources. Often available resources are barely sufficient to support existing services; there may be limited support to expand or improve existing programs or to develop new initiatives. Grants are invaluable in providing resources to support improvements in existing programs and efforts to develop, implement, and evaluate new programs.

Although a relatively high percentage of health and mental health professionals engage in grant writing activities in their careers, very few of these individuals receive systemic training in how to identify sources of grant support and apply for funding. Professionals typically must learn on the job the strategies required to secure funding that will enable them to become innovators in the field and effective systems change agents.

The purpose of this chapter is to discuss methods for identifying potential sources of grant support and strategies for preparing grant applications to obtain funding. This chapter includes a description of types of grants, potential sources of funding and resources for identifying grants, and components of effective grant applications. The chapter concludes with recommendations for getting started and moving through the initial stages of becoming a grant writer.

Types of Grants

Grants are available to support the professional activities of psychologists who are engaged in a wide range of professional activities. Most grant applications are unsolicited and tailored to address the mission and goals delineated by the sponsoring organization. In addition, grant applications may be a response to a program announcement (PA) by the sponsoring agency that delineates a range of priorities that may span one or more years and several competitions, or a request for applications (RFA) that refers to a specific competition and has highly specific parameters. Grants can support projects focused on a variety of activities, including service delivery, program development, training, career development, and research.

Service Delivery

Grants to support service delivery often address disparities in health care related to demographic factors; the projects may target underserved populations, such as individuals of low socioeconomic status, ethnic or racial minority status, rural or urban residence, or infant/preschool age (see Power, Eiraldi, Clarke, & Mazzuca, 2005; U.S. Department of Health and Human Services, 1999, 2001). These grants typically are designed to address gaps in service delivery by applying evidence-based strategies. Although there is a focus on providing evidence that services promote successful outcomes at the level of the child, there is also a strong emphasis on demonstrating improvements in the quality of service delivery over time using efficient and valid metrics of quality improvement (e.g., see Lynch-Jordan et al., 2010).

Program Development

Grants are available to support the development of programs in clinical and community settings, including schools. Typically, it is important to demonstrate that the program addresses a topic of public health significance based upon epidemiological findings and research on the developmental course of the problem if left untreated (Doll & Cummings, 2008). Further, it is helpful to describe clearly the theoretical and empirical basis for the program. A well-developed, comprehensive evaluation plan is essential. Ideally, the plan will include measures for assessing child outcomes and impact on important, naturalistic indictors of effectiveness (e.g., school attendance, academic grades in school, visits to the emergency room), as well as potential mediating variables (e.g., child, parent, and teacher engagement in intervention) and moderators (e.g., comorbid diagnostic status, age, gender).

Training

Funding for training in clinical practice and research is available through multiple private and public sources. These grants may be used to support training at the undergraduate, graduate, professional school, internship, residency, and fellowship levels. An example is the training program at Lehigh University and The Children's Hospital of Philadelphia in pediatric school psychology, funded by the U.S. Department of Education, Office of Special Education Programs (see Power, Shapiro, & DuPaul, 2003). Funds typically are used to support trainees and faculty (e.g., student tuition costs, stipends for trainees, partial salary support for faculty), although many training grants require that a high proportion of the funds be used for trainees. Obtaining a training grant often requires a well-developed plan for recruiting trainees from underrepresented ethnic/racial minority groups or disadvantaged backgrounds. A useful strategy for evaluating outcomes is to accumulate and examine a portfolio of permanent products generated by each trainee during the course of the project.

Career Development

Numerous funding opportunities are available to support the career development of health and mental health professionals. The greatest source of these funds is through federal agencies, such as the National Institutes of Health (NIH) and the Centers for Disease Control and Prevention (CDC), but career development awards are available through foundations, such as W.T. Grant and Spencer, as well as professional associations. The focus of these grants is generally on supporting the development of researchers in the early stages of their careers. Applicants need to submit a well-developed, cogent agenda for their career development that spells out a training plan to acquire skills in content and methodology, including course work, advanced seminars, in-depth mentoring, and professional readings guided by mentors. In addition, applications for early career awards typically include a proposal to conduct one or a series of research investigations that will enable the candidate to achieve training goals delineated in the application. Career development awards are also available for academicians at the midcareer and senior levels to support research and mentoring activities appropriate for professionals at these stages.

Research

There is a wealth of available resources to support the research of scholars at every level of professional development. Grants are available for model building, measure development, intervention development and feasibility testing, pilot testing of the efficacy and effectiveness of interventions, clinical trials of interventions, and dissemination research. Table 8.1 describes examples of types of awards funded by two federal agencies, NIH and the Institute of Education Sciences (IES). The term of these awards typically varies from 1 to 5 years, and the amount generally ranges from $50,000 to $500,000 for

Table 8.1 Examples of Available Mechanisms for Funding Intervention and Prevention Initiatives through the National Institutes of Health (NIH) and the Institute of Education Sciences (IES)

Grant Mechanism	Term	Amount	Purpose
NIH R03—Small Grants	1–2 years	Directs= $50,000/yr	Collection of preliminary data and analysis of secondary data
NIH R21—Exploratory Grants	2 years	Directs = $275,000/2 yrs	Research in early stages of project development
NIH R34—Clinical Trial Planning Grants	1–3 years	Directs = $100,000–$150,000/yr	Development of elements of a clinical trial (R01)
NIH R01—Research Project Grants	3–5 years	Directs = up to $500,000/yr	Discrete, specified research projects
IES Goal 1—Exploration Projects	1–2 years	Total = $100,000–$350,000/yr	Examine association between outcomes and malleable factors
IES Goal 2—Development Research	2–3 years	Total = $150,000–$500,000/yr	Development of innovative programs
IES Goal 3—Efficacy Research	3–4 years	Total = $250,000–$750,000/yr	Evaluate efficacy of fully developed programs
IES Goal 4—Dissemination Research	4–5 years	Total = $500,000–$1.2 mil/yr	Evaluate effectiveness of wide-scale implementation of efficacious programs
IES Goal 5—Measurement Research	2–4 years	Total = $150,000–$400,000/yr	Develop and validate assessment methods

Note: The amounts indicated for NIH grants reflect direct expenses only. For NIH grants, indirect expenses typically are funded in addition to direct expenses. The amounts indicated for IES grants reflect total costs, including direct and indirect expenses.

direct expenses per year. For federal awards, expenses allotted for indirect expenses (i.e., institutional administrative and operational costs) vary depending upon the rate negotiated by the institution and government agency. Consistent with most types of grants, a majority of applications for research grants are unsolicited, but there are a wealth of funding opportunities available through PAs and RFAs.

Sources of Funding

Numerous sources of grant support are available for professionals involved in service provision, training, and research. Types of support can be divided broadly into intramural (i.e., within one's institution) and extramural (i.e., outside of one's institution) sources.

Intramural Sources

Institutions often have sources of funding available to support program, training, and research initiatives. This is particularly the case in university and medical school settings. In universities, funding may be available at the department, school, or college level; and in hospitals, support may be provided at the division, department, or institutional level. Policies for obtaining these sources of funding vary widely across and within institutions. Some internal competitions are flexible with regard to length, required components, and formatting; whereas other competitions are highly formal, requiring proposals of a designated length, structure, and format. Although the length of the application review process varies, typically the turnaround on these applications is relatively brief (i.e., 1 to 3 months). Also, although the length of these awards is highly variable, most grants are for relatively short durations (i.e., 1 to 2 years).

Extramural Sources

The range of extramural resources available is vast. Sources of external support are both private and public.

Private. Thousands of grant opportunities are available through private corporations and foundations. Some of these entities fund only institutions located in their community or surrounding region, whereas others fund institutions from a broader region, nationally, or internationally. Corporations that fund health-related projects range from medium-size businesses to large, multinational corporations. Similarly, foundations that fund health programs range from small family trusts to large, high-profile foundations (e.g., Robert Wood Johnson, W.T. Grant, Annie E. Casey). Large, well-established foundations and corporations typically have a well-defined, structured process delineating the application and review process. Smaller corporations and family trusts have a process for applying for funds, but it may be less formal and structured. Further, larger corporations and foundations typically are able to fund more substantial awards involving multiple years.

Grants are available through private, nonprofit professional associations and research societies. For example, grants are often available through the Society of Pediatric Psychology (Division 54 of the American Psychological Association) and the Society for the Study of School Psychology to support dissertation research and early career development. These grants typically provide a relatively small amount of funding, but they can be invaluable in funding targeted research projects, building a line of research, and establishing a track record of securing grant funding.

Public. Publicly funded sources of support are available at the local (e.g., school district, town, county), state, and national levels. Typically grants at the national level are the most competitive and difficult to obtain because of the relatively high number of applicants. Federal and state grants generally are larger than local grants. Also, federal and state grants typically involve a more rigorous process of peer review that can take longer than local grants. Examples of federal agencies that fund health-related projects for children and adolescents include the NIH, IES, CDC, Health Services and Research Administration (HRSA), and Substance Abuse and Mental Health Services Administration (SAMHSA).

Identifying Sources of Funding

Numerous resources are available to professionals to identify sources of private and public funding. The following provides a description of some of these resources.

Offices of Research and Development

Universities and healthcare institutions typically have departments devoted to development and fundraising. Development officers can be invaluable in assisting professionals to identify sources of funding, in particular private grants from corporations and foundations.

Research Institutes and Centers

Universities and university-affiliated medical centers generally have institutes established to assist researchers in searching and applying for grants, in particular publicly funded awards. Training seminars and individual consultation is generally available to researchers through these centers.

Networks of Professionals

Social networks are invaluable in directing professionals to useful sources of information about grants. Professionals can find helpful guidance through mentors and colleagues within their institution and at other institutions. Further, professional organizations often provide forums for students and early career professionals to receive direction about how to identify resources to support their work.

Internet Resources

The Internet provides virtually limitless resources for identifying potential sources of public and private funding. To search for public sources, professionals can go to http://grants.gov/ and search under "Find Grant Opportunities." This site provides information about all discretionary grants offered by the 26 federal grant-making agencies in the United States. Table 8.2 provides a list of Internet sites for federal agencies that have grant opportunities for professionals focused on health and education. With regard to private sources of support, several excellent Internet-based search engines are available, including:

Foundation Center (http://fconline.foundationcenter.org) and
Big Online American (http://bigdatabase.com).

Table 8.2   Selected Internet Sites to Obtain Information about
Applying for Federal Grants

Federal Agency	Internet Site
All 26 federal grant-making agencies	http://grants.gov/
Agency for Healthcare Research and Quality	http://www.ahrq.gov/fund/grconix.htm
Centers for Disease Control and Prevention	http://www.cdc.gov/od/science/PHResearch/
Health Resources and Services Administration	http://www.hrsa.gov/grants/index.html
Institute of Education Sciences	http://ies.ed.gov/funding/
National Institutes of Health	http://grants.nih.gov/grants/oer.htm
Substance Abuse and Mental Health Services Administration	http://www.samhsa.gov/grants/apply.aspx

Elements of Successful Grant Applications

Although the elements of a successful grant application vary
depending upon the sources of support and types of grants
being pursued, there are several components that cut across
virtually all successful applications. This section provides
guidance about how to prepare competitive grant applications
for a broad range of funding opportunities.

Respond to the Priorities of the Funding Agency

The first and most important rule of thumb in preparing a
grant application is to make sure it is fully aligned with the
priorities of the funding agency. For cases in which the application is a response to a PA or RFA, it is essential for the proposal to meet the stated priorities. Further, successful applications carefully follow the format specified for the application.
Most granting entities have a well-delineated, written set of
priorities and guidelines. It is essential for applicants to study
these guidelines extremely carefully prior to preparing proposals and to review the available materials periodically to
ensure that the application fully aligns with expectations of
the funder. Application materials typically indicate a project
officer to contact when questions arise. It is generally a good
idea for applicants to contact the project officer with a list of
questions early on in the process of preparing an application.

Address a Topic of Public Health Significance

Successful grant proposals address an area of significant need related to the health and development of children and youth. The significance of the need is justified by providing epidemiological data regarding the prevalence of the disorder or disease, as well as identified risk and protective factors. In addition, the justification of need can be substantiated by describing research related to the developmental trajectory of children with the condition and the potential consequences of failing to treat the problem.

Describe the Innovation

To be successful with many grant applications, especially research awards, it is essential to clearly specify how the proposed project will make a unique contribution. For example, it is often a good idea to include a section beginning with the phrase, "This is the first study (project) that…." The applicant can then describe the multiple ways in which the project is innovative and addresses critical gaps in the knowledge base or in programming to address the targeted problem.

Provide a Cogent Theoretical and Empirical Foundation

Strong applications include a description of theoretical models that provide the conceptual basis for the project being proposed. For prevention and intervention projects, the conceptualization should take the form of a theory of change that describes mechanisms of action to explain how the proposed program can be effective. In addition, it is important to include a comprehensive and concise review of the empirical research pertaining to the proposed project. When the empirical literature on a topic is vast, it is important to describe recent, key studies or meta-analyses to elucidate the state of the current empirical research. This section should conclude with a succinct statement of what is known as well as the gaps in the science base to which the application responds.

Describe the Preliminary Work You Have Conducted

Grant reviewers typically like to see that applicants have a track record that lays the foundation for the work described in the application. For research grants, establishing a track record involves conducting preliminary studies. For other grants, it is important to convey that an infrastructure is currently in place and that preliminary efforts have been made to conduct the project. There is some irony in the process in that to get a grant to conduct a project, it is important to demonstrate that you have already made considerable progress with the project. The reality is that research and program development are incremental in nature; getting one project off the ground depends on success with previous efforts. Success with grant writing to some extent depends on the ability of the applicant to convey a cogent story about how the proposed project builds on previous work, substantially pushes forward an important line of work, and makes a critical and unique contribution to the field.

Clearly Specify the Goals or Aims of the Project

Successful grant applications typically include two to four clearly indicated goals or aims. This section of the application varies depending upon the type of grant being pursued. Service delivery, program development, training, and early career grant proposals generally include a statement of goals and objectives related to each goal. Objectives differ from goals in that objectives are more targeted and may be accomplished in a briefer time frame. Research grant applications generally provide a clear statement of aims. Most aims include a statement of testable hypotheses, but some aims are designed to develop a project or explore relationships among variables. This section of the grant application is critically important and therefore it is essential for each sentence to be well written and clearly stated. As a general rule of thumb, the goals or aims statement should be about one page in length and placed at the beginning of the proposal. A strong goals statement will pique the interest of reviewers and create an expectation that the project is important, innovative, and likely to result in substantial benefit.

Target Underserved or Understudied Populations

Most granting agencies have a commitment to channel resources to populations that are underserved or have not been sufficiently studied. These populations may include the economically disadvantaged, individuals of ethnic or racial minority status, persons with disabilities or chronic illnesses, very young children, or females (Kataoka, Zhang, & Wells, 2002). Information about specific populations being targeted for grants generally can be found in descriptions of the agency's funding priorities or in PAs and RFAs. Also, the project officer can be helpful in identifying characteristics of the population being targeted for grants.

Develop a Rigorous Project Methodology

The methodology section will vary as a function of whether the proposed project is a research study or a nonresearch project. For research investigations, a rigorous methodological plan including a description of: (a) the research design (e.g., experimental versus quasi-experimental; two-group comparison versus three-group comparison; type of control group, if appropriate; inclusion of one or more blocking variables or covariates); (b) participants, including eligibility criteria and recruitment strategies; (c) intervention or prevention strategies, the control group, if relevant, and intervention procedures; (d) measurement plan including assessment procedures; and (e) data analytic plan. The measurement plan should include a description of how both process (feasibility, acceptability, integrity, and participant engagement) and outcome variables will be assessed. For nonresearch projects, the methodology section will describe activities designed to address each project objective and the methods used to assess progress in meeting objectives. It is generally helpful for applicants to include a table linking project objectives, activities, and measurable outcomes.

Outline a Realistic Time Frame

Reviewers typically want to see a detailed outline of the time frame within which key components of the study will be completed. Sufficient time should be allotted to complete all elements of the study, allowing time for project start-up (recruiting staff, training staff members, obtaining approval from the Committee for the Protection of Human Subjects, if relevant, and forming essential partnerships) as well as project completion (data entry and checking, statistical analyses, presentation of findings, and preparation of manuscripts for publication). Further, it should be feasible to complete all of the projects specified within each time frame of the study. Presenting the time frame in graphic format typically is helpful for reviewers.

Plan for the Sustainability of the Program

A major concern of many granting agencies is that the program cannot be sustained after the period of funding has ended. Increasingly funding agencies are instructing reviewers to evaluate grant applications based upon the sustainability of the project. Plans to promote sustainability ought to be built into the project. One strategy is to incorporate resources indigenous to the school or community into the project. Indigenous resources may consist of personnel working within community settings, such as teachers, paraprofessionals, community leaders (Atkins, Graczyk, Fazier, & Abdul-Adil, 2006; Power, Dowrick, Ginsburg-Block, & Manz, 2004), as well as systems that provide a context for intervention in community settings. The idea is that by promoting staff investment, training community providers, and changing the infrastructure of key systems, the community is in a better position to sustain the intervention after funding. Another strategy is to incorporate partnership methods of program development and evaluation (Leff, Costigan, & Power, 2004; Nastasi, Moore, & Varjas, 2004). By involving community stakeholders in every stage of the process, the intervention is more likely to be acceptable to participants and implemented by them after funding expires.

Develop a Comprehensive Dissemination Plan

Reviewers generally want to see that a proposed initiative is going to have a substantial impact at a local, regional, or national level. As a general rule, it is important to include a brief section describing how the project can make a difference, targeted audiences for disseminating project findings, and dissemination strategies. Strategies might include presentations at local, regional, or national meetings, or publications in journals targeting a diverse range of readers. Further, dissemination efforts may be targeted for government officials, legislators, and administrators who are in a position to translate project findings into policy initiatives targeted at a broad population.

Assemble a Strong Project Team

The success of an application depends in part on whether the project team is likely to be effective in conducting the proposed project. Grant reviewers want to see that the project team is uniquely suited to conduct the proposed project. The selection of the project director or principal investigator is critically important. The project director must have the background and expertise to establish the infrastructure for the project, implement the study plan, resolve problems when they arise, evaluate process and outcomes, oversee the team, and disseminate findings. Also, the director must be willing to invest the time and energy needed to achieve project goals. In addition, a strong team is required to conduct the proposed project. The application must outline the contribution of each member of the team and describe how each individual adds unique value to the project. Most funding agencies require the inclusion of bio sketches or brief curricula vitae to demonstrate the qualifications of team members and their ability to contribute to the project. The format for the NIH bio sketches is included in Appendix A. For prevention and intervention studies, it is essential to include a sufficient number of individuals with the needed skills to provide the program, monitor integrity, collect data, verify data accuracy, and analyze data. It is often helpful to include project consultants who have relevant areas of expertise and can make specific contributions to the project (e.g., program design, measurement development, subject retention).

Demonstrate that Resources Are Adequate

Every project requires a wide range of resources to be successful. It is essential to demonstrate that existing resources are more than adequate to achieve project goals. Resources might include settings (e.g., schools, primary care sites, clinics) in which programs and studies will be conducted; systems for recruiting participants into projects; space for project staff; information systems to collect and manage incoming data; and statistical expertise to oversee data entry, checking, cleaning, and analyses. In addition, it is important to demonstrate that project leaders have the full support of administrators who control access to needed resources. Administrators may include school superintendents and principals; medical directors of clinical practices; department chairpersons; and officials in local, state, or federal government offices. Letters of support from key administrators generally should be provided to demonstrate the full support of these individuals who control access to critical resources. Letters indicating a long-standing, meaningful relationship with key partners generally

Table 8.3 Examples of Components of Letters of Support from Key
Contributors

Introductory statement indicating strong support of the application

Comments about why the project is important and can make a difference to the
    populations being served, including a statement about how this project addresses
    gaps not addressed by other projects

Description of the history of partnering with the applicant and comments about the
    nature and strength of the relationship

Description of the resources to be provided, including comments about the scope and
    depth of the resources

Summary statement highlighting the strength of the recommendation

have much more value than those indicating the promise of a
partnership in the future. Key elements of letters of support
are outlined in Table 8.3.

Develop a Realistic Budget

The budget request for a proposed project should be within
the parameters specified by the granting agency. Examining
the size of grant awards for previous projects funded by the
agency can be useful in identifying a reasonable total budget
request. Although it is often advisable to make a request below
the maximum allowable award, applicants need to request
resources that are essential to conduct the project in a successful manner.

Grant application budgets generally include two broad
categories: personnel and nonpersonnel. Personnel include
essential project staff working within the institution of the
principal agency applying for the award. Personnel expenses
consist of salary and fringe benefit support for project staff.
For training grant applications, stipends for trainees may be
included in the budget; applicants are advised to check the
proposal instructions to determine whether these costs should
be budgeted as personnel or nonpersonnel expenses. Project
consultants typically are included in the nonpersonnel
section. Project personnel from other agencies in a multisite
project typically are included in subcontracts and are budgeted as contractual costs. Nonpersonnel expenses consist of a
range of costs, including supplies, travel, stipends for participants in research studies, and consultant fees. All expenses
included in the budget need to be justified with explanations
for increasing or decreasing expenses on an annual basis over
the course of the grant.

Getting Started With Grant Writing

Writing grant applications can seem like an overwhelming challenge. Many students and professionals are hesitant to get started with grant writing because the process seems so complex and laborious. Based on our experience we make the following suggestions to individuals who are getting started with the process.

Put Yourself in the Right Context

Because learning to become a good grant writer is challenging, it is helpful to have resources for support. If possible, enroll in a training program that values grant writing, as evidenced by faculty who obtain grants, encourage students to get grants, and teach grant writing skills. If you have completed preservice training, try to find employment in settings that will provide resources for grant writing and offer you opportunities to contribute to grant applications with direction.

Work Closely With a Strong Mentor

Perhaps the best advice is to seek out midcareer and senior-level professionals who can provide mentoring. Effective mentors not only are good grant writers but they are also willing to invest in the development of students and early career professionals. These individuals typically have good reputations for mentoring among students. Also, good mentors typically have established track records as evidenced by grants obtained, publications, and presentations in collaboration with trainees and early career scholars.

Contribute to Grant Writing Efforts of Others

In most organizations, there are several professionals who dedicate time to grant writing and fundraising efforts. Identify these individuals, meet with them, and collaborate to find ways to assist them in their grant writing efforts. At the outset, there may be a role for beginners with regard to conducting literature searches, preparing the background section, researching prospective measures for outcome assessment, and preparing team bio sketches. Over time, additional opportunities and more challenging roles may become available.

Seek Out Peer Support

You are not alone in your efforts to learn how to become an effective grant writer. Identify peers at your institution and other organizations who are interested in learning to be strong grant writers and establish a mechanism to collaborate and support one another. Peers can help each other by offering encouragement, sharing lessons learned, reviewing each other's writing, and making suggestions.

Work Closely with the Project Officer

Many project officers are generous with their time and willing to support the development of trainees and early career professionals. It is important not to abuse the privilege of interacting with project officers: e-mail can be used to raise specific questions that can be addressed briefly; phone conversations are more appropriate for in-depth communications. It is important to prepare carefully for phone consultations; it is usually a good idea to share questions with the project officer a couple of days before the conversation. Project officers are often willing to review a draft of one or more sections of the application. Applicants can check to see whether the project officer would be willing to review the proposal to offer feedback, and if so, how much lead time is needed before grant submission.

Take a Risk: Apply for a Small Grant

A great way to learn about grant writing is to prepare an application yourself. Generally it is a good idea to start by preparing applications for small grants. It is quite likely that the proposal will not get funded, but the experience is invaluable. Also, many granting agencies, especially federal agencies, will provide detailed feedback that will be useful in preparing future proposals.

Start Working on the Application Early

For most grant competitions, completing the grant application requires many steps and involves the cooperation of numerous professionals within the institution. It is wise to allow as much time as possible, ideally 3 months or so, to prepare an application. Table 8.4 outlines suggested timelines for preparing a grant application. Note that the Sponsored Projects Office

Table 8.4 Suggested Timelines for Completing a Federal Grant
Application

Time Frame	Activity
12 weeks before due date	Make a decision to submit the application Study the Program Announcement (PA), Request for Applications (RFP), or grant guidelines carefully Notify Sponsored Projects Office at institution Begin working on Aims or Goals statement
10 weeks before due date	Identify members of the project team and secure commitments to participate Initiate work on budget section Collaborate with colleagues at other institutions, if applicable, to begin work on subcontracts
6 weeks before due date	Share a draft of brief proposal with project officer, if appropriate
4 weeks before due date	Complete a full draft of the narrative section of the grant application Request mentors and colleagues to review drafts of application Complete a draft of the budget and justification section and review with Business Manager
2 weeks before due date	Submit all grant application materials to Sponsored Projects Office for initial review Request additional feedback from mentors and colleagues
1 week before due date	Complete revisions to application materials as suggested by Sponsored Projects Office Respond to feedback from mentors and colleagues
1 day before due date	Make final revisions to application Submit the grant application Check to insure that application has been received and that there are no errors in application

in many institutions requires materials to be submitted 10 to 14 days in advance of submission in order to conduct a thorough review and insure that all issues have been addressed properly. Starting early also provides sufficient time to get feedback from the project officer of the granting agency and to obtain multiple, serial reviews from mentors and colleagues.

Act as If You Already Have a Grant

An irony of grant writing is that it often requires extensive background and expertise with a project before granting agencies are willing to provide grant funds for it. Therefore, it is important to conduct as much work on the proposed project as possible with the limited amount of resources available before the grant gets funded. Preliminary studies help to sort through feasibility issues and develop the infrastructure needed to conduct a successful project.

Be Persistent

At the outset, your rate of success may not be high. In fact, highly experienced and successful grant writers frequently fail to get projects funded. When projects are not funded, it is critical to remain optimistic, learn how to improve the application by reviewing feedback summary statements and conferring with project officers, and confer with colleagues and mentors. Good grant writers generally are highly tenacious and resilient professionals who are committed to learning and getting their projects funded.

Conclusions

Grants are invaluable for expanding resources to improve existing programs and develop innovative programs. Grants are available for a wide range of projects, including service delivery, program development, clinical and research training, career development in multiple phases, and research along the continuum from basic to applied. Virtually countless funding opportunities are available to professionals through private and public sources.

Information about available resources can be obtained through institution-based development offices and research institutes, professional associations and networks, and Internet resources. The elements of successful grant applications vary greatly depending upon type of grant and source of support, but hallmarks that cut across all applications include: (a) a clear, compelling response to the funding agency's priorities; (b) a focus on a topic of public health significance; (c) clear evidence that the proposed project is innovative; (d) a cogent theoretical justification including a description of mechanisms of action for prevention and intervention projects; (e) evidence of a successful track record in establishing and piloting the project; (f) a clear, cogent statement of goals or aims; (g) a focus on populations that have traditionally been underserved or underresearched; (h) a well-developed, rigorous methodology for conducting the project or study; (i) a feasible time frame for conducting the project; (j) a plan to promote sustainability; (k) a comprehensive dissemination plan; (l) a strong, integrated project team headed by a highly qualified project director; and (m) demonstration that available resources are clearly sufficient to successfully accomplish project goals.

Grant writing can seem overwhelming to trainees and early career professionals. For this reason, it is important for novices to work in a context that supports grant writing and seek out mentors who are strong grant writers and willing to invest in the professional development of others. Further, it is important to establish a network of support through peers and offer constructive feedback to one another. Ultimately, the best way to learn is to get started with grant writing by collaborating with others who are preparing applications and by taking the lead on a proposal for a small grant. Although grant writing, like publishing, can be a frustrating and often painstaking process, tenacity and openness to learning generally lead to highly successful outcomes.

Questions for Discussion

1. What ideas do you have for a grant? How can you build on your existing track record?
2. What are the obstacles you face in preparing grant applications and what can you do to overcome these barriers?
3. What are your assets and resources with regard to grant writing and how can you build on these?
4. Who can provide support to you with grant writing activities, including mentors and peers?

Additional Teaching Aids

PowerPoint slides pertaining to leadership development and which also contain information about grant writing guidelines are included in the attached CD.

References

Atkins, M. S., Graczyk, P. A., Frazier, S. L., & Abdul-Adil, J. (2003). Toward a new model for promoting urban children's mental health: Accessible, effective, and sustainable school-based mental health services. *School Psychology Review, 32,* 503–514.

Doll, B., & Cummings, J. A. (2008). *Transforming school mental health services: Population-based approaches to promoting the competency and wellness of children.* Thousand Oaks, CA: Corwin Press.

Kataoka, S. H., Zhang, L., & Wells, K. B. (2002). Unmet need for mental health care among U.S. children: Variation by ethnicity and insurance status. *American Journal of Psychiatry, 159,* 1548–1555.

Leff, S. S., Costigan, T. E., & Power, T. J. (2004). Using participatory action research to develop a playground-based prevention program. *Journal of School Psychology, 42,* 3–21.

Lynch–Jordan, A. M., Kashikar–Zuck, S., Crosby, L. E., Lopez, W. L., Smolyansky, B. H., Parkins, I. S., ... Powers, S. W. (2010). Applying quality improvement methods to implement a measurement system for chronic pain-related disability. *Journal of Pediatric Psychology, 35,* 32–41.

Nastasi, B. K., Moore, R. B., & Varjas, K. M. (2004). *School-based mental health services: Creating comprehensive and culturally specific programs.* Washington, DC: American Psychological Association.

Power, T. J., Dowrick, P. W., Ginsburg–Block, M., & Manz, P. H. (2004)..Partnership-based, community-assisted early intervention for literacy: An application of the participatory intervention model. *Journal of Behavioral Education, 13,* 93–115.

Power, T., Eiraldi, R., Clarke, A., Mazzuca, L., & Krain, A. (2005). Improving mental health service utilization for children and adolescents. *School Psychology Quarterly, 20,* 187–205.

Power, T. J., Shapiro, E. S., & DuPaul, G. J. (2003). Preparing psychologists to link the health and educational systems in managing and preventing children's health problems. *Journal of Pediatric Psychology, 28,* 147–155. PMID: 12556514.

U.S. Department of Health and Human Services. (1999). *Mental health: A report of the Surgeon General.* Rockville, MD: U.S. Department of Health and Human Services, Substance Abuse and Mental Health Services Administration, Center for Mental Health Services, National Institutes of Health, National Institute of Mental Health.

U.S. Department of Health and Human Services. (2001). *Mental health: Culture, race, and ethnicity: A supplement to mental health: A report of the Surgeon General.* Rockville, MD: U.S. Department of Health and Human Services, Substance Abuse and Mental Health Administration, Center for Mental Health Services, National Institutes of Health, National Institute of Mental Health.

APPENDIX

Biographical Sketch Format Used in NIH and Many Other Federal Grant Applications

BIOGRAPHICAL SKETCH

Provide the following information for the Senior/key personnel and other significant contributors.
Follow this format for each person. **DO NOT EXCEED FOUR PAGES.**

NAME	POSITION TITLE
eRA COMMONS USER NAME (credential, e.g., agency login)	

EDUCATION/TRAINING *(Begin with baccalaureate or other initial professional education, such as nursing, include postdoctoral training and residency training if applicable.)*

INSTITUTION AND LOCATION	DEGREE *(if applicable)*	MM/YY	FIELD OF STUDY

Please refer to the application instructions in order to complete sections A, B, C, and D of the Biographical Sketch.

A. Personal Statement

B. Positions and Honors

C. Selected Peer-reviewed Publications

D. Research Support

Nine

Critiquing Journal Articles and Preparing Manuscripts for Publication

Pediatric school psychologists frequently refer to the extant literature for information and guidance when working with individuals and their families, particularly when developing intervention strategies to address presenting concerns. These practitioners must be able to critically evaluate the research literature to aid in the selection of evidence-based strategies that will have the greatest likelihood of producing positive outcomes. One way to develop skills in critically evaluating research is to serve as a reviewer for a journal. The opportunity to engage in the review process allows for repeated practice in carefully considering manuscripts submitted for publication. This practice can ultimately result in improving one's own skills in conducting research and successfully submitting manuscripts for publication. As stated by Brown (2004), "There seems to be an 'art' to the publication process, which cannot simply be taught but must be practiced over time ..." (p. 3). The development of critical evaluation skills and abilities to contribute to the professional literature will ultimately result in building leaders in the field of pediatric school psychology.

This chapter is divided into two major sections: critiquing journal articles and preparing manuscripts for publication. Within the section on critiquing journal articles, critical components of journal articles and manuscripts are presented as a guide for evaluating strengths and shortcomings. Considerations for preparing a manuscript review are presented along with recommended resources to provide additional guidance for those who choose to engage in the journal review process. The second section of this chapter reviews the steps for preparing a manuscript for publication. Suggestions for selecting the most appropriate publication outlet and addressing the submission requirements of journals are discussed. Additionally, the editorial review process is explained and guidance is offered for interpreting and addressing editorial decisions. The information provided in this chapter is designed to help practitioners become more active consumers of, and contributors to, the research literature; assist research-oriented professionals with the development of skills related to manuscript reviewing; and demystify the publication process for trainees and early career professionals.

Critiquing Manuscripts and Journal Articles

Critiquing journal articles requires a consideration of numerous factors, including the public health significance and innovativeness of the study, its methodological rigor, the accuracy and strength of the findings, and the potential for the study to contribute to science and practice. Also, the organization and clarity of the manuscript is critically important. The following is a description of important points to consider in conducting a manuscript review or article critique. Readers are referred to publications prepared by the American Psychological Association (APA) for detailed information about what should be included in manuscripts, which is highly useful in critiquing manuscripts as well as preparing papers for publication (APA, 2010; APA Publications and Communications Board Working Group, 2008).

Evaluating the Strength of the Justification

The introductory section of a journal article is critical because it describes and explains the public health significance and unique ways in which the article makes a contribution to the scientific literature. This section is where readers develop their first impressions of an article. In other words, the introduction sets the tone for the remainder of the article. If this section is disorganized or lacking in attention to detail, the reader may suspect that the actual research presented in the article was conducted in a haphazard manner.

The introductory section should begin with a statement of the identified problem being addressed in the article. Specifically, the public health significance of the research should be presented by establishing the prevalence of the problem or condition addressed in the study, associated impairments, and developmental course. Finally, this part of the introduction should end with a statement of the unmet need. For example, if the identified problem is the lack of systems level collaboration for youth with chronic health conditions, the author would need to present data on the percentage of youth with chronic health conditions, how chronic health conditions are related to impairments across systems (family, school, community), and how the fragmentation among systems contributes to impairments in child functioning (e.g., lack of interdisciplinary collaboration may contribute to poor academic outcomes, problematic peer relationships, and limited adherence to required medical treatments). The author is then in a position to outline how the current study will address this need.

One of the critical components to consider when reviewing the introductory section of an article is whether the author has developed a strong rationale for the research. This rationale typically is presented through a concise yet thorough review of the relevant literature highlighting gaps in the research that need further investigation and presenting innovative ideas to expand the existing science base (DeBehnke, Kline, & Shih, 2001). Although it may be important to review some seminal works from the literature to build a base for the rationale, it is also critical that the information presented in the literature review is current. This demonstrates the author's awareness and understanding of the most recently published literature and how that research has informed their investigation.

It also is important to look for the theoretical framework or base upon which the research is derived (Drotar, 2009). Inclusion of this framework assists the reader in understanding how the study fits within the larger context of the field or profession, which can be helpful in establishing the importance of the project. For example, studies in the area of pediatric school psychology may be grounded in the biopsychosocial model, the medical model, cognitive-behavioral psychology, or child and adolescent development.

The introduction should conclude with a statement indicating the overall purpose of the study, and the specific research questions or aims to be addressed need to be clearly specified. If appropriate, hypotheses related to the research questions may be delineated as well. The introduction should then seamlessly transition to the methods section of the article.

Examining the Strength of the Methodological Plan

The methods described in the manuscript (e.g., participants, independent and dependent variables, procedures) should directly relate to the purpose of the study and stated research questions. If the study methods do not map directly to the questions driving the study, there may be a fatal flaw in the research. There are standard components or subsections that should be included in the method section of any empirical study (APA, 2010).

Participants.   Typically, the methods section of the manuscript begins with a thorough description of the participants. The sample size should be stated along with the process used to identify the participants. The population from which the sample has been selected and the methods used to select the sample (e.g., random sample, convenience sample, etc.) need to be described clearly. Also, specific inclusion and exclusion criteria must be presented. Details about the participants, such as age, gender, race/ethnicity, socioeconomic status, and any other demographic factors of relevance to the study, should be included in this section. If the sample in the study is a subsample of a larger population, the demographics of the study sample must be compared with those of the larger sample to demonstrate similarities. For example, if students from one elementary school in a district serve as participants in a study, and the authors wish to generalize the findings from their study to the larger elementary school population in that district, the authors must demonstrate that the students in the study sample are similar to the larger sample on specific demographic variables. In addition, the setting (e.g., classroom, physician's office, community clinic) where the study took place must be described. Common shortcomings in describing study participants include insufficient information about: (a) the demographics of the sample, (b) how the sample was derived from the population, and (c) how the sample compares to the larger population on key demographic variables.

Intervention Conditions.   If the study is an investigation of an intervention or prevention program, the next section typically describes the research design used to evaluate the effectiveness of the program (e.g., experimental design using a randomized clinical trial, quasi-experimental design, single-subject multiple baseline design). Chapter 6 describes the research designs commonly used in intervention and prevention studies conducted by researchers in pediatric school psychology. If the study is a randomized trial, it is strongly recommended that the guidelines specified in the 25-item Consolidated Standards of Reporting Clinical Trials (CONSORT) 2010 Checklist (www.consort-statement.org) be followed. As another example, if the study is a meta-analysis of the existing literature, the Meta-Analysis Reporting Standards (MARS) are recommended (APA Publications and Communications Board Working Group, 2008). Subsequently, the methods section describes the experimental intervention, including a description of its purpose and key components as well as information about the length, duration, format, and settings of the program. For example, this section specifies how many sessions are included, the length of each session, the formats used to provide sessions (e.g., individualized versus group sessions), and the setting in which the program is offered. Sufficient information should be presented so that independent readers can replicate the investigation.

Intervention studies using experimental and quasi-experimental designs include a control group, which should be described briefly after presenting the experimental condition. The type of control group selected (i.e., classroom of students that receives education "as usual," wait list group, active control condition that receives generic education and support, alternative evidence-based treatment) and justification for selecting the control condition should be described.

A major shortcoming of many manuscripts presenting intervention studies is that there is a failure to adequately describe methods to ensure that the program has been implemented with integrity. These methods typically include recruitment of intervention providers who meet established qualifications, extensive training of providers prior to the intervention, direct observation of intervention sessions with the provision of feedback to providers after sessions, and intensive supervision prior to each intervention session. Further, manuscripts describing intervention studies are often flawed in that they fail to report sufficient information about the integrity with which the intervention was implemented, including data about the adherence to intervention procedures and the quality of implementation (Perepletchikova & Kazdin, 2005).

Measurement Plan. The measures selected for the study should map directly to variables delineated in the research questions. Each measure must be explained in detail including information about the purpose of the tool as related to the research questions, why it was selected as opposed to other possible measures, and psychometric properties (e.g., reliability and validity). Although it is useful for authors to provide in-depth information about each measure's psychometric properties, space constraints typically place limits on how much information can be included. Nonetheless, sufficient information should be provided so that the reader is assured that the measure is an adequate tool for examining a targeted variable. In addition, assessment procedures and methods used to train research staff in the administration of measurement tools should be presented. For intervention and prevention studies, it is important to demonstrate that research staff involved in data collection are blind to the aims and design of the research investigation.

Analytic Plan.   The plan to analyze study data should include a description of each strategy selected and a justification of each decision. Often, there are multiple analytic strategies that can be used to examine a particular research question. The rationale for choosing a particular strategy and the advantages and potential limitations of the decision should be indicated briefly.

Each method of analysis should be described in a sufficient manner so that the reader understands the procedures. Journals differ substantially with regard to the sophistication of readers in being able to understand analytic methods. It is important for authors to provide an explanation that is tailored to the readership of a particular journal. More commonly used types of analyses (i.e., calculation of effect sizes) do not need to be described in as much detail as complex and less familiar types of analyses (i.e., hierarchical linear modeling, structural equation modeling, confirmatory factor analysis).

A common shortcoming is that manuscripts fail to report the statistical power associated with the sample size available for the study. A majority of studies have relatively small sample sizes and are powered to detect group differences that are large or very large. This is often not noted in the manuscript or described only in a peripheral manner in the limitations subsection of the Discussion. Another common problem is that analytic plans do not account for multiple group comparisons conducted as part of the analyses. Although it is not always necessary to adjust for multiple comparisons, such as when conducting preliminary or intervention development studies, it is important for authors to justify their decision not to make these adjustments.

Examining the Accuracy and Strength of the Findings

At the beginning of the Results section, it is often useful for authors to describe methods used for entering study data and conducting data checks to ensure accuracy. Virtually every analytic method is based upon statistical assumptions. Authors should provide assurance that assumptions for using each analytic method have been fulfilled. Also, missing data is a challenge with virtually every study. The amount of missing data across measures should be indicated and methods for addressing missing data in the analyses ought to be described (Baraldi & Enders, 2010).

The Results section typically includes statistical information about demographic and, if relevant, diagnostic variables pertaining to the participants. For intervention and prevention studies that include a control group, it is important to report the findings of group comparisons on demographic variables and other key factors (e.g., medical condition, comorbid mental health diagnoses, medication status). This information enables the reader to understand characteristics of the sample and determine whether one or more factors need to be accounted for in the analyses. For example, psychosocial intervention studies for children with mental health disorders need to account for the possibility that some of the children may be on psychotropic medication and there may be differences between groups on medication usage.

The organization of the main parts of the Results section may vary according to the requirements and standards of the journal to which the manuscript is submitted. It is usually helpful to organize the presentation of findings so that they clearly address each research question. Tables, figures, or graphs should be provided to present data in a way that readers can easily view. The reporting of effect sizes has become virtually a universal standard in the reporting of research findings. Although effect sizes typically are reported only when significant findings are indicated, it may be appropriate to report the magnitude of effects for exploratory or intervention development studies. Also, some journals are now requiring that confidence intervals for effect sizes be reported. Finally, although authors may be tempted to include interpretive comments in the Results section, Trusty (2011) cautions authors to only report study findings in this section and to avoid any interpretation of the results. Interpretation of findings is reserved for the final section of the manuscript.

Evaluating the Significance of the Study and Its Contribution to Science

The Discussion section of the manuscript provides authors an opportunity to describe the public health significance of the study and how the findings advance science by confirming what is expected but has not been proven or suggesting new areas to be explored. The Discussion should begin with a reminder of the purpose of the study followed by a brief review of the results. It is important for authors to interpret the results in light of their proposed hypotheses, if appropriate, as well as the extant literature presented in the introduction. If the obtained results are discrepant from expectations, the author should attempt to account for the discrepancy and make suggestions for further research to provide clarification.

A major purpose of the Discussion is to help the reader evaluate the question, "So what difference does this study make, and how does it contribute to the science base?" This is a major consideration for editors in determining whether a manuscript should be published. A study may be methodologically sophisticated and the manuscript may be presented in a highly organized and clear manner, but if the study does not address a question of importance and contribute findings that advance science, the paper may not be worthy of publication.

An important part of the Discussion is the description of the limitations of the study, particularly with respect to how methodological factors may have influenced the study outcomes. For example, if statistically significant findings were not found in relation to one or more research questions, the author may state that the sample size was not large enough to detect significance. As another example, the parameters of the sample virtually always place limitations on the generalizability of the findings. The limitations should be discussed with regard to factors that place limits on the internal or external validity of the study. In some cases, authors may be reticent to highlight the limitations of their study; however, this is a very important section of the article. As stated by Brown (2004), "Humility is essential to give your study credibility, which is best accomplished by frankly acknowledging design limitations and noting how future studies might proceed given such limitations" (p. 3). In fact, the identified limitations are highly useful in delineating next steps in a line of research.

It is critical to point out how the findings have relevance for practice in the profession. Journals differ markedly with regard to their interest in a description of practice implications. Articles in journals affiliated with professional associations (e.g., *Journal of Pediatric Psychology, Pediatrics, Journal of the Amerincan Academy of Child and Adolescent Psychiatry, Journal of Developmental and Behavioral Pediatrics, School Psychology Review*) typically include a paragraph or two that outlines how the findings can inform practice and research needed to further direct professional behavior. At the end of the Discussion, a culminating concluding paragraph should accurately state the results of the study with careful attention to not overstate the findings.

Considerations for Preparing a Manuscript Review

Many formats and styles are appropriate in preparing a manuscript review. Table 9.1 suggests one format that could be used. Regardless, there are several overarching principles to consider when writing a review. First, it is important to be respectful of the authors. Application of the Golden Rule, "Do unto others ..." is fully appropriate when framing out a review. For virtually every submitted manuscript, no matter how weak it may be, authors have made a substantial investment of time and effort to prepare the paper. In some cases, the manuscript may represent their first attempt to publish. Manuscript reviews should be prepared in a manner that is respectful and diplomatic. Also, it is important for reviewers to keep in mind that the nature of the review process is to identify and point out flaws. To be respectful of authors, it is important to point out strengths as well. We typically recommend that reviewers identify at least three strengths and that these be presented at the beginning of the review.

Second, the mark of a good review is not the number of methodological flaws detected in the study. A common practice among early career professionals is to focus on identifying study limitations and problems with manuscript presentation. These reviews often fail to evaluate the study in the broader context of its innovativeness and potential to make a contribution to the science base. A strong review strikes a balance between identifying limitations and considering the study's

Table 9.1   Outline for Preparing a Manuscript Review

Section	Description
Introductory paragraph	Provide a three- or four-sentence summary of manuscript
	Describe strengths of study/manuscript—identify at least three
Critique	Cite concerns, differentiating between major and minor concerns
	Provide one or more options for how to address each concern identified, when possible
Final paragraph	Provide a brief, two- or three-sentence summary of the review

importance and ability to make a unique contribution. For studies that are exploratory and address topics of major public health significance, there may be greater tolerance of methodological limitations than in studies that test well-justified hypotheses or seek to replicate prior findings. Regardless, it is always important for authors to describe the study clearly and in a well- organized manner following the publication guidelines of the APA (2010).

Third, evaluating the validity of a study's methods should consider issues pertaining to both internal and external validity. Obviously, a study's internal validity is absolutely essential to consider in evaluating the strength of the findings. Without internal validity, issues of external validity have little relevance. Nonetheless, a study with a high level of internal validity does not necessarily warrant publication. It is important for the study to have some relevance to the population of individuals from which the sample was derived. A consideration of external validity is important in answering the question, "So what does this study contribute?"

Fourth, not all concerns about a manuscript are equally important. Some concerns are major and deserve much more attention than others. Early career reviewers often engage in the practice of citing a litany of concerns without differentiating the importance of the issues. Interpreting a review like this may be challenging for editors because it puts them in a position of needing to determine the main concerns. Also, failure to identify the most salient concerns does not provide authors with direction about which issues deserve the most consideration for cases in which a revision and resubmission is indicated. Lovejoy, Revenson, and France (2011) share examples of reviewer comments illustrating many of the guidelines recommended in this section.

Benefits in Reviewing Manuscripts

Reviewing manuscripts and participating in the formal editorial review process provides a number of benefits including the opportunity to stay abreast of contemporary issues in one's field and fostering ideas for future research (Brown, 2004). In addition, thoroughly critiquing the research of others, and noting ways to communicate research most efficiently and effectively, can serve to enhance one's own writing (Nelson, 2011). If one has the opportunity to become a reviewer for a journal, there are resources available offering guidance on ethical issues related to the peer review process (Palermo, 2010), and do's and don'ts for writing critical reviews (see Drotar, 2010; Lovejoy et al., 2011; Nelson, 2011). Table 9.2 provides a checklist to reference for completing a manuscript review.

Table 9.2   Abbreviated Checklist for Preparing a Manuscript Review

Literature Review

- ✓ Is a clear statement of the problem presented?
- ✓ Does the author provide a convincing rationale for the study?
- ✓ Are the research questions clearly stated?
- ✓ Is the literature review comprehensive and current?

Methods

- ✓ Is the sample appropriate and adequate to address the research questions?
- ✓ Is the research design adequate to address the research questions?
- ✓ If appropriate, are the intervention or prevention strategies described in sufficient detail?
- ✓ Are the measures adequate and psychometrically sound?
- ✓ Are the procedures described clearly and in a manner that would allow the study to be replicated?
- ✓ Are there any major threats to internal or external validity in the design?
- ✓ Is the data analytic plan sufficient to address the research questions?

Results and Discussion

- ✓ Are the data adequate given the design of the study?
- ✓ Were statistical analyses described adequately and appropriate?
- ✓ Have the findings been discussed in relation to previous research?
- ✓ Were practical implications of the study presented?
- ✓ Were the limitations described sufficiently?
- ✓ Are the conclusions accurate and not overstated?
- ✓ Does the study make an important contribution to science?

Preparing Manuscripts for Publication

This section of the chapter reviews the steps to follow in preparing a manuscript for publication. Because the prior section provided a discussion of the specific sections within an article, the following section will focus on the process of manuscript preparation from deciding whether a study is worthy of publication to determining the best outlet for publication and submitting the manuscript to a specific journal. The review process is presented along with the steps that follow once an editorial decision is made.

How to Decide If Your Manuscript is Worthy of Publication

In determining whether a manuscript is worthy of publication, APA describes some of the characteristics of underdeveloped manuscripts that should be considered (APA, 2010). Among these concerns are unstated or unclear research questions; inadequate sample size; mismatch between research questions, study methods, and statistical analyses; and overall disorganization of the manuscript. In addition, the potential for a manuscript to be published depends upon the fit between the paper and the target population of the journal. Consulting with colleagues and peers is recommended for guidance throughout the manuscript preparation, submission, and review process.

Selecting an Appropriate Journal for Publication

Selecting the most appropriate journal for a manuscript is a critical step in the publication process. Time invested up front to find the best outlet for a manuscript will save significant time and effort in the long run. One of the first steps is to look for journals that have published articles on related topics, or journals that have a call for papers or a special series associated with the topic. Looking to the journals that were cited throughout the manuscript can be useful to start this process as well. Also, it may be important to consider the preferred audience for the manuscript. For example, if one is primarily interested in disseminating research to practitioners and researchers who conduct work related to primary care pediatrics, it is important to identify a range of publications that target this readership.

Once the publication outlets under consideration have been identified and narrowed, the next step is to investigate the specific journal websites for additional information to help make a decision. Find the mission statement of the journal to determine if the content of the manuscript is consistent with that journal's mission. Take time to read the description of the journal and look for information indicating the types of papers or research the journal typically publishes. For example, a journal may state that it publishes papers on a wide variety of topics or it may indicate that the journal has a specific and narrow focus.

In addition to the research topic, one needs to investigate if the journal publishes only certain types of research methods, such as a journal that only publishes qualitative studies. It is always helpful to look at sample publications from the journal, particularly if the outlet is unfamiliar because it is outside of your primary professional field. Journal editors consistently recommend that potential authors do their homework with respect to the fit between the manuscript and the journal, given that a mismatch often results in an outright rejection upon receipt (Drotar, 2009; Nelson, 2011).

Other issues to consider include the journal's acceptance rate and impact factor. To determine the competitiveness of a journal, one can look at the journal's acceptance and rejection rates. These rates often can be found on the journal's website as well as through a number of other sources that compile this type of information. For example, the APA publishes a yearly report of all affiliated journals indicating their rejection rates as well as circulation data. This information may help an author to gauge the likelihood of a manuscript being accepted by a particular journal. The journal impact factor is another consideration. The impact factor represents the average number of times articles from a journal within a given year have been cited in scientific papers published in the 2 (or 5) previous years. This information can be found in databases available through university libraries or by individual inquiries by searching the Web of Knowledge (http://wokinfo.com/).

Preparing the Manuscript for Publication

Once a particular journal has been selected, the next step is to carefully read the guidelines for authors on the journal's website. The guidelines provide important information such as the requested manuscript format (i.e., manuscript sections to include, font size), page length restrictions, and method of submission. There are often specific instructions for submitting tables, figures, and pictures. Additionally, information required for inclusion in an accompanying cover letter is indicated. It is critical to follow these guidelines and submit the manuscript accordingly to initiate the review process.

Once the manuscript is developed according to the author guidelines, it is recommended that the paper be carefully reviewed and proofread. It is usually very helpful to ask a colleague to review your paper and provide feedback prior to formal submission. A checklist presented in Brown (2004) offers details about the top 10 journal submission errors. This list is an excellent reference for both novice and experienced authors to help ensure the quality of the final manuscript and facilitate the review process. Also, the Checklist for Manuscript Submission presented in the *APA Publication Manual* (2010) is useful to ensure that the manuscript includes all the relevant elements. In addition to the manuscript, a cover letter must be submitted to the journal. The cover letter is written to the journal editor and typically attests to the fact that the research is original, the manuscript has not been submitted simultaneously to another journal for consideration, and the study took safeguards to protect human subjects and was conducted under the auspices of an Institutional Review Board. Other information that might be included, depending on the requirements of the journal, is the section of the journal for which the manuscript is to be considered (e.g., Brief Reports, Research into Practice, Special Series) and contact information for future correspondence (see DeBehnke, Kline, & Shih, 2001 for a checklist of items to include in a standard cover letter).

What Happens Next: The Review Process

Once a manuscript is formally submitted to a journal, the journal editor typically screens the manuscript to make certain that it complies with the required guidelines. The editor may reject the manuscript immediately if there are any significant concerns (e.g., the paper is not a good match for the mission of the journal, the paper is not prepared according to the required format, the sample size is inadequate to address study questions). If the manuscript passes through this first screening, it is then typically assigned to an Associate Editor, or Action

Editor, who then serves to manage the manuscript through the next phase of the review process. The Action Editor then recruits reviewers who have expertise related to the topic or methods used in the study, to carefully read the manuscript and provide a thorough evaluation of the paper along with a decision as to whether or not the manuscript warrants publication in the journal. The time frame for reviews may differ by journal, but reviewers typically are given at least 4 weeks to complete their review. The reviewers then submit their reviews and recommendations for publication to the Action Editor who, after weighing the reviewer's feedback along with their own evaluation, writes a decision letter that is then forwarded to the author.

Although journals may use a variety of different terms to categorize publication decisions, most typically fall into four main categories: reject, reject but recommend resubmission, tentatively accept, or accept. A decision to reject a manuscript indicates that there are major concerns with one of more parts of the study that cannot be addressed through a revision of the manuscript. A "reject but recommend resubmission" decision suggests that there are concerns with the study, but it is believed that the manuscript may be improved with significant revisions. It is important to note that this decision in no way guarantees that a revision of the manuscript will be accepted in the future. A decision to tentatively accept the manuscript indicates that the manuscript is a good fit for the journal and that minor revisions are needed prior to full acceptance. A decision to accept a manuscript, which is rarely rendered upon initial submission (Lovejoy et al., 2011), indicates that a manuscript is ready to advance to the production phase of publication.

Responding to Editorial Reviews

Depending upon the decision of the Action Editor, the author has several options. If the decision is positive (tentatively accept or accept), the author works with the Action Editor to make any requested revisions needed to finalize the manuscript. If the manuscript is rejected, but revision and resubmission are encouraged, the author must decide whether to address the requested revisions or submit to a different journal. Resubmitting a revised manuscript requires the author to carefully review and consider the recommendations of the Action Editor as well as the individual reviewers. It is important for authors to carefully consider each concern and recommendation, including those stated by the Action Editor and those indicated by each reviewer. The authors need to clearly indicate how they responded to each concern by modifying the manuscript or providing a justification for not doing so. In most cases the author is provided with a timeline by which the revised manuscript must be resubmitted for further consideration. When all revisions have been addressed, a cover letter is written to the Action Editor indicating how feedback/revisions were addressed and is sent back to the journal along with the revised manuscript (see Cummings & Rivara, 2002 for a recommended format for a resubmission cover letter).

Timeline

When a manuscript is accepted for publication in a given journal, the time frame from initial submission to publication varies greatly across disciplines and journals within a discipline. In general, journals in medicine have shorter lag times from submission to acceptance and acceptance to publication than psychology journals. In the fields of school psychology, pediatric psychology, and clinical child psychology, the lag time from submission to full acceptance may vary from 4 to 12 months, and the lag time from acceptance to publication can vary by an additional 2 to 18 months. The increasing emergence of electronic journals is serving to decrease average lag times to publication across disciplines.

Conclusion

Developing skills to critically evaluate articles and manuscripts submitted for publication is an invaluable investment of time for pediatric school psychologists. These skills will inform all areas of practice from problem identification to development of prevention and intervention strategies to program evaluation. One way to develop and further improve these evaluation skills is to serve as a journal reviewer. Carefully critiquing manuscripts submitted for publication and offering recommendations for improvement can ultimately result in the improvement of one's own writing. Pediatric school psychologists are encouraged to engage in the publication process to assist in educating others about best practices in working with youth with chronic health conditions. Although the publication process may appear daunting, particularly for novice researchers, following the suggestions and guidelines provided in this chapter will assist in successfully navigating the process.

Discussion Questions

1. The Introduction is one of the most important sections of an article or manuscript. What is the overall purpose of the introductory section and what specific components should be included in this section?
2. The Methods section must be written with sufficient detail so that the research can be replicated. List and discuss the specific subsections that must be included in the presentation of the methods.
3. What are some of the common mistakes made by reviewers when critiquing manuscripts?
4. The process of selecting a journal for manuscript submission may be time consuming, but it is a critical step in the publication process. Discuss the steps of this process, particularly as they relate to the type of research you conduct and your specific profession.

Additional Teaching Aids

PowerPoint slides pertaining to leadership development, preparing a manuscript review, and preparing a manuscript for publication are included on the attached CD.

References

American Psychological Association. (2010). *Publication manual of the American Psychological Association* (6th ed.). Washington, DC: Author..

American Psychological Association. (2011). *Preparing manuscripts for publication in psychology journals: A guide for new authors.* Washington, DC: Author.

American Psychological Association, Publications and Communications Board Working Group on Journal Article Reporting Standards. (2008). Reporting standards for research in psychology: Why do we need them? What might they be? *American Psychologist, 63,* 839–851.

Baraldi, A. N., & Enders, C. K. (2010). An introduction to modern missing data analyses. *Journal of School Psychology, 48,* 5–37.

Brown, R. T. (2004). A general approach to publication in the *Journal of Pediatric Psychology*: From the process of preparing your manuscript to revisions and resubmission [Editorial]. *Journal of Pediatric Psychology, 29,* 1–5.

Cummings, P., & Rivara, F. P. (2002). Responding to reviewers' comments on submitted articles. *Archives of Pediatric Adolescent Medicine, 156,* 105–107.

DeBehnke, D. J., Kline, J. A., & Shih, R. D. (2001). Research fundamentals: Choosing an appropriate journal, manuscript preparation, and interactions with editors. *Academic Emergency Medicine, 8,* 844–850.

Drotar, D. (2009). Thoughts on improving the quality of manuscripts submitted to the *Journal of Pediatric Psychology*: Writing a convincing introduction [Editorial]. *Journal of Pediatric Psychology, 34,* 1–3.

Drotar, D. (2010). Guidance for submission and review of multiple publications derived from the same study [Editorial]. *Journal of Pediatric Psychology, 35,* 225–230.

Lovejoy, T. I., Revenson, T. A., & France, C. R. (2011). Reviewing manuscripts for peer-review journals: A primer for novice and seasoned reviewers. *Annals of Behavioral Medicine, 42,* 1–13.

Nelson, T. (2011). Critiquing scholarship as formal review: The role and responsibilities of readers for academic journals. *Issues in Teacher Education, 20,* 5–16.

Palermo, T. M. (2010). Exploring ethical issues in peer review for the *Journal of Pediatric Psychology* [Editorial]. *Journal of Pediatric Psychology, 35,* 221–224.

Perepletchikova, F., & Kazdin, A. E. (2005). Treatment integrity and therapeutic change: Issues and research recommendations. *Clinical Psychology: Research and Practice, 12,* 365–383.

Trusty, J. (2011). Quantitative articles: Developing studies for publication in counseling journals. *Journal of Counseling and Development, 89,* 261–267.

Ten

Directions for Program Development, Research, and Training

With increasing emphasis on integrated health care, and the shift from providing behavioral health and medical care in silos to an interdisciplinary approach, pediatric school psychologists have opportunities to work in a variety of settings. Some are employed in schools where their role may include development of prevention programs, grant writing, program evaluation, parent education, and school–medical system liaison (Shaw, 2003). Pediatric school psychologists also may work in hospital settings where they may function in the role of consultation liaison, or assist in medical specialty clinics that provide support in the transition between hospital and school (Power, DuPaul, Shapiro, & Parrish, 1995). Primary care is another setting for the practice of pediatric school psychology. Professionals may be involved in colocation, collaborative care, and integrated care. Finally, some pediatric school psychologists engage in independent practice in the community.

Given the potential variety of roles and employment as a pediatric school psychologist, training programs are charged with the task not only of providing the foundational knowledge and skills related to this profession, but also preparing trainees for employment in a variety of settings through practica and internships. This chapter provides an overview of preservice and in-service training recommendations for the subspecialty of pediatric school psychology as well as networking strategies to create opportunities for professional practice. This chapter also discusses directions for future research in the area of pediatric school psychology and ways in which professionals with this unique set of knowledge and skills can impact prevention efforts and service delivery strategies to promote positive outcomes for youth with physical and mental health conditions.

Recommendations for Preservice Training

When considering the development of a pediatric school psychology training program, one must acknowledge the depth and breadth of skills as well as the experiences required for this training. As such, we recommend that such a program be offered only at the doctoral level. Another consideration is whether the training can be integrated within an existing doctoral program or must be initiated as a new, stand-alone program. If the training can be integrated into an existing program, the process of program development may be less challenging, assuming that internal and external resources can be accessed to support the program. The challenge may be greater in terms of accessing needed resources if this is a new program. However, the positive aspect of developing a new program may be the flexibility offered when one is not attempting to fit a program into something that is already established. Depending upon the situation, a strategic plan will need to be developed that encompasses all aspects of the proposed training including pediatric psychology, community psychology, public health, systems level collaboration, action research, leadership development, and grant writing (Power, 2000).

Developing a Strategic Plan

To develop a strategic plan, one must turn to the existing literature to determine what is recommended in terms of specific knowledge and skills in pediatric school psychology. In addition to the general training areas listed above, Shaw (2003) suggests the following key skills as necessary in pediatric psychology training: understanding the financial components related to health care, including insurance and Medicaid reimbursement and billable hours; knowledge of specific medical conditions and their impact on academic, behavior, and mental health outcomes for youth; awareness of the disease processes and pharmacological treatments, including the clinical effects and side effects of medications; knowledge of evidence-based, psychosocial prevention and intervention strategies to address pediatric health issues; and skills to access external funding. This list of recommended key areas can help one begin to identify existing courses and training experiences that would meet these areas and plan for the development of new courses and clinical experiences not currently available.

As part of this strategic plan, existing resources within one's training institute should be considered. For example, if there is a medical school affiliated with the institution or a teaching hospital in the community, one may be able to network with faculty and pediatricians in these institutions to discuss potential areas of collaboration that would be beneficial to all involved. Similarly, reaching out to colleagues in departments such as school psychology, clinical psychology, community psychology, psychiatry, nursing, and public health may be fruitful in establishing joint opportunities for knowledge and skill development.

The next logical step is to communicate with representatives from all of these programs and institutions to discuss the benefits of joint training and the positive outcomes for all. Discussions related to sharing resources, administrative oversight, and benefits of increasing student course enrollment are important topics for discussion. Additionally, developing a shared mission is critical to ensuring commitment and accountability.

An important initial step in planning is to focus on funding. Short-term funding goals need to be determined for initiation of the program whereas long-term goals are necessary to plan for maintenance of the program. Consideration should be given to faculty support for course offerings, development and support for practicum experiences, and funding for students (i.e., assistantships and tuition waivers). There are a number of sources for funding that may be available including institutional, state, and federal grants. The reader is referred to chapter 8 of this text for information regarding types of funding sources and guidance for writing a successful grant application.

Once these foundational pieces have been established, the specific details of the training curriculum can then be determined. This training curriculum should include doctoral level courses focused on topics needed for this specialization specific to medical topics, health psychology, behavioral medicine, and leadership development. For example, in addition to the required school psychology doctoral coursework focusing on advanced consultation, supervision, and intervention, students in the pediatric school psychology subspecialty training area at the University of South Florida (USF) complete courses in pediatric health issues in the schools, pediatric psychopharmacology, psychological assessment of infants and toddlers, advanced practicum, and a doctoral seminar in pediatric school psychology (Bradley-Klug & Armstrong, 2011). These students also actively participate in a research group investigating issues relevant to pediatric school psychology (see Appendix A for an overview of the USF Pediatric School Psychology Training Program). In the Lehigh University pediatric school psychology program (Power, Shapiro, & DuPaul, 2003), students enroll in courses pertaining to evidence-based interventions for children with chronic health conditions; intervention development and applications in pediatric settings, prevention science, and comprehensive school health programs; prevention program development and applications in multiple settings; child psychopathology, pediatric psychopharmacology; theory and practice of organizational change; early intervention; and ongoing seminars related to leadership, research, and supervision (see Appendix B for an overview of the Lehigh University Pediatric School Psychology Training Program).

In addition to coursework focused on building knowledge, specific practical experiences must be integrated into the training curriculum. These training experiences may range from shadowing a pediatric school psychologist in the first year of the program to completing an advanced clinical practicum in the fourth year. Additional types of experiences might include attending and presenting at medical grand rounds at a local hospital, completing an applied or research-based assistantship in a clinical setting, and completing a doctoral-level internship in a setting that offers applied experiences and supervision in pediatric school psychology. Given the diversity of settings where one may by employed as a pediatric school psychologist, students should have the opportunity to apply their skills in school, hospital (tertiary care, primary care), and community-based private practice settings.

A third and equally important aspect of a comprehensive training program in pediatric school psychology involves research opportunities and requirements. Students must have the opportunity to collaborate with colleagues in research endeavors related to topics of importance in this area as well as be required to complete their dissertation on a critical topic in pediatric psychology. One way to foster a research climate in this type of training program is through the establishment of faculty- or student-initiated research groups. These groups can be broad based and focus on pediatric psychology in general or be more narrowly focused on topics such as promoting systems-level communication and collaboration for youth with chronic illness. Students should be required to actively participate in these groups and can receive mentoring and experiences in such activities as grant writing, reviewing manuscripts for publication, preparing and presenting posters and papers at conferences, writing manuscripts for publication, and developing empirical investigations from identification of the research questions to dissemination of study results. This also is a venue for students to develop their dissertation research and receive ongoing feedback from faculty as well as their peers.

Upon completion of all preinternship requirements, students should be required to complete an internship in a setting that offers additional knowledge, training, and supervision related to pediatric school psychology. There are a number of nationally accredited clinical internships in pediatric psychology that offer these experiences. However, these internships are highly competitive and not all students who seek these internship sites will be offered the opportunity to receive their training there. Alternatively, developing or accessing internship training opportunities in settings such as schools, hospitals, university- or community-based clinics, or private practice settings with doctoral level supervision in pediatric (school) psychology should be explored. Postdoctoral training in this specialty is strongly recommended and is required in most states for licensure. Postdoctoral positions in pediatric school psychology or related areas (e.g., pediatric psychology) provide individuals with a variety of clinical and research experiences under supervision. These types of positions may be located in teaching hospitals, medical centers, or in schools of health or social sciences based in university settings.

Recommendations for In-Service Training

The section above focuses on the development of training programs for students who are currently matriculated in a graduate program. However, for practitioners who already have completed their advanced degree, it is important to consider professional development options for those individuals to gain knowledge and experience in pediatric psychology. Similarly, many existing programs may not have the resources available to develop a pediatric school psychology area of training and students in these programs need to consider alternative ways to develop the knowledge and skills related to this subspecialty.

Practitioners also may access information related to working with youth with chronic health conditions through professional conferences. In addition to conferences specific to one's profession, interdisciplinary conferences offer professional development opportunities. For example, the Collaborative Family Healthcare Association (CFHA) is an interdisciplinary organization that promotes integrated health care from a systems level perspective. CFHA hosts a conference each year and encourages individuals from a variety of disciplines (e.g., physicians, nurses, psychologists, researchers) to attend and present. This type of conference offers a novel opportunity for networking across disciplines. Teleconferences and Web-based conferences also are available on topics related to providing services for youth with chronic illness.

Professional development opportunities also may be available through online courses offered by programs that either have a pediatric psychology training program or related programs such as public health or leadership. Oftentimes these courses are offered for nondegree seeking students who can participate in the online courses without matriculation into a specific program.

Networking with community-based primary care providers also may result in opportunities for additional training. Similarly, local teaching or children's hospitals offer ongoing presentations and grand rounds on topics that may be related to pediatric school psychology. Many of these presentations are videotaped and available for review if one cannot attend, so the potential options are limitless.

Launching a Career and Creating Professional Opportunities

Once you have completed your preservice training in pediatric school psychology, several challenges are presented. These include launching your career in a planful manner, connecting with health providers in the community, and forming partnerships with community agencies.

Launching Your Career

Upon embarking on one's career, a critical step is to establish a strong mentoring plan. Mentors typically are senior-level professionals who have achieved success in areas related to your career goals, and who are willing to share time to invest in your professional development. Typically it is helpful to have more than one mentor and perhaps to include a professional outside of the local community who can offer alternative perspectives. Advisors in graduate school, internship, and fellowship programs can continue to serve as mentors, and they can be invaluable in linking you with others who can serve in this role. In the context of the mentoring relationship, it is important to establish long-term goals (i.e., 5-year and 10-year), short-term goals (i.e., yearly), and a specific set of activities to achieve the goals. Of course, the goals and activities can change over the course of time in response to changing priorities, professional opportunities and experiences, and advice from mentors.

Once you have developed the skills to serve as a pediatric school psychologist, the next step is to market those skills within the setting where you currently practice as well as in the community at large. One particular target audience in the community is pediatricians. Forging the link between psychology and medicine can be challenging. For example, a recent study found that pediatricians retain a traditional view of school psychologists and perceive school psychologists' main role to be that of assessment and design of behavioral interventions. Importantly, pediatricians who were unaware of the breadth of training of school psychologists were generally unlikely to communicate and collaborate with these professionals (Bradley-Klug, Sundman, Nadeau, Cunningham, & Ogg, 2010). Thus, it is important for pediatric school psychologists to market their specific skills and offer suggestions for areas in which to collaborate.

Networking with Community Agencies

Networking with others requires development of an outreach strategy. One of the first steps is to make a list of the community agencies to contact. The next step is to consider the options for contacting these agencies, such as by phone, e-mail, brochure, or face-to-face meeting. A combination of these methods may result in the best option. One also must consider the skills to be marketed through these contacts and suggestions for collaboration. Finally, providing your contact information is essential.

Depending on your training, scope of practice, and career goals, community agencies to contact may include schools, local pediatricians, community mental health agencies, local hospitals, local psychologists in independent practice, and advocacy organizations (e.g., Autism Speaks). Contacting these agencies by phone or e-mail may be the most efficient method, but not necessarily the most effective. In many cases, this type of communication requires that a message be left and depends upon the individual on the receiving end to respond. As such, this may result in one-way communication that is short-lived.

Development of a handout or brochure to market specific skills of interest to individual agencies is worthy of consideration. This written document allows for the inclusion of detailed information and the brochure can be delivered in person. Items to consider including in a handout or brochure are your work hours, phone numbers where you can be reached during these hours, and a number where you can be reached after hours if necessary. If the telephone number for your business has an automated system, be sure there is an option for the caller to easily identify your extension or name. Also, recognize that the hours of those in other professions may not be the same as yours, so providing after hours contact information is recommended. Consider posting this type of information on your professional or business website as well.

Another way to market your knowledge and skills in the community is to volunteer to conduct seminars or training workshops at local medical schools or hospitals (i.e., grand rounds). Hosting an after-hours event in the community also would be a method for initiating networks with local professionals. Another potential contact would be through a local early career professionals' network. Typically affiliated with the local Chamber of Commerce, these young professionals groups are emerging across the nation and often organize monthly meetings to exchange ideas, share interests, and offer professional development opportunities for members.

Another method for use in facilitating and maintaining collaboration with community organizations is through telehealth. Using telecommunications technology, such as Web conferencing, may be most beneficial in rural areas where more traditional methods of traveling to meeting sites for interdisciplinary conferences may not be cost-effective or feasible.

Whatever methods are chosen for networking, suggestions for areas of collaboration that will be beneficial to all involved must be made apparent. Examples of these areas include developing educationally based prevention programs, intervention and treatment planning, progress monitoring of treatment to improve outcomes, monitoring treatment adherence, encouraging parent involvement, and sharing treatment plans to avoid duplication of services.

Educating Parents in Systems Level Communication and Collaboration

Consistent with a developmental-ecological model (Kazak, Rourke, & Navsaria, 2009), a critical function for pediatric school psychologists is to strengthen the family system and advocate for the needs of families. The previous sections focused on networking with community agencies. However, one of the most important groups to include in this networking strategy is parents. One way to initiate communication and collaboration with families is through parent support groups and organizations in the community. Information on these groups and organizations, such as contact names, meeting locations, and meeting times, can be gathered from local hospitals, community-based physicians, and local religious organizations. However, although not all parents are members of these types of organizations, the school system is an organization where all parents have a connection. Pediatric school psychologists may have the opportunity to speak with parents about the importance of sharing information with school personnel and may work toward developing trust with parents through participation in school events. Also, pediatric school psychologists can contribute to advocacy efforts at a local, state, and national level to develop and advance policies that support families and child development.

Directions for Future Research

Intervention

There are a number of areas in pediatric school psychology that require further research, including investigations related to specific conditions. However, there are some issues that cut across illnesses that would benefit from further research. Regardless of the setting in which a pediatric school psychologist is employed, the issues of pediatric pain, treatment adherence, traumatic stress, and mental health conditions are pervasive.

Pain. It is estimated that between 25 and 30% of youth experience chronic or recurrent pain, with the most commonly reported symptoms being headaches, abdominal pain, and back pain (Hicks, von Baeyer, & McGrath, 2006). Pain symptoms can interfere with school attendance, academic performance, social interactions, ability to participate in athletic activities, and overall quality of life. Symptoms of pain may be affected by stress, anxiety, changes in emotions, and sleep. Thus, due to the potential for functional impairments caused by pain as well as the variability of pain symptoms, research is needed to develop methods to prevent the onset of pain as well as to control these symptoms in the context of a variety of situations.

Although there are a number of interventions that may be used to treat pain such as cognitive behavioral strategies, medication, biofeedback, physical therapy, and behavioral interventions, the efficacy of packaged interventions programs compared to single interventions require additional research (Dahlquist & Nagel, 2009). Likewise, the cost–benefit ratio of various treatment options needs to be investigated. Studies looking at alternative methods of treatment, such as online treatments (see Hicks et al., 2006) warrant further investigation not only for their potential cost effectiveness, but also for the benefits of a Web-based program for families who do not have easy access to medical professionals. Relatedly, variables contributing to treatment integrity and adherence need to be included in these investigations. Studies also need to consider the relationship between various pain management strategies, cultural factors, the protective responses of parents (Simons, Claar, & Logan, 2008), and management of pain in the school setting (Logan, Coakley, & Scharff, 2007).

Adherence. Commonly associated with taking a prescribed medication, adherence encompasses consistent implementation of a treatment plan that might include exercise, a specific dietary regimen, hygiene, and other activities contributing to health. Studies assessing treatment adherence report 50% or fewer youth adhere to prescribed treatments (La Greca & Mackey, 2009). At issue with the report of these data is the way adherence is assessed. The most cost effective methods for determining adherence are youth or parent reports and pill counts. However, these methods are fraught with problems due to subjectivity of the measures. Other methods such as drug assays or electronic monitoring devices may be considered intrusive and cost prohibitive. Thus, research is needed to determine the most effective and efficient ways to assess and monitor treatment adherence, particularly in the pediatric population.

Numerous factors have been identified in the literature as affecting adherence including regimen complexity, side effects of treatment, duration of treatment, potential for disruption of lifestyle, social support, mental health status, adolescent decision making competence, and the relationship of individuals with their prescribing primary care physician (Miller & Drotar, 2007; Quittner, Modi, Lemanek, Levers-Landis, & Rapoff, 2008; Stewart, 1996). Although factors have been studied that appear to influence self-care behaviors (e.g., disease knowledge, reinforcement, peer support), more recent studies suggest that a combination of strategies may result in the highest levels of adherence (Wu & Roberts, 2008). Future research should focus on what packaged strategies result in the most positive outcomes as well as the variables (i.e., gender, ethnicity, socioeconomic status) that may influence the effectiveness of these interventions. The incorporation of electronic technologies in treatment adherence strategies also deserves attention in future studies, as simply sending text message reminders to youth with Type 1 diabetes has been shown to improve self-care behavior (Franklin, Waller, Pagliari, & Greene, 2006).

Traumatic Stress. The topic of posttraumatic stress, including both the symptoms (PTSS) and the disorder (PTSD), in relation to medical illness and injury has raised numerous questions. Part of this controversy is related to variability in the presence of PTSS and PTSD symptoms across studies. Manne (2009) recommends taking a broader perspective on this topic beyond simply looking at prevalence rates, to focusing on factors that moderate or mediate these symptoms such as pain management, recurrence of illness, child's understanding of the illness, and family support. This broader perspective aligns with the developmental-ecological model (Kazak et al., 2009), emphasizing a systemic approach to understanding relationships among variables. Similarly, parents of youth with chronic health conditions also may experience traumatic stress (Greening & Stoppelbein, 2007), and the relationship of parental stress to youth coping is worthy of further investigation.

Posttraumatic growth (PTG) refers to an individual's reported positive change as the result of a traumatic experience such as a medical illness. The majority of the research on PTG has been with survivors of cancer. For example, this phenomenon was explored by Barakat and colleagues (2006) who interviewed adolescent survivors of cancer and their parents to determine if they reported any positive outcomes as a result of their experiences with this disease. Eighty-five percent of the adolescents reported at least one positive outcome with a third of those expressing more than four positive changes. Additionally, a large majority of mothers and fathers also reported positive outcomes. Some of the positive experiences included changing the way one thinks about life, developing new plans for the future, and treating other people differently. Research is needed to determine the variables that influence the ability of individuals to be resilient in the face of adversity, as well as the relationship of PTG to other types of chronic illness. Because PTG is reportedly associated with positive mental health outcomes (Helgeson, Reynolds, & Tomich, 2006), development of strategies to promote PTG in youth and their families is critical.

Mental Health Conditions.   The comorbidity of mental health conditions with pediatric chronic illness varies across conditions. For example, approximately 33% of children with Type 1 diabetes meet criteria for depression (Jaser, Whittemore, Ambrosino, Lindemann, & Grey, 2008), and prevalence rates for depression in children with epilepsy have been reported to range from 10 to 30% (Wagner, Smith, Ferguson, Horton, & Wilson, 2009). In contrast, studies investigating the presence of psychosocial conditions in children with juvenile rheumatoid arthritis compared to healthy children report no significant deficits (Rapoff, Lindsley, & Karlson, 2009), and multiple investigations of the prevalence of mental health concerns in survivors of pediatric cancer indicate that the rates are similar to the general population (Bradley-Klug & Sundman, 2010).

Data indicating relatively little difference in psychosocial conditions between youth with pediatric health conditions and healthy youth are somewhat controversial as it is difficult to fathom that individuals dealing with medical conditions can remain mentally healthy. This controversy has raised questions about the tools used to assess mental health as well as questions about the types of adaptive styles used by some children that might cause them to underreport their mental health status. Youth categorized as employing a repressive adaptive style of responding, identified by Phipps and colleagues (2006), demonstrated high levels of restraint and low levels of reported distress. Therefore, these youth are unlikely to report mental health concerns. Clearly, additional research investigating the relationship of physical and mental health outcomes in the pediatric population is warranted.

Prevention

As indicated throughout this book, pediatric school psychology is characterized by a strong emphasis on prevention. The focus on prevention includes research and practice related to universal, selective, and targeted programming.

Universal Programming. Rather than waiting for a child or adolescent to demonstrate symptoms of illness, a more contemporary approach to providing services to all children is to focus on prevention through universal programming. At the level of universal programming, screenings and preventive strategies can be applied for all populations to prevent the onset of illness and promote health. For example, it is recommended that children be screened for sleep problems and disorders prior to entry into kindergarten based upon research indicating that approximately 12 to 15% of children have a sleep disorder that impacts their educational outcomes (Luginbuehl & Bradley-Klug, 2008). This means that it would be useful for school personnel to incorporate questions related to sleep into their existing screening measures. It also requires educators to have a plan for what to do for children who are found to be at-risk for a sleep disorder (e.g., provide parent training, refer the family to a community resource, etc.).

Examples of universal programming to prevent the development of sleep problems include providing parent training about the importance of sleep for children and adolescents, as well as teaching parents behavioral techniques to promote good sleep hygiene. Similarly, given the serious public health concern related to childhood overweight and obesity, many schools now conduct universal screenings of all youth by assessing their body mass index (BMI) and notifying caregivers of the results. Universal strategies such as examining the nutritional content of school meals and offering students healthy food choices throughout the school day are ways in which educational systems are currently addressing the concern of childhood obesity. Although screening is promoted to identify students who may have an underlying health condition, this process is limited not only by a lack of tools but also by limited mechanisms in place to carry out this type of screening. Research is needed to examine other types of universal screening and programming that could be implemented. Program evaluation data also are needed to determine the effectiveness of these efforts and offer any revisions necessary to promote positive health-related outcomes.

Selective and Targeted Programming. Selective programming is designed for youth who are at-risk for the development of a particular disorder due to membership in a particular group (e.g., low socioeconomic status, elevated level of adverse family circumstances). Research has shown that individuals at perhaps the greatest risk are those who are repeatedly exposed to adverse psychosocial circumstances regardless of whether they are detected by a screener at a particular point in time. Thus, it is important to initiate prevention efforts as early as feasible at a broad level, and to target individuals at increased risk by virtue of socioeconomic risk or psychosocial vulnerability (Shonkoff, Boyce, & McEwen, 2009). Targeted programming is designed for those individuals who demonstrate current signs of risk for disorder by virtue of the presence of known risk factors or their score on a screening measure. Strategies can be developed for these individuals to reduce risk or prevent the emergence of the disorder. Pediatric school psychologists can work with educators as well as community-based professionals to identify screening measures and the pediatric populations that would benefit from screening as well as the related prevention strategies.

Advances in Technology

The use of technology in our society is rapidly growing, and virtual interactions are becoming a very common form of communication. *E-Health* is a term that has emerged in the medical literature and refers to Internet-assisted strategies as well as health information technology interventions (Knapp, 2010). Likewise, information communication technologies (ICTs) are being developed to improve the ability to disseminate information about evidence-based practices (Bacigalupe, 2011; Knapp et al., 2011). Parents and youth can now access health care information directly from the Internet, and in many cases do so based upon ease of access and limited cost. A study by Knapp and colleagues (2011) reported that 81% of the low-income families in their sample had access to and used the Internet. Thus, previous concerns that technology would not be available to families from particular demographically diverse backgrounds appear to be fading.

Telehealth (also referred to as telepractice, telepsychology, or telemental health) encompasses numerous technology-based forums such as e-mail, videoconferencing, and Web-based education (Novotney, 2011). Information related to diagnosis, disease process and symptoms, impact on the child, and treatments can be easily accessed by all individuals involved in the care of a child with a chronic illness. For example, Izquierdo et al. (2009) designed an intervention for children ages 5 to 14 with Type 1 diabetes that made use of an educational telemedicine unit to videoconference the school nurse, child, and diabetes team every month. Children's levels of hemoglobin A1c and quality of life were also assessed every 3 months for one year. Compared to a control group, students who received the telehealth intervention had decreased levels of hemoglobin A1c and had higher ratings on a quality of life questionnaire (Izquierdo et al., 2009).

Internet-based interventions also fall under the category of telehealth and are being investigated for use as an alternative to traditional treatments. Palermo and colleagues (2009) investigated the effectiveness of an Internet-based cognitive behavior therapy strategy to treat chronic pain among children aged 11 to 17 years. In addition to receiving medical care, participants in a treatment group completed an 8-week Internet-based program that provided training in relaxation techniques, cognitive strategies, communication strategies, and sleep interventions. Children also kept a daily diary and reported the helpfulness of the skills they learned. When compared to a control group who only received medical care, children who completed the online intervention reported a significant reduction in pain intensity and fewer activity limitations.

Social networking is yet another strategy emerging in the health care literature. Today's youth interact on a regular basis through network services such as e-mail and instant messaging. Battles and Wiener (2002) investigated the effects of an interactive online community, STARBRIGHT World (SBW), on levels of pain, mood, anger, loneliness, problem behavior, and willingness to return to treatment among seriously ill children aged 8 to 19 years. The majority of the children were infected with HIV. The program was designed to allow participants to talk and connect to other chronically ill children, play games, and learn about their medical condition. Though the intervention did not reduce levels of pain, participants reported less loneliness, worry, and withdrawn behavior as a result of engaging in the online community.

Consideration should be given to how technology may be used to address issues such as education of the disease process, treatment adherence, treatment application, and monitoring of treatment effects. Such methods may be especially helpful for families that live in rural communities and have less immediate access to on site health care facilities (Hicks et al., 2006). As stated by Bacigalupe (2011), "social technologies defy the financial, geographical, and logistical barriers that exist in creating a context for ongoing interaction, collaborative learning, fast access to information, and transparency" (p. 5). As such, technology may have a significant place in the future of pediatric school psychology.

It should be noted that the practices related to telehealth are not without concern. Licensure issues related to practice across state lines are being discussed at the national level among organizations such as the American Psychological Association (APA). Additionally, there are concerns about privacy related to the use of technology. The provision of services through technology has now been approved for third party reimbursement by some insurance companies (Novotney, 2011), but currently this type of service may not be an option for all clients. Although technology provides a new and exciting addition to the provision of health care, professional guidelines and training are necessary to protect the rights of clients and ensure the ethical behavior of professionals.

Interdisciplinary Models of Care

Due to the many factors impacting an individual with a chronic health condition and the multiple systems involved, an interdisciplinary team approach is needed in order to provide optimal service delivery. This team may include individuals such as the affected youth, caregivers, psychologist, primary care physician, social worker, psychiatrist, school nurse, and mental health counselor. Alternative methods of providing collaborative care are currently being proposed in the health care literature as part of the patient-centered medical home initiative. Collaborative care is an approach involving the coordination of services across providers and systems of care that focuses on the whole patient rather than just the presenting disease (Peek, Baird, & Coleman, 2009). An integrated approach to care has been found to reduce the number of necessary appointments, decrease the length of treatment, and ultimately decrease health care costs (Novotney, 2010). Although this type of service delivery is not a new concept, several approaches to collaborative care have been advanced more recently: colocation and embedded service delivery (Hunter & Goodie, 2010). Colocation is a model that involves the provision of behavioral health services on location within the primary care setting, yet these services remain separate. Embedded service delivery represents a model whereby the behavioral health care professional and primary care provider work together as members of a team. These examples of integrated service delivery offer readily available access to interdisciplinary care for patients and have promising long-term benefits for improving the quality of services and outcomes for children. However, research is needed to determine the efficiency and effectiveness of these models with the pediatric population especially with regard to the impact on educational outcomes for youth.

The Future of Pediatric School Psychology

Advances in health care and medical technology have resulted in more children surviving illness and entering the educational system. Similarly, with the development of more sensitive assessment tools, the mental health needs of youth are being uncovered at an increasing rate. Because children and adolescents spend a significant portion of their day in the school setting, there is a critical need for psychologists who can address concerns that cut across the health, school, and family systems. In addition, the rapid increase in prevalence of chronic health conditions and the exorbitant costs of health care have highlighted the critical importance of prevention efforts. The pediatric school psychologist can serve as an integral part of the collaborative health care team, providing unique knowledge and skills related to educational issues as well as knowledge of mental and physical health issues. Pediatric school psychology is in its embryonic stages; the demand for care that emphasizes preventive services that are coordinated across systems affirms the critical need for these experts and creates conditions for the rapid development of this specialty.

Discussion Questions

1. What are the recommended areas of training, in both foundational knowledge and clinical skills, necessary to develop expertise in pediatric school psychology?
2. Pediatric school psychology is a relatively new subspecialty area that may be unfamiliar to professionals in the schools and community. What can one do to market one's knowledge and skills in pediatric school psychology in order to facilitate systems-level communication and collaboration?
3. There are a number of directions for future research presented in this chapter. Discuss three of these areas focusing on how they cut across illnesses and the specific recommendations for future research related to each.
4. How might advances in technology improve the practice of pediatric school psychology? Be sure to discuss the potential advantages of technology, as well as the disadvantages, with respect to providing services to individuals with chronic health conditions.

Additional Teaching Aids

Guidelines for training and career development are included on the attached CD.

References

Bacigalupe, G. (2011). Is there a role for social technologies in collaborative health care? *Families, Systems, and Health, 29,* 1–14.

Barakat, L. P., Alderfer, M. A., & Kazak, A. E. (2006). Posttraumatic growth in adolescent survivors of cancer and their mothers and fathers. *Journal of Pediatric Psychology, 31,* 413–419.

Battles, H. B., & Wiener, L. S. (2002). STARBRIGHT world: Effects of an electronic network on the social environment of children with life-threatening illnesses. *Children's Health Care, 31(1),* 47–68.

Bradley-Klug, K. L., & Armstrong, K. H. (2011). *Preparing pediatric school psychologists for work with children with special care needs.* Manuscript in preparation.

Bradley–Klug, K. L., & Sundman, A. (2010). Late effects of childhood cancer: Implications for school psychologists. *School Psychology Forum, 4,* 13–24.

Bradley–Klug, K. L., Sundman, A., Nadeau, J., Cunningham, J., & Ogg, J.(2010). Communication and collaboration with schools: Pediatricians' perspectives. *Journal of Applied School Psychology, 26,* 263–281.

Dahlquist, L. M., & Nagel, M. S. (2009). Chronic and recurrent pain. In M. C. Roberts (Ed.), *Handbook of pediatric psychology* (4th ed., pp. 152–170. New York: Guilford.

Franklin, V. L., Waller, A., Pagliari, C., & Greene, S. A. (2006). A randomized controlled trial of Sweet Talk, a text-messaging system to support young people with diabetes. *Diabetic Medicine, 23,* 1332–1338.

Greening, L., & Stoppelbein, L. (2007). Brief report: Pediatric cancer, parental coping style, and risk for depressive, posttraumatic stress, and anxiety symptoms. *Journal of Pediatric Psychology, 32,* 1272–1277.

Helgeson, V. S., Reynolds, K. A., & Tomich, P. L. (2006). A meta-analytic review of benefit finding and growth. *Journal of Consulting and Clinical Psychology, 74,* 797–816.

Hicks, C. L., von Baeyer, C. L., & McGrath, P. J. (2006). Online psychological treatment for pediatric recurrent pain: A randomized evaluation. *Journal of Pediatric Psychology, 31,* 724–736.

Hunter, C. L., & Goodie, J. L. (2010). Operational and clinical components for integrated–collaborative behavioral health care in the patient–centered medical home. *Families, Systems, and Health, 28,* 308–321.

Izquierdo, R., Morin, P. C., Bratt, K., Moreau, Z., Meyer, S., Ploutz-Snyder, R., ... Weinstock, R. S. (2009). School-centered telemedicine for children with type 1 diabetes mellitus. *The Journal of Pediatrics, 155,* 374–379.

Jaser, S. S., Whittemore, R., Ambrosino, J. M., Lindemann, E., & Grey, M. (2008). Mediators of depressive symptoms in children with Type 1 diabetes and their mothers. *Journal of Pediatric Psychology, 33,* 509–519.

Kazak, A. E., Rourke, M. T., & Navsaria, N. (2009). Families and other systems in pediatric psychology. In M. Roberts & R. Steele (Eds.), *Handbook of pediatric psychology* (pp. 656–671). New York: Guilford.

Knapp, C. (2010). E–health in pediatric palliative care. *American Journal of Hospice and Palliative Medicine, 27,* 66–73.

Knapp, C., Madden, V., Marcu, M., Wang, H., Curtis, C., Sloyer, P., & Shenkman, E. (2011). Information seeking behaviors of parents whose children have life–threatening illnesses. *Pediatric Blood & Cancer, 56,* 805–811.

La Greca, A. M., & Mackey, E. R. (2009). Adherence to pediatric treatment regimens. In M. Roberts & R. Steele (Eds.), *Handbook of pediatric psychology* (pp. 130–152). New York: Guilford.

Logan, E. E., Coakley, R. M., & Scharff, L. (2007). Teachers' perceptions of and responses to adolescents with chronic pain syndromes. *Journal of Pediatric Psychology, 32,* 139–149.

Luginbuehl, M., & Bradley–Klug, K. L. (2008). Assessment of sleep problems in a school setting. In A. Ivanenko (Ed.), *Sleep and psychiatric disorders in children and adolescents* (pp. 109–138). New York: Informa Healthcare.

Manne, S. (2009). Commentary: Adopting to a broad perspective on posttraumatic stress disorders, childhood medical illness and injury. *Journal of Pediatric Psychology, 34,* 22–26.

Miller, V. A., & Drotar, D. (2007). Decision–making competence and adherence to treatment in adolescents with diabetes. *Journal of Pediatric Psychology, 32,* 178–188.

Novotney, A. (2010). Integrated care is nothing new for these psychologists. *Monitor on Psychology, 41,* 41–43.

Novotney, A. (2011). A new emphasis on telehealth: How can psychologists stay ahead of the curve—and keep patients safe? *Monitor on Psychology, 42,* 40–44.

Palermo, T. M., Wilson, A. C., Peters, M., Lewandowski, A., & Somhegyi, H. (2009). Randomized controlled trial of an Internet-delivered family cognitive-behavioral therapy intervention for children and adolescents with chronic pain. *Pain, 146,* 205–213.

Peek, C. J., Baird, M. A., & Coleman, E. (2009). Primary care for patient complexity, not only disease. *Families, Systems, & Health, 27,* 287–302.

Phipps, S., Larson, S., Long, A., & Rai, S. N. (2006). Adaptive style and symptoms of PTSS in children with cancer and their parents. *Journal of Pediatric Psychology, 31,* 298–309.

Power, T. J. (2000). The school psychologist as community-focused, public health professional: Emerging challenges and implications for training. *School Psychology Review, 29,* 557–559.

Power, T. J., DuPaul, G. J., Shapiro, E. S., & Parrish, J. M. (1995). Pediatric school psychology: The emergence of a subspecialty. *School Psychology Review, 24,* 244–257.

Power, T. J., Shapiro, E. S., & DuPaul, G. J. (2003). Preparing psychologists to link the health and educational systems in managing and preventing children's health problems. *Journal of Pediatric Psychology, 28,* 147–155.

Quittner, A. L., Modi, A. C., Lemanek, K. L., Levers–Landis, C. E., & Rapoff. M. A. (2008). Evidence-based assessment of adherence to medical treatments in pediatric psychology. *Journal of Pediatric Psychology, 33,* 916–936.

Rapoff, M. A., Lindsley, C. B., & Karlson, C. (2009). Medical and psychosocial aspects of juvenile rheumatoid arthritis. In M. Roberts & R. Steele (Eds.), *Handbook of pediatric psychology* (pp. 366–380). New York: Guilford.

Shaw, S. R. (2003). Professional preparation of pediatric school psychologists for school–based health centers. *Psychology in the Schools, 40,* 321–330.

Shonkoff, J. P., Boyce, W. T., & McEwen, B. S. (2009). Neuroscience, molecular biology, and the childhood roots of health disparities: Building a new framework for health promotion and disease prevention. *Journal of the American Medical Association, 301,* 2252–2259.

Simons, L. E., Claar, R. L., & Logan, D. L. (2008). Chronic pain in adolescence: Parental responses, adolescent coping, and their impact on adolescents' pain behaviors. *Journal of Pediatric Psychology, 33,* 894–904.

Stewart, M. A. (1996). Effective physician–patient communication and help outcomes: A review. *Canadian Medical Association Journal, 152,* 1423–1433.

Wagner, J. L., Smith, G., Ferguson, P. L., Horton, S., & Wilson, E. (2009). A hopelessness model of depression symptoms in youth with epilepsy. *Journal of Pediatric Psychology, 34,* 89–96.

Wu, Y. P., & Roberts, M. C. (2008). Meta-analysis of interventions to increase adherence to medication regimens for pediatric otitis media and streptococcal pharyngitis. *Journal of Pediatric Psychology, 33,* 789–796.

APPENDIX A

Overview of University of South Florida Pediatric School Psychology Program

Key Components of Training
- Effective interdisciplinary communication and collaboration
- Understanding the impact of pediatric health issues on the academic, behavior, and mental health outcomes for youth
- Understanding the disease process
- Developing familiarity with the patient-centered medical home concept
- Developing knowledge of evidence-based, psychosocial prevention and intervention strategies

Specialized Coursework
- In addition to doctoral level course work in the USF School Psychology Program, students complete the following additional courses:

    ○ Pediatric Health Issues in the Schools
    ○ Seminar in Pediatric Psychology
    ○ Psychological Assessment of Infants & Toddlers*
    ○ Pediatric Psychopharmacology*

Required Additional Experiences
- Shadowing (first-year students)
- Advanced Practicum in Pediatric School Psychology
- Applied Clinical Assistantship in Department of Pediatrics or related setting
  - Available Clinical Rotations
    - Early Steps Program: Infant Toddler Developmental Specialist (ITDS)
    - Parent Training
    - Neurodevelopmental Medicine
    - Infectious Disease Clinics
    - Children's Cancer Center
    - St. Joseph's Hospital
    - Rothman Center for Neuropsychiatry
- Pediatric Grand Rounds
- Pediatric School Psychology Research Group
- Internship

Recommended Additional Experience
- Postdoctorate in pediatric psychology

*Availability of these courses varies based on funding

APPENDIX B

Overview of Lehigh University Pediatric School Psychology Program

Key Components of Training
- Practica in university-affiliated and community sites
- Emphasis on services to diverse, low income children and families
- Emphasis on applied research
- Emphasis on research and practice in primary care settings
- Didactic and practicum experiences
- Focus on prevention and intervention
- Practica in health and school settings

Specialized Coursework
- Medical aspects of disabilities
- Comprehensive school health programs

- Prevention of health problems and health promotion
- Leadership development and systems change
- Early intervention
- Pharmacology
- Working in culturally and linguistically diverse environments

Specialized Practica

- Provide typical school psychological services within school settings
- Collaborate with team of professionals to provide health care services in medical and school settings
- Serve as liaison between schools and health care settings to provide integrated care

Index

CD Contents

---

1   Slides of Background and Overview

2   Slides of Understanding Health Problems and Developing Interventions

3   Slides for Health Promotion and Illness Prevention

4   Slides for Strategies for Leadership Development

5   Case Study on Interventions for Health Conditions

6   Case Study in Program Development

7   Guidelines for Program Development and Evaluation

8   Guidelines for Measurement Development

9   Guidelines for Grant Writing

10   Guidelines for Manuscript Review

11   Guidelines for Manuscript Development

12   Guidelines for Training